FROMMER'S
WALKING TOURS
PARIS

BY
LISA LEGARDE

PRENTICE HALL TRAVEL

NEW YORK • LONDON • TORONTO • SYDNEY
TOKYO • SINGAPORE

FROMMER BOOKS

Published by Prentice Hall General Reference
A division of Simon & Schuster Inc.
15 Columbus Circle
New York, NY 10023

Copyright © 1993 by Simon & Schuster Inc.

Library of Congress Cataloging-in-Publication Data
Legarde, Lisa.
    Paris/by Lisa Legarde.
       p. cm.—(Frommer's walking tours)
    Includes bibliographical references and index.
    ISBN 0-671-79764-6
    1. Paris (France)—Tours. 2. Walking—France—Paris—Guidebooks.
  I. Title. II. Series.
DC708.L395   1993
914.4'36104839—dc20   93-6988
                                                      CIP

Design by Robert Bull Design
Maps by Ortelius Design

FROMMER'S EDITORIAL STAFF
Vice President/Editorial Director: Marilyn Wood
Senior Editor/Editorial Manager: Alice Fellows
Senior Editor: Lisa Renaud
Editors: Charlotte Allstrom, Thomas F. Hirsch, Peter Katucki, Sara Hinsey Raveret, Theodore Stavrou
Assistant Editors: Margaret Bowen, Christopher Hollander, Ian Wilker
Editorial Assistants: Gretchen Henderson, Bethany Jewett
Managing Editor: Leanne Coupe

Manufactured in the United States of America

CONTENTS

LIST OF MAPS

SAFETY ADVISORY

Whenever you're traveling in an unfamiliar city or country, stay alert. Be aware of your immediate surroundings. Wear a moneybelt and keep a close eye on your possessions. Be particularly careful with cameras, purses, and wallets, all favorite targets of thieves and pickpockets.

INVITATION TO THE READERS

In researching this book, I have come across many wonderful sights, shops, and restaurants, the best of which I have included here. I am sure that many of you will also discover appealing places as you explore Paris. Please don't keep them to yourself. Share your experiences, especially if you want to bring to my attention information that has changed since this book was researched. You can address your letters to:

Lisa Legarde
Frommer's Walking Tours: Paris
Prentice Hall Travel
15 Columbus Circle
New York, NY 10023

Introducing Paris

Paris has always aroused the passions of its visitors. To Henry James it was "the greatest temple ever built to material joys and the lust of the eyes"; Hemingway described it as "a moveable feast," that, if you were lucky enough to experience as a young man would stay with you for the rest of your life. Mark Twain was less positive about it: "The French talk funny, eat frogs, and don't bathe. One shouldn't trust the water and all French women can become spectacles of depravity. The streets were cleaner in St. Louis." For D. H. Lawrence it was "a nasty city," and Virginia Woolf found it a "hostile, brilliant alien city." Still, they felt compelled to visit. And happily, millions of people remember Paris as Oscar Hammerstein did—"The last time I saw Paris, her heart was warm and gay, I heard the laughter of her heart in every street café." Whether they loved or hated Paris, something always drew them back.

From the Middle Ages, when students came to listen to the great philosopher Abelard, to the 20th century, when expatriate American writers and artists discovered the Left Bank, Paris has always acted as a magnet. Through the centuries writers, painters, poets, and philosophers have been drawn to the City of Light's beauty, intellectual ferment, dedication and devotion to art and ideas, and to its joie de vivre, which translates daily life into an art form as any visit to a charcuterie, a bakery, a florist, a milliner, a jeweler, a chocolatier, or a market will confirm.

Before you begin strolling the streets and making your own acquaintance with the city, it will help to have a broad outline of its history. Today, Paris consists of 20 *arrondissements,* each with a character and ambience of its own. In fact, many contain today what were once separate villages, like Auteuil and Passy. The city's growth can be traced in a series of concentric circles that radiate out from the original nucleus on the Ile de la Cité, each one marking a particular period of Paris's expansion. Ever since the first wall was built around the Ile de la Cité in the late 3rd century later ones were added, each marking the expanding perimeters of the city: those of Philippe Auguste in 1180, Charles V in 1370, and Louis XIII in the 1630s. Only odd remnants of the first can be seen today—in the Marais and St. Paul—but an outline of the later walls can still be traced, running from the Bastille in the east to the Cour Carrée at the Louvre in the west. Under Louis XIII the walls were extended to embrace the Tuileries palace and gardens. When Louis XIV, the "Sun King" who dominated Europe, felt secure enough to tear these walls down they were replaced by the *Grands Boulevards*—des Capucines, des Italiens, and de la Madeleine, to name only three. Another wall, punctuated by 52 toll gates designed by Claude-Nicolas Ledoux, was built at the perimeter of the city between 1784 and 1789 by the Fermiers Généraux, import tax collectors. This wall became an object of hatred, one of the insults to the common people that helped foment the French Revolution. It was demolished several decades later along with most of the toll gates. A later wall which followed the route of today's boulevards des Marechaux was built by Louis Adolphe Thiers between 1841 and 1845; it failed the test of the Franco-Prussian War, and its parts were ceded to the city of Paris or destroyed.

Today a circle of boulevards, for the most part coinciding with the ramparts of the 14th, 16th, and 17th centuries, encloses most of old Paris except for a southern portion that extends beyond the boulevard St-Germain. Outside the Grands Boulevards lie the *faubourgs,* or old suburbs, around which runs another circle of boulevards corresponding to the 18th-century ramparts. Beyond those boulevards stretch still other suburbs to the boulevards that line the fortifications of the late 19th-century period.

FROM GALLIC-ROMAN LUTETIA TO MEDIEVAL PARIS

The Seine has always played a major role in the city's life. Indeed, it was the river that was the crucible of the early city, for here on the Ile de la Cité a small Gallic trading post, Lutetia Parisiorum, was established at the end of the third century B.C. The city's birth by the river is still remembered in its coat of arms—a boat with the inscription *Fluctuat Nec Mergitur* ("It floats and does not sink"). The river, however, did not protect Lutetia from the armies of Julius Caesar, who defeated the Gallic leader, Vercingétorix, in 52 B.C., and made the settlement an urban outpost of the Roman Empire, situated on the main trading routes between Mediterranean and northern Europe. These trade routes traveled the same paths as today's rue St-Jacques on the Left Bank and the rue St-Martin on the Right

Bank. Under Roman rule, the city expanded across the river to the Left Bank, particularly on and around the Montagne-Ste-Geneviève. Today, the two great monuments from this period that can still be seen are the baths at Cluny and the Arènes de Lutèce, where you can imagine the gladiators battling before audiences seated on the ring of tiered stone seats.

Some of the most enduring elements of French culture emerged in Paris as the Roman Empire waned and the Middle Ages began. Christianity was introduced around A.D. 250 by Saint Denis, the first bishop of Paris; his persecution and martyrdom is recalled in the name *Montmartre*. When the Romans retreated the city fell under the threat of barbarian invasion and so a wall protecting the Ile de la Cité was erected in the late 3rd century; the citizens of Paris were often forced to retreat from the barbarians to the fastnesses of these walls. In the 5th century fears ran high that the Huns were planning to attack the city, and legend has it that only the prayers of Genevieve, patron saint of Paris, saved the city from the invaders. France began to stabilize as a distinct, independent kingdom when Clovis I, the first Merovingian king, defeated the last Roman governor of Gaul in 486 and also turned back the Visigoths and the Alemanni.

In 508 Clovis made Paris his capital. After his death there followed a period of fratricidal strife that arose from Clovis's division of his kingdom. The dynasty collapsed and the Carolingians were able to usurp the throne. The first Carolingian king, Charles Martel, defeated the Saracens on a battlefield between Tours and Poitiers in 732. He was succeeded by his son Pépin the Short, and he in turn by his son, the great Charlemagne, who established an extensive empire but spent most of his time in Aix-la-Chapelle. After the death of his son Louis I, the kingdom was rent by another period of fratricidal strife, and Carolingian might declined to the point that Paris was besieged by the Norsemen from 885 to 886.

When the Carolingian dynasty died out, the nobles chose Hugh Capet, the count of Paris, as king in 987, and he made Paris his capital. His 11th- and 12th-century successors—Robert II, Henry I, Philip I, Louis VI, and Louis VII—all solidified and extended the monarchy's power. During this period a series of village settlements began to form around several abbeys—the church of St-Germain l'Auxerrois, the Abbey St-Germain-des-Prés, the abbey of Ste-Geneviève and the abbey of Notre Dames-des-Champs, to name only a few. Under Philippe Auguste (1179–1223) these settlements were enclosed within a rampart that dates from 1190 on the Right Bank and from about 1209 on the Left Bank. Streets were laid out, a fort was built (the Louvre), and several churches, including Notre Dame, were begun.

Meanwhile, four mendicant orders established themselves on the Left Bank—the Jacobins in 1219, the Cordeliers in 1230, the Augustin friars in 1293 on the quai des Grands-Augustins, and the Carmelites in 1319 in the place Maubert. A large number of schools were also established in the late 13th and 14th centuries, including that founded by Robert de Sorbon in 1253 which became a fountainhead of theological learning legendary for its great scholars

Albertus Magnus and Saint Thomas Aquinas. This revival of learning reached its height in the 13th century, as scholars and students arrived from all over Europe with Latin as their *lingua franca*—hence the name Latin Quarter. The city's reputation as a leading theological center was enhanced by the major role that France played in the Crusades—a role personified by Saint Louis (Louis IX, 1226–70), who built Paris's brilliant jewel box, the Sainte-Chapelle, to store such treasures from the Holy Land as the Crown of Thorns (now housed in the Treasury of Notre Dame and shown once a year on Good Friday). His successors Philip III (1270–85) and Philip IV (1285–1314) further strengthened the monarchy, but the rest of the 14th century was consumed by the Hundred Years' War, which lasted from 1337 to 1453.

The seeds of this strife between England and France had been laid in 1152 when Eleanor of Aquitaine, Louis VII's divorced wife, married the Duke of Normandy, the future King Henry II of England. Her dowry included vast lands in France and so the battle for France was enjoined. The Burgundians joined the English; famine and the Black Death made things worse; the English entered Paris and crowned Henry VI king of England and France in Notre Dame and effectively occupied the country from 1419 to 1436. France's situation deteriorated until Joan of Arc bolstered the courage of the French king and inspired the French army to drive the English from France in 1453.

Also during this dark period, Paris experienced the declaration of its first commune (municipal corporation). During the 13th century the Right Bank had developed into Paris's commercial center as well as its royal seat and municipal center, and a municipal authority had been established in the position of merchant provost. In 1358 Merchant Provost Etienne Marcel took advantage of the chaos to declare the city an independent commune and to lead a peasant revolt against the dauphin, who later became Charles V.

PARIS IN THE 16TH CENTURY

After the long interruption of the Hundred Years' War, the consolidation of the monarchy's power resumed under Louis XI (1461–83), Charles VIII (1483–98), Louis XII (1498–1515), and most of all under Francis I (1515–47). France's first great Renaissance prince and a New Monarch, Francis I tore down the fort at the Louvre and transformed it into a magnificent palace to which the monarchy moved permanently later—an action that moved the center of power away from the east around the Palais de Justice to the west around the Louvre.

When Henry II made his solemn entry into Paris in 1549 after the death of Francis I, it marked the triumph of the Renaissance. Work on the Louvre was continued, and in 1564 Catherine de Médicis began the construction of the Tuileries. The city began to take on a modern look as streets were straightened, house facades were built of stone, quays were constructed, the Pont Neuf was begun; amenities like theaters were also introduced. But the stability was not to last, for the Wars of Religion (1562–98) did not spare the city during the reigns of the last two Valois kings, Charles IX (1560–74) and Henry III (1574–89). They tore Paris asunder. The St. Bartholomew's Day Massacre in 1572 saw Paris awash in blood as thousands of Protestants were killed; on the Day of the Barricades in 1588, Henry III was forced to flee. Henry of Navarre, the legal heir of Henry III and a Protestant, laid siege to the city. He was opposed by the Catholic League, led by the Guise family. It terrorized the city. Henry defeated the League but was forced to convert to Catholicism before being allowed to enter Paris on March 22, 1594, when he is rumored to have said "Paris bien vaut une messe" (Paris is worth a Mass).

One of the most beloved of French kings, Henri IV (1589–1610), and his minister the Duc de Sully were responsible for building the place Royale (later place des Vosges), which became the cornerstone of the later development of the Marais as the aristocratic quarter in the 17th century. He also laid out the place Dauphine, built the quai de l'Horloge, and enlarged the Cour Carrée at the Louvre to four times its size, adding the Grande Galerie and the Pavillon Henri IV, which housed the Galerie d'Apollon. Under him France's prosperity was restored and religious tolerance encouraged.

FROM LOUIS XIII TO LOUIS XVI

Upon Henry IV's assassination by a Catholic fanatic in 1610, Louis XIII (1610–43) succeeded and the city expanded even more. He joined over two unoccupied islands in the river which became the Ile St-Louis. He extended the walls that Charles V had built running from the Bastille in the east to the Cour Carrée in the west to include the Tuileries. To the west of the Tuileries, the regent Marie de Médicis laid out the cours la Reine, a favorite route for fashionable carriages. She also built the Palais du Luxembourg, or Luxembourg Palace (1615). Louis XIII's brilliant minister, Cardinal Richelieu, established the Académie Française (French Academy), built the Palais Cardinal (later Palais Royal), and also destroyed the power of the Huguenots. Richelieu was followed by the equally brilliant Jules Mazarin, who endowed the Collège Mazarin in the Hôtel de L'Institut, which now houses the Académie Française. His own palace later became the Bibliothèque Nationale.

The power of the monarchy was further centralized during the long reign of Louis XIV (1643–1715). During his minority the Fronde (a protest led by the *parlement* and nobles) and the resultant disturbances caused the court to leave Paris in 1649. He returned in 1652 but moved the court first to St-Germain-en-Laye and later to Versailles. Aided by his two great ministers, Jean-Baptiste Colbert and François Louvois, Louis XIV made France a great military power feared throughout Europe. Paris and Versailles, in particular, became the showcases for this power. Although he shunned Paris he gave much to the city. He added the magnificent colonnade to the Louvre;

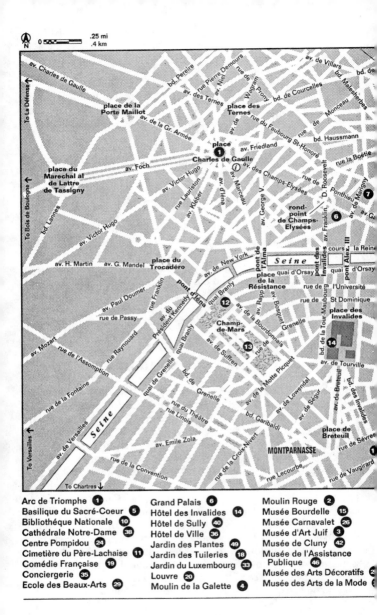

Arc de Triomphe ❶
Basilique du Sacré-Coeur ❺
Bibliothéque Nationale ❿
Cathédrale Notre-Dame ㊳
Centre Pompidou ㉔
Cimetière du Père-Lachaise ⓫
Comédie Française ⓳
Conciergerie ㉟
Ecole des Beaux-Arts ㉙

Grand Palais ❻
Hôtel des Invalides ⓮
Hôtel de Sully ㊵
Hôtel de Ville ㊱
Jardin des Plantes ㊾
Jardin des Tuileries ⓲
Jardin du Luxembourg ㉝
Louvre ⓴
Moulin de la Galette ❹

Moulin Rouge ❷
Musée Bourdelle ⓯
Musée Carnavalet ㉖
Musée d'Art Juif ❸
Musée de Cluny ㊷
Musée de l'Assistance
  Publique ㊻
Musée des Arts Décoratifs ❷
Musée des Arts de la Mode ❻

he laid out the Grands Boulevards along the axis traced by Louis
XIII's earlier walls. The Tuileries palace was completed, sumptuously
decorated, and its gardens—redesigned by André Le Nôtre—
expanded along the tree-lined Champs-Elysées (1667). He laid out
the place Vendôme and place des Victoires; he built the Hôtel des
Invalides—a retreat for sick soldiers—and the pont Royal, as well as
the Observatory and the Gobelins factory. Louis XIV's desertion of
Paris alienated its citizens and prepared the ground for the ideas that

PARIS ORIENTATION

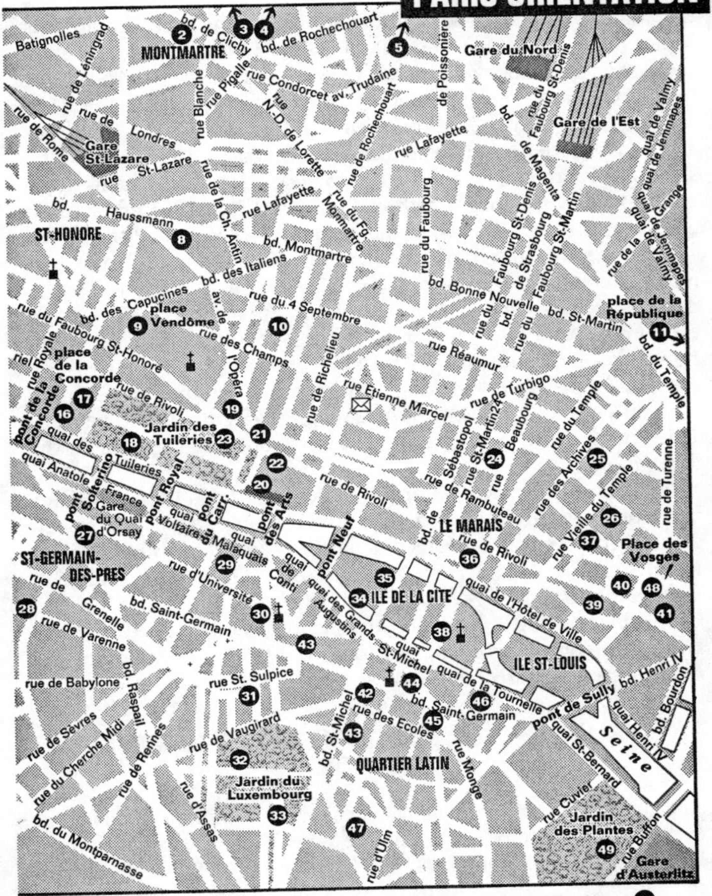

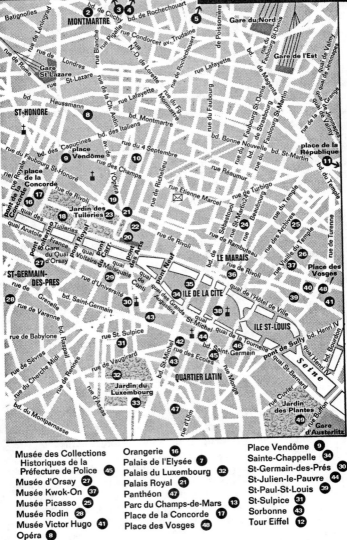

Musée des Collections Historiques de la Préfecture de Police 45
Musée d'Orsay 27
Musée Kwok-On 37
Musée Picasso 25
Musée Rodin 28
Musée Victor Hugo 41
Opéra 8
Orangerie 16
Palais de l'Elysée 7
Palais du Luxembourg 32
Palais Royal 21
Panthéon 47
Parc du Champs-de-Mars 13
Place de la Concorde 17
Place des Vosges 48
Place Vendôme 9
Sainte-Chappelle 34
St-Germain-des-Prés 30
St-Julien-le-Pauvre 44
St-Paul-St-Louis 39
St-Sulpice 31
Sorbonne 43
Tour Eiffel 12

---

sparked and kindled the revolution. When his reign ended, however, France was still feared throughout Europe, although the many wars that had established its hegemony had severely weakened its financial strength.

Louis XV's long reign, from 1715 to 1774, continued the three trends that had been developing under Louis XIV—expansion, war, and financial decline. Under Louis XV the place Louis XV (later place de la Concorde) was laid out; the rue Royale was created in 1732; and the Madeleine church was begun in 1764. The great boulevards began to be lined with fine mansions and houses, as well as such theaters as the Comédie Italienne (1780), which occupied the site of today's Opéra Comique. The Théâtre Française opened in 1782. On the Left Bank the École Militaire and the Champ-de-Mars date from 1751; St-Sulpice was completed and a new church was begun on the site of the Panthéon. People flocked to the gardens of the Palais Royal and to its new galleries, which had been added in 1761 and housed entertainments of all sorts, including cafés, shops, and a wax works.

During the 18th century, the financial strain of pomp, glamor, and military conquest began to show. The treasury continued to be drained by wars—the War of the Austrian Succession (1740–48) and the Seven Years' War (1756–63). The support of the American Revolution by Louis XVI (1774–92) further depleted the treasury; eventually, in 1788, the king was forced to summon the States General—the old parliamentary assembly—for the first time since 1614, placing him in a weak position and opening the door to the Revolution.

Still, during the two great reigns of Louis XIV and Louis XV, Paris had dominated the Western world, nourishing some of Europe's greatest architects and intellectual figures—architects J. H. Mansart under Louis XIV; and François Mansart, J. G. Soufflot, and J. A. Gabriel under Louis XV; dramatists Molière, Racine, and Pierre Corneille; composers Rameau, Jean-Baptiste Lully, and Christophe Gluck; painters Fragonard, Watteau, and François Boucher; and philosophers Voltaire and Montesquieu.

FROM THE REVOLUTION TO THE SECOND EMPIRE

The summoning of the States General set into motion the chain of events that led to the Revolution. The States General was transformed into the National Assembly (1789). In July 1789 a Paris mob stormed the Bastille, and three days later Louis XVI was forced at the Hôtel de Ville to kiss the new French tricolor. In October the king was hauled from Versailles to the Tuileries, and a constitutional monarchy was established in 1791. War with much of Europe followed, accompanied by the growth of radical factions in France during 1792. The Tuileries was stormed by revolutionary troops and a Parisian mob on August 10, 1792, and the king was removed to the Temple as a prisoner. He and his queen, Marie Antoinette, were beheaded in the place de la Concorde in 1793. Robespierre presided over the Reign of Terror (1793–94) until it was ended by the 9th Thermidor on July 27, 1794, and a reaction ushered in the Directory (1795–99), which was terminated by Napoléon Bonaparte's coup d'état.

Napoléon moved into the Tuileries, and for his convenience the arcades on the rue de Rivoli were introduced (1801). He crowned himself emperor in 1804 in the Cathédrale Notre Dame, then embarked on a series of campaigns that took him to Egypt and to Moscow until he was defeated at the battle of Waterloo in 1815. Napoléon gave the city many of its most grandiose monuments. He started the Arc de Triomphe and completed the Madeleine, which was meant to serve as a "temple of glory." He also commissioned his favorite architects, Percier and Fontaine, to build the Arc de Triomphe du Carrousel. The Bourse des Valeurs (1808–26), was also begun, in the style of a Greek temple. It was also Napoléon who really set the Louvre on its course as an art museum. The art booty that he acquired in his many military campaigns was displayed there and became the core of the later museum's collection.

In 1814 Louis XVIII (1814–24) was restored to the throne, and the city began its enormous 19th-century growth. By 1841 the population was 935,000, up from 547,000 in 1801; in 1861 it had soared to 1,696,000 and by 1881 reached 2,270,000. Industrialization took hold; industrial exhibitions were held, and the first railway arrived in Paris in 1837. It was a period of great social change and democratization, which may have helped cause two revolutions. The first, in 1830, replaced Charles X, who had tried to restore absolute monarchy, with Louis Philippe (1830–48). Another, in 1848, brought Louis-Napoléon Bonaparte to power, first as president of the Second Republic and subsequently as Emperor Napoléon III, in 1852.

During his long reign as emperor, from 1852 to 1870, Napoléon III reshaped Paris under the authority of his préfect of the Seine, Baron Georges-Eugène Haussman, who razed whole neighborhoods to cut the wide boulevards and avenues that Parisians walk along today. The new gates of the city were the railroad stations—the Gare de Lyon, the Gare du Nord, the Gare Montparnasse, and the Gare St-Lazare—and Haussman laid out boulevards and avenues for their easy access, including the boulevard de Strasbourg and the rue de Rennes. In the process great crossroads were created, such as the rue de l'Etoile, the place de l'Opéra, and the place de la République. During the Second Empire 24 parks, including the Bois de Boulogne, parc de Monceau, and the parc des Buttes-Chaumont, were created, a system of horse-drawn omnibus transportation was begun, Les Halles constructed, and a sewage system was laid. For many of us this era marks the beginning of modern Paris—the Paris that is still recognizable today.

In this Paris lived and worked the intellectual giants of the day—Balzac, Baudelaire, Dumas, Hugo, Sand, Chopin, Berlioz, Delacroix, Ingres, Daumier, and Manet, to name only a few who frequented the new boulevards with their cafés, music halls, and theaters (including the Opéra, which was relocated to its present site in 1875, and the Opéra Comique). Offenbach and Gounod were the favorites at the opera; the crowd pleasers at the theater were comedies by Dumas and Labiche. Famous courtesans reveled in their social prominence, capturing the hearts of even the emperor. One of these was La Paiva, who amassed such a vast fortune that she was able to build a veritable palace on the Champs-Elysées. Everyone came to Paris for pleasure—the French from the provinces, who came by train to shop, go to the theater and sit in the plush red cafés lit with gilt chandeliers, and the English, who came to indulge every pleasure and then went home to complain. The animated life that filled the boulevards, from the porte St-Denis to the Madeleine—especially on the boulevard des Italiens, between the rue de Richelieu and the rue de la Chausée-d'Antin—is what comes to mind still when one thinks of Paris—the Paris that we know so well from the paintings by Manet, Renoir, and the other Impressionists, as well as other French artists and photographers. Here were concentrated the most fashionable cafés, theaters and restaurants—above all, the Café Tortoni at the corner of rue Taitbout, where Manet had lunch practically every day before walking in the Tuileries, and to which everyone who was anyone in Paris repaired before and after the theater. The city was the art capital of Europe, and its achievements were showcased in the International Exhibitions of 1855, 1867, 1878, 1889, and 1900, the occasions for the building of the Trocadéro (1878), the Eiffel Tower (1889), and the Grand Palais and Petit Palais (1897–1900). Everyone came to admire this Paris—the modern city par excellence.

FROM THE PARIS COMMUNE TO WORLD WAR I

The Empire ended disastrously in the Franco-Prussian War (1870–71). Paris was besieged for four months and the Germans entered the city. Napoléon was taken prisoner at the Battle of Sedan and after the Germans withdrew a communist uprising took place; which was quickly and bloodily suppressed, but not before the mob had torched the Tuileries, burning all but the Pavillon de Flore to the ground. The last of the Communards were executed at Père-Lachaise cemetery. The Third Republic was declared, which lasted for 60 years; new cabinets came and went while the country underwent more rapid social and industrial change, which in turn spawned revolutionary cultural and artistic movements.

Under the Third Republic French painters made France the world center of art. The change from the Romantic era to the modern era was clearly marked with the death of writer Victor Hugo in 1885. Hugo had been the great romantic symbol of 19th-century France. His body lay in state under the Arc de Triomphe for 24 hours, and thousands flocked to pay their last respects. But change had been coming for a while, as evidenced in the works of such realist painters as Manet and Courbet and in the novels of Zola, which had been stirring great controversy. In particular Manet's *Le Déjeuner sur L'Herbe,* shown at the Salon des Refusés in 1863 (created by Napoléon III to display works rejected by the Salon, the annual exhibition of works sponsored by the Académie Française) had shocked people for both its subject matter and technique. Manet, Pissarro, Renoir, Cézanne, Monet, Morisot, Degas, Sisley, and 21 other artists, calling themselves the Société Anonyme, held their first exhibition in 1874 in a studio at 35 boulevard des Capucines, which they borrowed from Nadar the photographer. It was greeted with revulsion. The paintings were dismissed as mere muddy scrapings and the artists described as madmen. Louis Leroy, in *Charivari,* dubbed the show the "Exhibition of the Impressionists," and the name stuck. In 1876 a second exhibition was held, showing 24 works by Degas, 12 by Pissarro, 18 by Monet, and 15 each by Sisley and Renoir. Again the critics howled. Albert Wolff described the show as a "horrifying spectacle," and its artists as five or six lunatics afflicted with the madness of ambition. He complained vehemently about each artist; of Renoir, he recommended someone "try to explain to M. Renoir that a woman's torso is not a mass of decomposing flesh with those purplish green stains which denote a state of complete putrefaction in a corpse." Only one or two enlightened critics, including Charpentiers and Chocquet, realized that 19th-century life called for new art and new literature.

By the 1890s the Impressionists had arrived—at least in Paris. Similar experimentation was occurring in music by such composers as Faure, Debussy, Ravel, and Dukas; in the sciences with Berthelot, Pasteur, and the Curies; and in literature by Proust, who published the first volume of his revolutionary novel *A la Recherche du Temps Perdu* in 1913. In 1898 Samuel Bing opened his shop, Art Nouveau, and its name became synonymous with the fluid, sinuous decorative style that dominated the first decade of the century and can still be most easily seen at such grand restaurants as Maxim's (1890) on the rue Royale or out on the street at the one or two remaining Hector Guimard entrances to the métro (which opened in 1900).

France's transformation to a modern industrial nation also produced a far more democratic society, giving rise to an urban proletariat that flocked to the cafés, restaurants, café-concerts, and dance halls. These were the people that the Impressionist and realist painters documented in their art—shop girls, milliners, barmaids, and prostitutes who frequented the cafés and dance halls. By the turn of the century Paris had 27,000 cafés, about 150 café-concerts and thousands of restaurants, a phenomenal number considering there were only 50 at the end of the 18th century. Cultural life centered on the cafés along the Grands Boulevards and in Montparnasse and Montmartre. Manet, Zola, Fantin-Latour, Nadar, Monet, Pissarro, and Renoir gathered at the Café Guerbois (from 1869 to 1873) at the beginning of the avenue de Clichy in Montmartre and later at the Nouvelle-Athènes in the place Pigalle.

The café-concert was one of the inventions of the late 19th century that contributed to the city's reputation for gaiety and sociability. Here, people came when they liked, dressed as they liked, ate and drank as they watched the show, commented throughout, and joined in the singing. Maurice Chevalier and Mistinguett both started their careers in such places. On the boulevards there was the Eldorado and the Scala, while in Montmartre was the Moulin Rouge, built in 1889, immortalized by Toulouse-Lautrec, and host to many a famous artist, including Colette, La Goulue, and Jane Avril. It had a large ballroom with tables in the gallery and a garden where one could watch the "girls" riding donkeys. The Folies Bergère on the rue Richer, begun as the Café du Sommier Élastique, became famous throughout Europe in the 1890s. Poets and painters frequented Le Chat Noir in Montmartre and Aristide Bruant's Le Mirliton. But the frivolity, fun, and frolic of the café-concerts and the dance halls were to die down for a while when, in August 1914, the troops marched off singing the "Marseillaise."

FROM 1920 TO THE PRESENT

During World War I the Germans failed to reach Paris, but France bore the brunt of the fighting, and at the end of the war premier Georges Clemenceau won heavy war reparations and insisted on imposing a tough treaty on the Germans at Versailles. Postwar Paris in the twenties became a magnet for young Americans. Prohibition had been passed in the United States in 1919, and nativism and isolationism dominated American politics; whereas Paris was fun and also the art capital of the world. It had already given birth to Impressionism and Art Nouveau in the 19th century, cubism (1907–14), dadaism (1915–22), and now surrealism and Art Deco in the 1920s. The young Americans came in droves from the early twenties to the late thirties, gathering on the Left Bank in the cafés of Montparnasse—the Dôme, the Sélect, and La Coupole. In the forties and fifties, the bohemians moved to the boulevard St-Germain, where they frequented the Deux Magots, Café de Flore, and Brasserie Lipp, all still thriving on the boulevard St-Germain today.

In the 1930s economic depression throughout Europe and appeasement of Hitler led to the outbreak of World War II. Hitler's troops broke through the Maginot line and Paris was occupied on June 14, 1940. The Germans established their headquarters at the Hotel Lutetia on the boulevard Raspail. The Vichy government, led by Marshal Pétain, in theory ran unoccupied France, but in fact collaborated with the Germans, while General Charles de Gaulle became leader of the Free French and organized *le maquis* ("the resistance") throughout the country. The Allies landed in Normandy in June 1944, and Paris was finally liberated on August 25, 1944; the next day General de Gaulle paraded down the Champs-Elysées. By the end of the year the Germans had been expelled from France. De Gaulle headed a provisional government prior to the official proclamation of the Fourth Republic.

The Fourth Republic saw the violent end of colonial French rule around the world, in Madagascar, Indochina, and North Africa, where the Algerian war of liberation led to the collapse of the Fourth Republic. De Gaulle was recalled to head the Fifth Republic in 1958 to resolve the crisis created when a right-wing military coup in Algeria threatened France. In 1962, after a referendum in France, Algeria gained its independence. The decade ended with more turmoil. In May 1968 workers were striking around the country; at the same time in Paris students took to the streets rebelling against France's antiquated educational system. In 1969 Georges Pompidou became president. During his tenure the Centre Pompidou, or Beauborg, was begun, along with the Tour Montparnasse. The tower was a preview of what was to come as the 1980s transformed the architectural unity of Paris with the addition of the Centre Pompidou and Forum des Halles, the Institute du Monde Arab, the Opera de la Bastille, I. M. Pei's controversial pyramids at the Louvre, the Grande

Arche de la Défense, and the complex at La Villette. François Mitterand, France's first socialist president, was elected in 1981. In 1989 Paris celebrated two great birthdays: the bicentennial of the French Revolution and the centennial of the Eiffel Tower, both great gifts to the culture of the Western world, both symbols of hope, progress, and change that express the ability of human beings to renew their spirits—and Paris's unique ability to transform itself into a new city of light for each generation.

Getting to Know Paris

Paris may be one of the largest cities in Europe, but after a little orientation you'll find that it's a surprisingly easy metropolis to get around in. This chapter collects the practical information you'll need to make your visit an enjoyable, hassle-free success, including tips on traveling to Paris, an introduction to transportation within the city, a brief rundown of the city's layout and neighborhoods, and an A-to-Z guide to services in Paris that will help you find what you need at a glance.

GETTING THERE

BY PLANE

The flying time to Paris from New York is about 7 hours; from Chicago, 9 hours; from Los Angeles, 11 hours; from Atlanta, 8 hours, from Miami, 8½ hours; and from Washington, 7½ hours.

THE MAJOR AIRLINES One of the best choices for passengers flying to Paris from both the southeastern United States and the Midwest is **Delta Airlines** (tel. 800/241-4141), whose network greatly expanded after its adoption of some of the routes of the now-defunct Pan Am. From such cities as New Orleans, Savannah, Phoenix, Columbia (S.C.), Birmingham, and Nashville, Delta flies to

Atlanta, connecting every evening with a nonstop flight to Orly Airport in Paris. Delta also operates a daily nonstop flight to Paris from both Cincinnati and New York's JFK. Both of these leave late enough in the afternoon to permit easy transfers from much of Delta's vast North American network. An additional recent acquisition from Pan Am involves nonstop flights to Orly four times a week from Orlando, Florida.

Another excellent choice for Paris-bound passengers is **United Airlines** (tel. 800/538-2929), with nonstop flights from Chicago, Washington, D.C., Los Angeles, and San Francisco to Paris's Charles de Gaulle Airport. United also offers attractive promotional fares—especially in the low and shoulder seasons—to London's Heathrow from at least seven major North American hubs. From London, it's an easy train and hovercraft connection to Paris, a fact that tempts many passengers to spend a weekend in London either before or after their visit to Paris.

American Airlines (tel. 800/624-6262) offers daily nonstop flights to Paris (Orly) from Dallas/Fort Worth, Raleigh/Durham, Chicago, and New York's JFK.

Continental Airlines (tel. 800/231-0856) offers daily nonstop flights to Paris's Orly from its hubs in Newark (N.J.) and Houston.

TWA (tel. 800/221-2000) operates frequent (usually daily) nonstop service to Paris's Charles de Gaulle from Boston, St. Louis, New York's JFK, and Washington, D.C.'s Dulles. TWA also offers service to Paris (with one touchdown en route in Washington, D.C.) from Los Angeles.

Aircraft belonging to the **Air France Group** (tel. 800/237-2747) fly frequently across the Atlantic. Formed by a merger in the late 1980s that combined three of France's largest nationalized airlines: Air France, UTA (*Union des Transports Aériens*), and France's internal domestic airline, Air Inter. At press time, the conglomerate flew from both Newark (N.J.) and New York's JFK to both Charles de Gaulle and Orly in Paris. The group also flies to Paris from about 10 U.S. cities (including Los Angeles and San Francisco), as well as from Mexico City (via Houston), Montréal, and Toronto.

USAir (tel. 800/622-1015) offers daily nonstop service from Philadelphia International Airport to Paris's Orly. Because Philadelphia is one of USAir's most important hubs, connections are excellent throughout the airline's North American network.

REGULAR AIRFARES Fares and conditions for the flights of each of the airlines listed above are highly competitive. All of them offer a consistently popular **advance-purchase excursion (APEX)** fare that requires a 30-day advance payment and a minimum stay of between 7 and 21 days. In most cases this ticket, although reasonably priced, is nonrefundable or only partially refundable and requires you to pay a penalty if you change flight dates or destination.

Most airlines divide their year roughly into seasonal slots, with the least expensive fares offered between November 1 and March 14. Shoulder season, the period between the high and low seasons, is only slightly more expensive and includes all of October, which many veteran tourists consider the ideal time to visit France. Shoulder season also extends from mid-March to mid-June.

A regular **economy-class** ticket will allow you to catch most any flight, depending on seat availability, without regard to advance-booking requirements and without penalty for last-minute changes in your itinerary. **Business class** offers wider seats, more leg room, and sometimes—but not always—the advantages of first class.

OTHER GOOD-VALUE CHOICES Proceed with caution through the next grab bag of suggestions. What constitutes "good value" keeps changing in the airline industry. It's hard to keep up, even if you're a travel agent. Fares change all the time, and what was the lowest possible fare one day can change the very next day when a new promotional fare is offered. So be aware of how volatile the situation is.

Bucket Shops The name originated in the 1960s, when mainstream airlines gave the then-pejorative term to resellers of blocks of unsold tickets consigned to them by major transatlantic carriers. "Bucket shop" has stuck as a label, but it might be more polite to refer to them as "consolidators." They exist in many shapes and forms. In its purest sense, a bucket shop acts as a clearinghouse for blocks of tickets that airlines discount and consign during normally slow periods of air travel.

Charter operators (see below) and bucket shops used to perform separate functions, but their offerings in many cases have been blurred recently. Many outfits perform both functions.

Tickets are discounted anywhere from 20% to 35% of the full fare. Terms of payment can vary, anywhere from 45 days before departure to last-minute sales offered in a final attempt by an airline to fill a semiempty craft.

Bucket shops abound from coast to coast, but just to get you started, here are some names. Look also for their small one-column ads in your local newspaper's travel section.

One of the biggest U.S. consolidators is **Travac,** 989 Sixth Ave., New York, NY 10018 (tel. 212/563-3303 or toll free 800/TRAV-800), which offers seats throughout the U.S. to most cities in Europe.

Out West, you can try **Sunline Express Holidays, Inc.,** 607 Market St., San Francisco, CA 94105 (tel. 415/541-7800 or toll free 800/SUNLINE).

Since dealing with unknown bucket shops might be a little risky, it's wise to call the Better Business Bureau in your area to see if complaints have been filed against the company from which you plan to purchase a ticket.

Charter Flights For reasons of economy—never for convenience—some travelers opt for charter flights to France or to one of the countries bordering it.

Strictly speaking, a charter flight occurs on an aircraft reserved months in advance for fixed-time transit to some predetermined point. Before paying for a charter, check carefully the restrictions on your ticket or contract. You may be asked to purchase a tour package and pay far in advance. You'll pay a stiff penalty (or forfeit the ticket entirely) if you cancel. Also, charters are sometimes cancelled when the plane isn't filled. In some cases, the charter ticket seller will offer you an insurance policy for your own legitimate cancellation (hospital certificate or death in the family, for example).

There is no way to predict if a charter flight or a bucket shop will cost less than an APEX or promotional ticket on a regularly scheduled airline. You have to investigate at the time of your trip.

Some charter companies have proved unreliable in the past, leaving passengers stranded. I prefer to deal with subsidiaries (or at least affiliates) of major international carriers. Some of these include the following.

Jet Vacations, 1775 Broadway, New York, NY 10019 (tel. 212/247-0999 or 800/538-0999), is a wholly owned subsidiary of Air France and an obvious charter-line choice for Paris. Committed to filling as many seats on Air France flights as possible, and operating from many cities including New York's JFK, Newark (N.J.), Boston, Washington, D.C. (Dulles), Chicago, Miami, Houston, Los Angeles, and San Francisco, it has no objections to selling one-way tickets to Paris, space available, up until a few days before takeoff of any given flight.

BY TRAIN

If you're already in Europe, you may want to go to Paris by train, especially if you have a Eurailpass. Even if you don't, the cost is relatively low.

Visitors from London may want to consider a British/French joint rail pass, linking the two most popular vacation spots on the Continent—Britain and France. Called **BritFrance Railpass,** it is available to North Americans, providing unlimited train travel in Britain and France, plus a round-trip ticket for travel across the English Channel via hovercraft. You may choose a total of any 5 days of unlimited rail travel during a 15-day consecutive period or 10 days during a single month—on both British and French rail networks. Passes are available at any office of FrenchRail, Inc. (tel. 800/848-7245) or at BritRail Travel International (tel. 212/575-2667) in New York City.

BY BUS

Bus travel to Paris is available not only from London but also from most major cities on the Continent. European Railways operates **Europabus** and **Eurolines.** These bus lines link Paris to major cities. In Great Britain, bus tickets are sold at all National Express offices. In Paris, the contact is Eurolines, 5 av. de la Porte de la Villette, 75019 Paris (tel. 1/40-38-93-93). If you're in Germany, contact Europabus at Mannheimerstrasse 4, 6000 Frankfurt (tel. 069/23-07-35). In the United States, contact DER Tours at 800/782-2424.

BY SHIP

The days of sailing to Paris in the style of Marilyn Monroe and Jane Russell in *Gentlemen Prefer Blondes* are long gone.

The only ocean liner that makes scheduled transatlantic crossings is the **Queen Elizabeth 2** (QE2), the star and flagship of the British Cunard line. Its most frequent itinerary is between New York and England's Channel port of Southampton. From Southampton, you can go by ferry or hovercraft to France, or take a train to London, perhaps taking in a play, museums, and some shopping before flying over to Paris. Cunard offers 27 transatlantic crossings, from April to early December, between New York and Southampton.

Fares are extremely complicated, based on cabin standard and location and the season of sailing. Call a travel agent or a Cunard representative at 800/221-4770. In New York City, call 212/880-7500.

BY FERRY FROM ENGLAND

About a dozen companies run hydrofoils, ferries, and hovercrafts across *La Manche,* as the French call the Channel. Services operate day and night. Most carry cars, but some hydrofoils carry passengers only. Hovercraft or hydrofoils make the trip in just 40 minutes, while slow-moving ferries might take hours, depending on conditions.

The major routes are between Dover and Folkestone and Calais and Boulogne (about 12 trips a day). Depending on weather conditions, prices and timetables can vary. It's always important to make a reservation, because ferries are crowded.

Call **British Rail International** (tel. 071/834-2345), **P&O** (tel. 081/575-8555), or **Sealink** (tel. 023/364-7047) in England. Special fares are offered, but they change frequently. It's better to contact a travel agent—say, in London—to book your ticket for you. A good travel agent will help you sort out the maze of ferry schedules and find a suitable option.

ORIENTATION

ARRIVING

BY PLANE

Paris has two major international airports: **Orly,** 8½ miles from Paris, and **Charles de Gaulle** (also called Roissy), 14¼ miles from the city. A shuttle operates between the two airports about every 30 minutes, taking 50 to 75 minutes to make the journey. At Orly catch this bus at Exit B.

For information about transportation to Charles de Gaulle Airport, call 47-58-20-18; for Orly, call 45-50-32-30. For airport flight information, call Charles de Gaulle at 48-62-12-12 and Orly at 47-67-12-34.

CHARLES DE GAULLE AIRPORT At Charles de Gaulle Airport, foreign carriers use Aérogare 1, and Air France uses Aérogare 2. From Aérogare 1, you take a moving walkway to the passport checkpoint and the Customs area. The two terminals are linked by a shuttle bus (*navette*).

The **shuttle bus** connecting Aérogare 1 with Aérogare 2 also transports passengers to the Roissy rail station, from which fast **RER trains** leave every 15 minutes to such Métro stations as Gare du Nord, Châtelet, Luxembourg, Port-Royal, and Denfert-Rochereau.

You can also take an **Air France shuttle bus**—to the Arc de Triomphe, for example. That ride, depending on traffic, takes less than 45 minutes. The shuttle departs about every 12 minutes between 5:45am and 11pm.

Taxis into the city will cost 150F ($27.75) to 200F ($37), depending on traffic. At night (from 8pm to 7am), fares more than double.

Buses to Charles de Gaulle Airport leave from the terminal in the basement of the Palais des Congrès at Port Maillot every 15 minutes to Aérogare 2 and every 20 minutes to Aérogare 1. The trip takes about 30 minutes, but during rush hours allow another half hour.

ORLY AIRPORT Orly also has two terminals—Orly Sud (south) for international flights and Orly Ouest (west) for domestic flights. They are linked by a shuttle bus.

Air France buses leave Orly Sud every 12 minutes between 5:45am and 11pm from Exit 1, heading for Gare des Invalides. At Exit D, you can board Bus 215 for place Denfert-Rochereau in the south of Paris.

A **shuttle bus** leaves Orly about every 15 minutes for the RER train station, Pont-de-Rungis/Aéroport-d'Orly, from which RER trains take 30 minutes into the city center.

You can also take a **shuttle bus** from Orly Sud to the Orly train station, where high-speed RER trains leaving every 15 minutes will take you to all the central stops along the Seine. En route you can transfer to any Métro line.

A **taxi** from Orly to the center of Paris costs about 130F ($24.05), more at night. Don't take a meterless taxi from Orly Sud—it's much safer to get a metered cab from the line, which is under the scrutiny of a police officer.

Buses *to* Orly Airport leave from the Invalides terminal to either Orly Sud or Orly Ouest every 15 minutes, taking about 30 minutes.

BY TRAIN

There are six major train stations in Paris: **Gare d'Austerlitz,** 55 quai d'Austerlitz, 13e (servicing the southwest with trains to the Loire Valley, the Bordeaux country, and the Pyrénées); **Gare de l'Est,** place du 11 November 1918, 10e (servicing the east, with trains to Strasbourg, Nancy, Reims, and beyond to Zürich, Basel, Luxembourg, and Austria); **Gare de Lyon,** 20 boulevard Diderot, 12e (servicing the southeast with trains to the Côte d'Azur, Provence, and beyond to Geneva, Lausanne, and Italy); **Gare Montparnasse,** 17 boulevard Vaugirard, 15e (servicing the west, with trains to Brittany); **Gare du Nord,** 18 rue de Dunkerque, 15e (servicing the north with trains to Holland, Denmark, Belgium, and the north of Germany); and **Gare St-Lazare,** 13 rue d'Amsterdam, 8e (servicing the northwest, with trains to Normandy).

For **general train information** from any of these stations, call 45-82-50-50 from 7am to 10pm daily. **To make reservations,** call 45-65-60-60 daily from 8am to 8pm. Buses operate between stations.

Note: The stations and the surrounding areas are usually seedy and frequented by pickpockets, hustlers, prostitutes, and drug addicts. Be alert, especially at night.

Each of these stations also has a Métro stop, making the whole city easily accessible. Taxis are also available at every station at designated stands. Look for the sign that says "TETE DE STATION."

BY BUS

Most buses arrive at **Gare Routière International,** 8 place Stalingrad, 19e (tel. 42-05-12-10; Métro: Stalingrad). Call 40-38-93-93 for information about international routes.

BY CAR

Driving a car in Paris is definitely not recommended. Parking is difficult and traffic is dense. If you do drive, remember that Paris is encircled by a ring road called the *périphérique.* Always obtain detailed directions to your destination, including the name of the exit on the périphérique (exits are not numbered). Avoid rush hours.

Few hotels, except the luxury ones, have garages, but the staff will usually be able to direct you to one nearby.

The major highways into Paris are the A1 from the north (Great Britain and Benelux); the A13 from Rouen, Normandy, and other points of northwest France; the A109 from Spain, the Pyrénées, and the southwest; the A7 from the French Alps, the Riviera, and Italy; and the A4 from eastern France.

TOURIST INFORMATION

The main **tourist information office** is at 127 Champs-Elysées, 8e (tel. 47-23-61-72), where you can secure information about both Paris and the provinces. The office is open daily from 9am to 8pm.

Welcome Offices in the city center will also give you free maps, brochures, and *Paris Monthly Information,* an English-language listing of all current events and performances.

CITY LAYOUT

Paris is surprisingly compact. Occupying 432 square miles (six more than San Francisco), it is home to 10 million people. As mentioned, the River Seine divides Paris into the **Right Bank** (Rive Droite) to the north and the **Left Bank** (Rive Gauche) to the south. These designations make sense when you stand on a bridge and face downstream, watching the waters flow out toward the sea—to your right is the north bank to your left the south. Thirty-two bridges link the Right and Left banks, some providing access to the two small islands at the heart of the city, **Ile de la Cité**—the city's birthplace and site of Notre-Dame—and **Ile St-Louis,** a moat-guarded oasis of sober 17th-century mansions. These islands can cause some confusion to walkers who think they've just crossed a bridge from one bank to the other, only to find themselves caught up in an almost medieval maze of narrow streets and old buildings.

MAIN ARTERIES & STREETS Between 1860 and 1870 Baron Haussmann forever changed the look of Paris by creating the legendary **boulevards:** boulevards St-Michel, St-Germain, Haussmann, Malesherbes, Sebastopol, Magenta, Voltaire, and Strasbourg.

The "main street" on the Right Bank is, of course, the **Champs-Elysées,** beginning at the Arc de Triomphe and running to the place de la Concorde. Haussmann also created avenue de l'Opéra (as well as the Opéra), and the 12 avenues that radiate starlike from the Arc de Triomphe giving it its original name, place de l'Etoile (renamed place Charles-de-Gaulle following the general's death). Today it is often referred to as place Charles-de-Gaulle-Etoile.

Haussmann also cleared Ile de la Cité of its medieval buildings, transforming it into a showcase for Notre-Dame. Finally, he laid out the two elegant parks on the western and southeastern fringes of the city: **Bois de Boulogne** and **Bois de Vincennes.**

FINDING AN ADDRESS The city of Paris is divided into 20 municipal wards called "arrondissements," each with its own mayor, city hall, police station, and central post office. Some even have remnants of market squares. Most city maps are divided by arrondissement, and all addresses include the arrondissement number (written in Roman or Arabic numerals and followed by "e" or "er"). Paris also has its own version of a zip code. Thus the proper mailing address for a hotel is written as, say, 75014 Paris. The last two digits, 14, indicate that the address is in the 14th arrondissement, in this case, Montparnasse.

Numbers on buildings running parallel to the River Seine most often follow the course of the river—that is, east to west. On perpendicular streets, numbers on buildings begin low closer to the river.

ARRONDISSEMENTS IN BRIEF

Paris's 20 arrondissements each possess a unique style and flavor. One of your first tasks will be deciding which district appeals most to you and finding accommodations there. Then try and visit as many areas as you can.

1st Arr. Located on the Right Bank, the 1st has the most popular attractions, including the Louvre, the Forum des Halles (now transformed into a modern shopping mall), Sainte-Chapelle,

Conciergerie, and the Jardin des Tuileries. Two of the most prestigious addresses are place Vendôme (site of the Hôtel Ritz) and Palais Royal, a section of elegant buildings and galleries surrounding the gardens to the north. (See tours 1, 2, and 9)

2nd Arr. Home to the Bourse des Valeurs, or stock exchange, the 2nd is in fact primarily a working-class district. Highlights include rue de la Paix, a traditional street of goldsmiths and furriers, and the Bibliothèque Nationale. The Right Bank district lies mainly between the Grands Boulevards and the rue Etienne-Marcel. (See tour 9)

3rd Arr. This embraces much of The Marais ("the marsh"), one of the best-loved Right Bank neighborhoods of Paris. Many of the buildings date from the Middle Ages, and much of the old has been saved and restored. Highlights include the Musée Picasso. (See tour 7.)

4th Arr. This area contains the Hôtel de Ville (city hall) and such major attractions as Notre-Dame (on Ile de la Cité), the Centre Pompidou, and place des Vosges, site of the Musée Victor Hugo. It also includes Ile Saint-Louis with its aristocratic town houses, courtyards, and antiques shops. (See tours 1, 2, and 4)

5th Arr. Known as the Latin Quarter, its attractions include the Sorbonne, the Panthéon, the Musée de Cluny, and the Jardin des Plantes. When people refer to the Left Bank they usually mean the 5th and 6th arrondissements—an area filled with students, cafés, bistros, and street life. (See tours 4 and 5.)

6th Arr. This is the heartland of Paris publishing and, for some, the most colorful part of the Left Bank. Waves of earnest young artists can be seen emerging from the Ecole des Beaux-Arts. This is one of the best areas for good budget hotels and restaurants. Highlights include the Jardin du Luxembourg and place St-Germain-des-Prés. (See tour 4.)

7th Arr. The home of the Eiffel Tower is primarily an upscale Right Bank residential and government-diplomatic area. Other highlights on the Left Bank side include Napoléon's Tomb and the Invalides Musée de l'Armée. Next to the Invalides is the city air terminal. (See tour 4.)

8th Arr. The 8th is the heart of the Right Bank and its prime showcase is the Champs-Elysées, linking the Arc de Triomphe with the delicate Obelisque on place de la Concorde. Here you'll find the fashion houses, the most elegant hotels, expensive restaurants and shops, and the most fashionably attired Parisians. Other landmarks include the Palais de l'Elysée, home of the French president; the Church of the Madeleine; the Faubourg Saint-Honoré; and the Parc de Monceau. (See tour 8.)

9th Arr. Visited primarily because of its Grands Boulevards, such as boulevard des Capucines and boulevard des Italiens, the 9th also includes the Quartier de l'Opéra and the strip joints of Pigalle (the infamous "pig alley" for the G.I.s of World War II). Other major

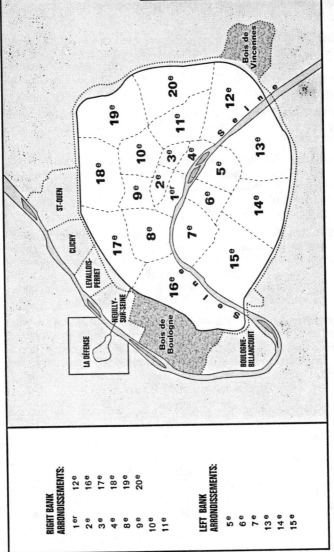

RIGHT BANK ARRONDISSEMENTS:
1er 12e
2e   16e
3e   17e
4e   18e
8e   19e
9e   20e
10e
11e

LEFT BANK ARRONDISSEMENTS:
5e
6e
7e
13e
14e
15e

attractions are the Musée Grevin (the major waxworks of Paris) and the Folies Bergère. (See tour 9.)

10th Arr. The Gare du Nord and Gare de l'Est are both in this commercial district. Movie theaters and porno houses often dot this area.

11th Arr. Increasingly fashionable, this is the site of place de la Bastille and the new Bastille opera house. For many decades, it has been a working-class district, attracting immigrants from all over the world.

12th Arr. Very few tourists come here, but when a famous French chef opened the restaurant Au Trou Gascon *tout le monde* showed up. Its major attraction is the Bois de Vincennes, a popular patch of woodland with boating lakes, a racecourse, and a zoo. The Gare de Lyon is located here, too.

13th Arr. This primarily working-class district grew up around the famous Gobelins tapestries works. The Gare d'Austerlitz is a landmark.

14th Arr. Montparnasse, home of the "lost generation," is well known to tourists. Stein, Toklas, Hemingway, and other American expatriates gathered here in the 1920s. After World War II it ceased to be the center of intellectual life in Paris, but the memory lingers on in its cafés. (See tour 3.)

15th Arr. Beginning at Gare Montparnasse, the 15th stretches all the way to the Seine. In land mass and population, it's the largest quartier of Paris, but it attracts few tourists and has few attractions, except for the Parc des Expositions and the Institut Pasteur. In the early 20th century, many artists—Chagall, Léger, and Modigliani—lived in this arrondissement in "The Beehive." (See tour 3.)

16th Arr. Originally the village of Passy, where Benjamin Franklin lived most of his years in Paris, this district is still reminiscent of Proust's world. Highlights include the Bois de Boulogne; the Jardin du Trocadéro; the Musée de Balzac; the Musée Guimet (famous for its Asian collections); and the Cimetière de Passy, resting place of Manet, Talleyrand, Giraudoux, and Debussy.

17th Arr. Although partly in the 8th, Parc Monceau flows into the 17th. This is the home of the Palais des Congrès and Porte Maillot Air Terminal.

18th Arr. The 18th is the most famous outer *quartier* of Paris, embracing Montmartre, associated with such legendary names as the Moulin Rouge, the Basilica of Sacré-Coeur, and the place du Tertre. Utrillo was its native son, Renoir lived here, and Toulouse-Lautrec adopted the area as his own. The most famous enclave of artists in Paris, the Bateau-Lavoir, of Picasso fame, gathered here. Max Jacob, Matisse, and Braque all came and went from here. Today, place Blanche is known for its prostitutes, and Montmartre is filled with honky-tonks and terrible restaurants. Go for the attractions and the *memoires*. The most famous flea market, Marché aux Puces de Saint-Ouen, is another landmark. (See tour 10.)

19th Arr. Today visitors come to what was once the village of La Villette to see the new Cité des Sciences et de l'Industrie, a spectacular science museum and park. The district also includes Les Buttes-Chaumont, a park where kids can enjoy puppet shows and donkey rides.

20th Arr. Its greatest landmark is Père-Lachaise Cemetery, resting place of Edith Piaf, Marcel Proust, Oscar Wilde, Isadora Duncan, Sarah Bernhardt, Gertrude Stein, Colette, and many, many others. (See tour 11.)

MAPS

If you're staying more than two or three days, purchase an inexpensive, pocket-size book that includes the "plan de Paris" by arrondissement available at all major newsstands and bookshops. Most of these guides provide you with a Métro map, a fold-out map of the city, and indexed maps of each arrondissement, with all streets listed and keyed.

GETTING AROUND

Paris is a city for strollers whose greatest joy in life is rambling through unexpected alleyways and squares. Given a choice of conveyance, make it your own two feet every time possible. Only when you're dead tired and can't walk another step, or in a roaring hurry to reach an exact destination, should you consider the following swift and prosaic means of urban transport.

BY PUBLIC TRANSPORTATION

DISCOUNT PASSES If you're staying for a week or longer, purchase one of several long-term passes, any of which allows unlimited travel on the city's Métro and buses within Paris city limits. Bring an ID photograph with you to apply for the card, and ask for one at any Métro ticket counter.

Another possibility is to purchase a *Le Paris-Visite* pass, a tourist pass valid for three or five days on the public transportation system, including the Métro, city buses, even RER (Réseau Express Régional) trains. (The RER contains both first- and second-class compartments, and the pass lets you travel in first class.) As a special bonus, the funicular ride to the top of Montmartre is also included. The card is available at RATP (Régie Autonome des Transports Parisiens), tourist offices, or at the main Métro stations. It can also be purchased at **Marketing Challenges,** 10 East 21st Street, New York, NY 10010 (tel. 212/529-8484).

BY SUBWAY

The **Métro** (tel. 43-46-14-14 for information) is the most efficient means of transportation, and it's easy to use. Each line is numbered and the final destination of each is clearly marked on subway maps, on the trains themselves, and in the underground passageways. Most stations display a map of the system at the entrance. Figure out the route from where you are to your destination, noting the stations

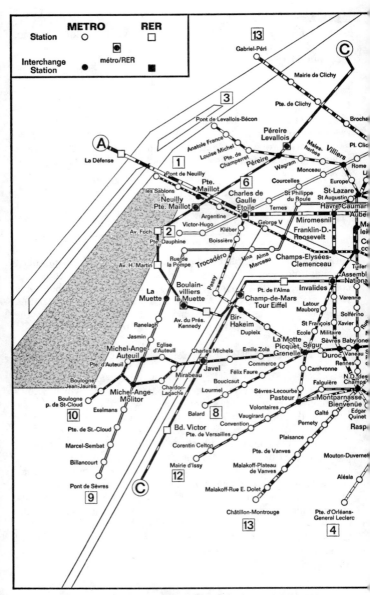

where you will have to change. To make sure you catch the right train, find your destination, then visually follow the line it's on to the end of the route and note its name. This is the *direction* you follow in the stations and see on the train. Transfer stations are known as *correspondances*. (Note that some require long walks—Châtelet is the most notorious.)

Most trips will require only one transfer. Many of the larger stations have maps with pushbutton indicators that will help you plot

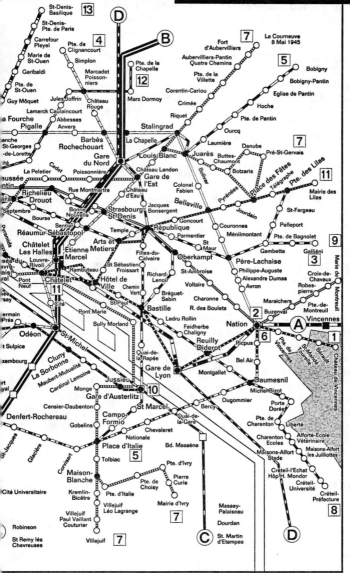

your route more easily by lighting up automatically when you press the button for your destination. A ride on the urban lines costs the same to any point.

On the Sceaux, the Noisy-Saint-Léger, and the Saint-Germain-en-Laye lines serving the suburbs, fares are based on distance. A *carnet* (ticket book) is the best buy.

You can also purchase *Formule 1,* allowing unlimited travel on the city's network of subways for one day.

At the turnstile entrances to the station, insert your ticket in the turnstile and pass through. At some exits tickets are checked, so hold on to your ticket. There are occasional ticket checks on the trains, platforms, and passageways, too.

If you are changing trains, get out and determine toward which *direction* (final destination) on the next line you want to head, and follow the bright-orange "CORRESPONDANCE" signs until you reach the proper platform. Don't follow a "SORTIE" sign, which means "Exit," or else you'll have to pay another fare to resume your journey.

The Métro starts running daily at 5:30am and closes around 1:15am. It's reasonably safe at any hour, but beware of pickpockets.

BY BUS

Bus travel is much slower than the subway. Most buses run from 6:30am to 9:15pm (a few operate until 12:30am, and a handful operate during the early-morning hours). Service is limited on Sunday and holidays. Bus and Métro fares are the same and you can use the same *carnet* tickets on both. Most bus rides require one ticket, but there are some destinations requiring two (never more than two within the city limits).

At certain bus stops, signs list the destinations and numbers of the buses serving that point. Destinations are usually listed north to south, and east to west. Most stops along the way are also posted on the sides of the buses. To catch a bus, wait in line at the bus stop. Signal the driver to stop the bus and board in order. During rush hours you may have to take a ticket from the dispensing machine, indicating your position in the line.

If you intend to use the buses frequently, pick up a RATP bus map at the office on place de la Madeleine, 8e; at the tourist offices at RATP headquarters, 53 bis, quai des Grands Augustins, 75006 Paris, or write to them ahead of time. For detailed information on bus and Métro routes, call 43-46-14-14.

BY TAXI

It's impossible to secure one at rush hour, so don't even try. Taxi drivers are strongly organized into an effective lobby to keep their number limited to 14,300.

Watch out for the common rip-offs. Always check the meter to make sure you're not paying the previous passenger's fare. Beware of cabs without meters, which often wait for tipsy patrons outside nightclubs—always settle the tab in advance. Regular cabs can be hailed on the street when their signs read "LIBRE." Taxis are easier to find at the many stands near Métro stations.

BY CAR

Don't even consider driving a car in Paris. Streets are narrow and parking is next to impossible. Besides, most visitors don't have the nerve, skill, and ruthlessness required.

If you insist on ignoring my advice, here are a few tips: Get an excellent street map and ride with a co-pilot because there's no time to think at intersections. "Zone Bleue" means that weekdays and Saturdays you can't park without a parking disc, obtainable from garages, police stations, and hotels. Parking is unrestricted in these zones Sunday and holidays. Attach the disc to your windshield, setting its clock to show the time of arrival. Between 9am and noon and from 2:30 to 5pm you may park for one hour, from noon to 2:30pm for 2½ hours.

Watch for the gendarmes, who lack patience and consistently countermand the lights. Horn-blowing is absolutely forbidden except in dire emergencies.

RENTALS The major car-rental companies usually match one another's price schedules and rental conditions. Of the major worldwide competitors, the cheapest weekly arrangements, as of this writing and subject to change, are offered by Avis and Budget, followed by Hertz and National. These relative advantages change (sometimes radically) as the categories of car become more luxurious, but in almost every case, the best deal involves a weekly rental with unlimited mileage and an advance reservation *from within North America* at least two business days in advance. Shop around before you commit yourself, knowing that it pays to ask questions.

Warning: All car-rental bills in France are subject to a 22% government tax, among the highest in Europe.

Renting a car in Paris (and France) is easy. You need a valid driver's license and must be at least 21 years old for the cheaper models, and at least 25 for the more expensive vehicles. Renters must also present a valid passport and a valid credit card unless payment is arranged in North America before leaving home. It usually isn't obligatory, but some small companies sometimes require an international driver's license.

A collision-damage waiver (CDW), will eliminate most (or all, depending on the company) of your financial responsibility in the event of theft or accidental damage to your car. It's a good idea to take it, although certain credit-card issuers will agree—if the imprint of their credit card appears on the original rental contract—to pay for any accident-related liability. (This varies broadly from company to company and must be confirmed individually with your credit-card issuer.)

Avis (tel. 800/331-1084) has offices in Paris at both Orly and Charles de Gaulle airports, as well as an inner-city headquarters at 5 rue Bixio, 7e (tel. 45-50-32-31), near the Eiffel Tower. The best rates are given to drivers who reserve a car at least two business days before leaving North America.

Budget Rent-a-Car (tel. 800/527-0700) has 29 locations inside Paris.

Hertz (tel. 800/654-3001) has about a dozen locations as well as offices at Orly and Charles de Gaulle. The company's main office in Paris is at 27 rue St-Ferdinand, 17e (tel. 45-74-97-39). A discounted weekly rental must be reserved at least two days in advance. Be sure to ask about any promotional discounts the company might be offering.

National Car Rental (tel. 800/227-3876) is represented in Paris by **Europcar,** whose largest office lies at 145 avenue Malakoff, 16e (tel. 45-00-08-06). It also has offices at both of the Paris airports and at another dozen or so locations within the city. Its headquarters can rent you a car on the spot, but to qualify for the cheaper weekly rental you must reserve at least two days in advance by calling the number above.

BY BICYCLE

To ride a bicycle through the streets and parks of Paris, perhaps with a *baguette* tucked under your arm, might have been a fantasy of yours since you saw your first Maurice Chevalier film. If the idea appeals to you, you won't be alone: The city in recent years has added many miles of right-hand lanes specifically designated for cyclists, and hundreds of bike racks scattered throughout the city. (When these aren't available, many Parisians simply chain their bike to the nearest available fence or lamp post.) Cycling is especially popular within Paris's larger parks and gardens.

One of the largest companies in Paris concerned with bicycle rentals is the **Bicy-Club,** 8 place de la Porte-de-Champerret, 17e (tel. 47-66-55-92; Métro: Porte-de-Champerret), which maintains at least a half-dozen rental outlets within the parks and gardens of the Paris region, usually on weekends and holidays between March and November. Two of the company's most popular outlets include a kiosk behind the Relais du Rois, route de Suresnes, in the Bois de Boulogne, and another kiosk in the Bois de Vincennes near the entrance to the Parc Floral, near the Esplanade du Château.

FAST FACTS: PARIS

American Express Offices are located at 11 rue Scribe, 9e (tel. 47-77-77-07), which is close to the Opéra (also the Métro stop). Hours are 9am–5:30pm Mon–Fri. The bank window is open Sat 9am–5pm, but you can't pick up mail until Monday. Other offices are at 5 rue de Chaillot, 16e (tel. 47-23-61-20; Métro: Alma-Marceau), 83 bis, rue de Courcelles, 17e (tel. 47-66-09-00; Métro: Courcelles), and 38 av. de Wagram, 8e (tel. 42-27-58-80; Métro: Ternes).

Area Code Paris's telephone area code is 1, followed by the eight-digit number. No other provinces have area codes. However, to dial long distance anywhere within France, you must first dial 16.

Banks American Express may be able to meet most of your banking needs. If not, banks in Paris are open 9am–4:30pm Mon–Fri. A few are open on Saturday. Ask at your hotel for the location of the bank nearest to you. Shops and most hotels will cash your traveler's checks, but not at the advantageous rate a bank or foreign exchange office will give you, so make sure you've allowed enough funds for *le weekend.*

Bookstores Paris has several English-language bookstores carrying American and British books and maps and guides to the city and other destinations. Try **Brentano's,** 37 av. de l'Opéra, 2e (tel. 42-61-52-50; Métro: Opéra), open Mon–Sat 10am–7pm; or **Galignani,** 224 rue de Rivoli, 1e (tel. 42-60-76-07; Métro: Tuileries), open Mon–Sat 10am–7pm. Most famous of all is **Shakespeare and Company,** 37 rue de la Bûcherie, 5e (no phone; Métro or RER: St-Michel). It's open daily 11am–midnight.

Business Hours French business hours are erratic, as befits a nation of individualists. Most **museums** close one day a week (often Tues). They are generally closed on national holidays. Usual hours are 9:30am–5pm. Some museums, particularly the smaller and less-staffed ones, close for lunch from noon–2pm. Most French museums are open Sat; many are closed Sun morning but are open Sun afternoon. Again, refer to the individual museum listings. Generally, **offices** are open Mon–Fri 9am–5pm, but don't count on it. Always call first. **Stores** are open from 9 or 9:30am (often 10am) to 6 or 7pm without a break for lunch. Some shops, particularly those operated by foreigners, open at 8am and close at 8 or 9pm. In some small stores the lunch break can last three hours, beginning at 1pm.

Cameras/Film See "Photographic Needs," below.

Cigarettes Bring in as many as Customs will allow if you're addicted to a particular brand, because American cigarettes are very expensive in France. A possible solution is to learn to smoke French cigarettes. Don't expect them to taste anything like your familiar brand, but you may acquire a liking for the exotic. One of the most popular French cigarettes is called Gauloise Bleu.

Currency Exchange For the best exchange rate, cash your traveler's checks at banks or foreign-exchange offices, not at shops and hotels. Most post offices will also change traveler's checks or convert currency. Currency exchanges are also found at Paris airports and train stations. One of the most central currency-exchange branches in Paris is at 154 av. des Champs-Elysées, 8e (tel. 42-25-93-33; Métro: George-V). It's open Mon–Fri 9am–5pm and Sat and Sun 10:30am–6pm. A small commission is charged.

Dentists If a toothache strikes you at night or in the early hours of the morning (and doesn't it always?), telephone 43-37-51-00 anytime between 8pm and 8am Mon–Fri. On Saturday, Sunday, and holidays, you can call this number day or night. You also can call or visit the **American Hospital,** 63 bd. Victor-Hugo, Neuilly (tel. 46-41-25-25). A bilingual (English-French) dental clinic is on the premises. **Métro:** Pont de Levallois or Pont de Neuilly. **Bus:** 82.

Doctors Some large hotels have a doctor attached to their staff. If yours doesn't, I recommend the **American Hospital,** 63 bd. Victor-Hugo, Neuilly (tel. 46-41-25-25). The emergency room is open 24 hours daily with 43 outpatient and inpatient specialists housed under one roof. **Métro:** Pont de Levallois or Pont de Neuilly. **Bus:** 82.

Drugstores Go to the nearest *pharmacie*. If you need a prescription during off-hours, have your concierge get in touch with the nearest Commissariat de Police. An agent there will have the address of a nearby pharmacy open 24 hours a day. French law requires that the pharmacies in any given neighborhood designate which one will remain open all night. The address of the one that will stay open for that particular week will be prominently displayed in the windows of all other drugstores. One of the most centrally located all-night pharmacies is **Pharmacy Dhery,** 84 av. des Champs-Elysées, 8e (tel. 45-62-02-41). **Métro:** George-V.

Embassies & Consulates If you lose your passport or have some such emergency, the consulate can usually handle your individual needs. An embassy is more often concerned with matters of state between France and the home country represented. Hours and offices of the various foreign embassies and consulates follow. **United States:** The embassy at 2 av. Gabriel, 75008 Paris (tel. 42-96-12-02), is open Mon–Fri 9am–4pm. Passports are issued at its consulate at 2 rue St-Florentin (tel. 42-96-12-02, ext. 2531), which lies off the northeast section of place de la Concorde (Métro: Concorde). To get a passport replaced costs about $42. In addition to its embassy and consulate in Paris, the United States also maintains the following consulates: 22 cours du Maréchal-Foch, 33080 Bordeaux (tel. 56-52-65-95); 7 quai Général-Sarrail, 69454 Lyon (tel. 72-40-50-58); 12 bd. Paul-Peytral, 13286 Marseille (tel. 91-54-92-00); and 15 av. d'Alsace, 67082 Strasbourg (tel. 88-35-31-04). **Canada:** The embassy is at 35 av. Montaigne, 75008 Paris (tel. 47-23-01-01), open Mon–Fri 9–11:30am and 2–4pm. The Canadian Consulate is around the corner at 16 rue d'Anjou (same phone). New passports are issued at the latter address (Métro: F.D. Roosevelt or Alma-Marceau). **Great Britain:** The embassy is at 35 rue du Faubourg St-Honoré, 75383 Paris (tel. 42-66-91-42), open Mon–Fri 9:30am–1pm and 2:30–6pm (Métro: Concorde or Madeleine). **Australia:** The embassy is at 4 rue Jean-Rey, 75015 Paris (tel. 40-59-33-00), open Mon–Fri 9:15am–12:15pm and 2–4:30pm (Métro: Bir-Hakeim). **New Zealand:** The embassy is at 7 bis, rue Leonard-de-Vinci, 75016 Paris (tel. 45-00-24-11), open Mon–Fri 9am–1pm and 2:30–6pm (Métro: Victor-Hugo).

Emergencies For the **police,** call 17; to **report a fire,** 18. For an ambulance, call the fire department at 45-78-74-52; a fire vehicle rushes cases to the nearest emergency room. **S.A.M.U.** (tel. 45-67-50-50) is an independently operated, privately owned ambulance company. Or contact **S.O.S. Médecin** (tel. 47-07-77-77) for a mobile doctor with car radio. You can reach the police at 9 bd. du Palais, 4e (tel. 42-60-33-22; Métro: Cité).

Etiquette If you make a reservation at a restaurant, keep it or call in good time to cancel. Always refer to your waiter as *"monsieur,"* not *"garçon."* When entering a shop or café, nod and greet strangers with a "Monsieur" or "Madame." Be aware of your voice level in public places—the French are. Refrain from smoking between courses in restaurants. Avoid discussing money, salaries, size of houses, and horsepower of U.S. cars compared with French cars. Discussions about World War II, the Algerian revolution, religion, or politics can sometimes spark violent controversy, especially at gatherings of extended families.

Eyeglasses   Lissac Brothers (Frères Lissac) is one of the city's largest chains, with at least 18 branches in greater Paris. On the Right Bank, go to 112–114 rue de Rivoli, 1e (tel. 42-33-44-77; Métro: Louvre), and on the Left, to 51 bd. St-Michel, 5e (tel. 43-54-24-07; Métro: St-Michel). There's a surcharge for same-day service. Always carry an extra pair.

Hospitals   The **American Hospital,** 63 bd. Victor Hugo, Neuilly (tel. 46-41-25-25), operates 24-hour emergency service. **Métro:** Pont de Levallos or Pont de Neuilly. **Bus:** 82.

Language   In the wake of two World Wars and many shared experiences, not to mention the influence of English movies, TV, and records, the English language has made major inroads and is almost a second language in some parts of Paris. An American trying to speak French might even be understood. The world's best-selling phrase books are published by Berlitz—*French for Travellers* has everything you'll need.

Libraries   There are many. The **American Library,** 10 rue du Général Camou, 7e (tel. 45-51-46-82; Métro: Alma-Marceau), founded in 1920, allows nonmembers to read for 30F ($5.55) per day. **Bibliothèque Publique Information,** Centre Pompidou, place Georges-Pompidou, 3e (tel. 42-77-12-33; Métro: Rambuteau), has books in English. There's also a video and listening room. You can read on the premises, but you can't check out books. It's open Mon–Fri noon–10pm and Sat and Sun 10am–10pm.

Newspapers/Magazines   English-language newspapers are available at nearly every kiosk (newsstand) in Paris. Published Monday through Saturday, the *International Herald-Tribune* is the most popular paper with visiting Americans and Canadians. Kiosks are generally open daily 8am–9pm.

Photographic Needs   All types of film are available in Paris at fairly modest prices. Unless you're going to be in France for an extended period, I don't recommend that you process your film here, for it takes time. Ask at your hotel for the nearest camera shop.

Police   Call 17. The principal Prefecture is at 7 bd. du Palais, 4e (tel. 42-60-33-22; Métro: Cité).

Post Office   The main post office (P.T.T.) for Paris is **Bureau de Poste,** 52 rue du Louvre, 75001 Paris (tel. 40-28-20-00; Métro: Louvre). Your mail can be sent here *poste restante* (general delivery) for a small fee. Take an ID, such as a passport, if you plan to pick up mail. It's open daily 8am–7pm for most services, 24 hours a day for telegrams and phone calls. Stamps can be purchased also at your hotel reception desk (usually) and at *café-tabacs* (tobacconists).

Restrooms   If you are in dire need, duck into a café or brasserie to use the lavatory. It's customary to make some small purchase if you do so. Paris Métro stations and underground garages usually contain public lavatories, but the degree of cleanliness varies. France still has many "hole-in-the-ground" toilets, so be forewarned.

Safety Whenever you're traveling in an unfamiliar city or country, stay alert. Be aware of your immediate surroundings. Wear a moneybelt and keep a close eye on your possessions. Be particularly careful with cameras, purses, and wallets, all favorite targets of thieves and pickpockets.

In Paris, be aware of child pickpockets. They roam the French capital, preying on tourists around sights such as the Louvre, Eiffel Tower, and Notre-Dame, and they especially like to pick your pockets in the Métro, sometimes blocking you off from the escalator. A band of these young thieves can clean your pockets even while you try to fend them off. Their method is to get very close to a target, ask for a handout (sometimes), and deftly help themselves to your money or passport.

Shoe Repairs Ask at your hotel for a nearby repair shop or try **Central Crepins,** 48 rue de Turbigo, 3e (tel. 42-72-68-64; Métro: Etienne-Marcel), which performs at least some of its sewing by hand and does very competent repair work. It's open Mon–Fri. Or try **La Cordonnerie Pulin,** 5 rue Chaveau-Lagarde, 8e (tel. 42-65-08-57; Métro: Madeleine), open Mon–Sat; closed Aug.

Telegrams/Telex/Fax Telegrams may be sent from any Paris post office during the day (see "Post Office," above) and anytime from the 24-hour central post office. In sending telegrams to the United States, the address is counted in the price, there are no special rates for a certain number of words, and night telegrams cost less. If you're in Paris and wish to send a telegram in English, call 42-33-44-11. The 24-hour public Telex office in Paris is at 103 rue de Grenelle, 7e (tel. 45-50-34-34; Métro: rue-du-Bac). By phone, you can dictate a Telex by calling 42-47-12-12. You can also send Telex and Fax messages at the main post office in each arrondissement of Paris.

Telephone Public phone booths are found in cafés, restaurants, Métro stations, post offices, airports, and train stations and occasionally on the streets. Some of these booths work with tokens called *jetons,* which can be purchased at the post office or from the cashier at any café. (It's usually customary to give a small tip if you buy them at a café.) Pay telephones accept coins of ½, 1, 2, and 5F; the minimum charge is 1F (20¢). Pick up the receiver, insert the *jeton* or coins, and dial when you hear the tone, pushing the button when there is an answer. The French also use a *telecarte,* a telephone debit card, which can be purchased at rail stations, post offices, and other places. Sold in two versions, it allows callers to use 50 or 120 charge units by inserting the card in a phone booth. They cost 40F ($7.40) and 96F ($17.75), respectively.

If possible, avoid making calls from your hotel, which might double or triple the charges.

When you're calling long distance within France, dial 16, wait for the dial tone, and then dial the eight-digit number of the person or place you're calling. To reach Paris from one of the Provinces, dial 16 and 1, then the eight digit number. To call the U.S. or Canada, first dial 19, listen for the tone, then slowly dial 1, the area code, and the seven-digit number. To place a collect call to North America, dial 19-33-11, and an English-speaking operator will assist you. Dial 19-00-11 for an American AT&T operator.

For information, dial 12.

Time French summer time lasts from around April to September, and runs one hour ahead of French winter time. Depending on the time of year, France is six or seven hours ahead of Eastern Standard Time in the United States.

Tipping Tipping is practiced with flourish and style in France, and, as a visitor, you're expected to play the game. All bills, as required by law, show *service compris*, which means the tip is included; customary practices of additional gratuities are as follows.

Waiters: In restaurants, cafés, and nightclubs, service is included; however, it is customary to leave something extra, especially in first-class and deluxe establishments, where 10% to 12% extra is often the rule. In inexpensive places, 8% to 10% will suffice.

Porters: Usually a fixed fee is assessed, about 5F (95¢) to 10F ($1.85) per piece of luggage. You're not obligated to give more; however, many French people do, ranging from .50F (10¢) to 2F (35¢).

Theater ushers: Give at least 2F (35¢) for seating up to two persons.

Hairdressers: The service charge is most often included; otherwise, tip at least 15%, more in swankier places.

Guides: In museums, guides expect 5F (95¢) to 10F ($1.85).

Cloakroom attendants: Often the price is posted; if not, give at least 2F (35¢) to 5F (95¢).

Hotels: The service charge is added, but tip the bellboy extra—from 6F ($1.10) to 20F ($3.70) for three bags (more in deluxe and first-class hotels). A lot depends on how much luggage he has carried and the class of the establishment. Tip the concierge based entirely on how many requests you've made of him or her. Give the maid about 20F ($3.70) if you've stayed for three or more days. The doorman who summons a cab expects another 5F (95¢), likewise your room-service waiter, even though you've already been hit for 15% service. Incidentally, most small services around the hotel should be rewarded with a 5F (95¢) tip.

Transit Info For information on the city's public transportation, stop in at either of the two offices of the Services Touristiques de la RATP—at 53 bis, quai des Grands-Augustins, 6e (tel. 40-46-42-12; Métro: St-Michel), or at place de la Madeleine, 8e (tel. 43-46-14-14; Métro: Madeleine).

Useful Telephone Numbers Police 17; fire 18; emergency medical assistance 15.

Yellow Pages As in North America, the *Yellow Pages* are immensely useful. Your hotel will almost certainly have a copy, but you'll need the help of a French-speaking resident before tackling the French Telephone Company's (PTT's) *Yellow Pages.*

Some words aren't too different from the English. *Pharmacie* (pharmacy), *antiquités* (antiques), *théâtres* (theaters), and *objets d'art* may be easy to decipher. But other words, such as *cordonniers* (shoemakers and shoe-repair shops) and *horlogerie* (watch-repair shop), might be less obvious. Ask someone at the reception desk of your hotel for translations if needed.

Don't ever assume that someone on the other end of the phone speaks English. You may have to ask a French-speaking person to make the call for you.

WALKING TOUR 1

The Quays of the Seine

Start: The intersection of rue des Prêtres-St-Germain-l'Auxerrois and rue de l'Amiral-de-Coligny. (Métro: Louvre-Rivoli or Pont-Neuf.)
Finish: Pont Neuf.
Time: Two to three hours, depending on how much time you spend in churches, shops, and museums.
Best Time: Any time of day, but if you're interested in shopping at the bookstalls along the quay, or in any of the shops for that matter, it's best to go in the early afternoon.

A relatively straightforward, short walk along the Seine is probably just what you need on your first day in Paris. You'll get your bearings by visiting parts of both the Right and Left bank neighborhoods that border the river, and you'll get to see some of the loveliest views in all of Paris.

This romantic stroll takes you by interesting shops, wonderful mansions, and the oldest church in Paris. Try to imagine as you walk what the banks of the river were like before the quays were built—when the houses here overhung the Seine and the river was the center of trade and commerce.

From where you're standing, go into place du Louvre, where you'll find:

1. St-Germain l'Auxerrois at 2 place du Louvre, a church named for Germain, the bishop of Auxerre, a "healer" who was so good at curing people that he is said to have raised disciples from the dead.

Of the original structure, built in the Romanesque style, only the 12th-century tower still stands. A feature on the exterior is the Gothic porch on the west side of the church. The porch is one of only two of its kind in the entire city of Paris, and given the number of churches you're going to discover while walking these tours during your stay in Paris, you'll find that to be a somewhat amazing fact (The other is on the Sainte-Chapelle). Also note from the outside the bell tower. The 38-bell carillon was the only one in the city of Paris saved from the melting pots of the Revolution. It was the very same carillon (along with the Tour de l'Horloge on the Ile de la Cité) that rang out the signal that began the massacre of St. Bartholemew's Day, when the Catholics butchered over 3,000 sleeping Huguenots.

The organ case on the interior came from the Sainte-Chapelle and was constructed in 1756. The royal pew, canopy and all, was made by Charles Le Brun for the royal family in 1684.

The architect Louis Le Vau and sculptor Antoine Coysevox are buried within the church. Molière was married here, and this is also where he had his son baptized.

Continue around and back out to quai du Louvre. Turn left along quai du Louvre, and on your right you'll see the Louvre. We won't be going into the Louvre on this tour; instead, go left across the:

2. **Pont des Arts,** a pedestrian bridge. Take this opportunity to stand in the middle of it and take in the views in both directions (Notre Dame is on your left as you cross).

The bridge, which took its name from the Palais des Arts (the original name of the Louvre), was built between 1802 and 1804 as a pedestrian toll bridge. The first cast-iron bridge built in Paris, it was a pleasure to walk across then because of the wonderful gardens that were maintained on it. You are not standing on the original bridge, which was closed in 1970 because it was considered too dangerous. It was reopened after a two-year restoration project (1982–84) and the only major differences are that this one is built of steel and has only five, rather than the original nine, arches, making it more navigable to boats and barges.

Just as you come across the bridge, directly in front of you is the:

3. **Palais de l'Institut de France,** at 23 quai de Conti. Louis Le Vau is responsible for this masterwork, which he designed specifically to line up with the Cour Carrée directly across the pont des Arts. It took nearly 30 years to construct (1663–91) but was well worth the wait.

One of the academic groups that calls this palace home is the Académie Française, which was founded by Richelieu in 1635 specifically to compile and update a dictionary of the French language. There are only 40 members, and in order for someone new to be elected, someone must first die, and the electee must write the eulogy for his predecessor. Many people imagine members of the Académie have included France's best writers, but that's not necessarily true—Baudelaire, Proust, and Flaubert were never admitted. The fact is that it's rare for a great writer to be admitted at all. Basically, if you sat in on one of the meetings what you'd probably find is a bunch of old guys arguing over which words should be included in the dictionary.

Here too, in the same building, is the Mazarin library. It was with Cardinal Mazarin's money that the Palais de l'Institut de France was built, and his books are housed in the East Pavilion of the building. Mazarin's private library became the first public library in France in 1643, when he decided to open it to scholars once a week initially and eventually every day of the week. Surprisingly, during the Revolution, the collection was significantly enlarged because any books that were confiscated from private collections or from churches were added to Mazarin's already grand collection. It's next to impossible to gain access to the library unless you are a student or permanent scholar there, so it's best not to try, but do walk around and view the architectural design elements within the building, especially the magnificent staircase.

Right next door to the Institut (to the right if you're facing the river) is the:

4. **Hôtel de la Monnaie** (The Mint), at 11 quai de Conti. Quai de Conti, built between 1650 and 1760, was named for a family of princes that used to live in a building that occupied the spot on which the Mint now stands.

Hôtel de la Monnaie, built between 1771 and 1777 in the Louis XVI style of architecture, was designed by J. D. Antoine. It was his first important work, and he lived in the building from the time it was completed until his death. In front you'll see enormous Ionic columns and six allegorical statues that represent Prudence, Might, Justice, Trade, Peace, and Plenty. The statues were sculpted by Pigalle, Mouchy, and Lecomte.

From about 1878 to 1973 all French coins and medals were minted here. Currently there are only two active workshops, but you can go in and visit if you're interested in how it's all done.

Continue straight ahead on quai de Conti. At number 1 you'll come to the spot known as the:

5. **Curie intersection,** so-called because Pierre Curie, the scientist and husband of Marie Curie, was killed on this spot in 1906 by a runaway horse and carriage.

Also here, at the corner of quai de Conti and rue Dauphine, was the original Café Anglais, the first establishment in Paris to offer English newspapers and pamphlets and a favorite hangout of English writers.

Continue ahead onto the oldest quay in Paris, the:

6. **Quai des Grands-Augustins.** Built in 1313 under Philippe le Bel, the quay was named for one of the largest monasteries in France.

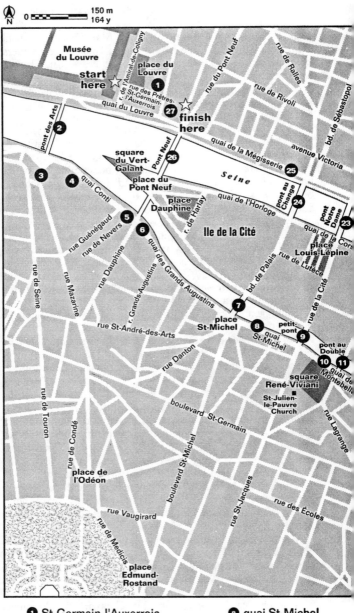

1 St-Germain-l'Auxerrois
2 pont des Arts
3 Palais de l'Institut de France
4 Hôtel de la Monnaie
5 Curie intersection
6 Quai des Grandes-Augustins
7 pont St-Michel
8 quai St-Michel
9 petit-pont
10 quai de Montebello
11 pont au Double
12 bouquinistes
13 quai de la Tournelle
14 pont de la Tournelle

THE QUAYS OF THE SEINE

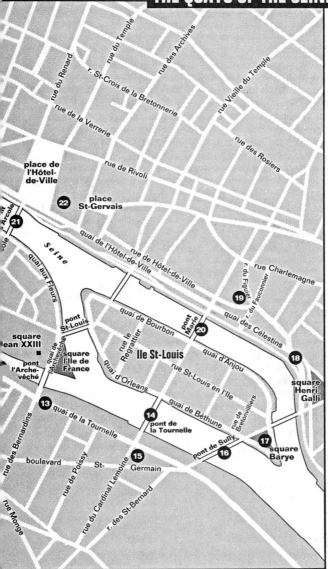

15 La Tour d'Argent
16 pont de Sully
17 square Barye
18 quai des Célestins
19 Hôtel de Sens
20 pont Marie
21 pont d'Arcole

22 Hôtel de Ville
23 pont Notre Dame
24 pont au Change
25 quai de la Mégisserie
26 Pont Neuf
27 La Samaritaine

Originally established in the 13th century by Saint Louis, the Saint-Augustin friars settled in the area in 1293. In 1588 a papal reform divided the monastery into the Grands and Petits Augustins. The Petits Augustins were forced to leave, but the Grands Augustins remained. Unfortunately, the monastery and its Gothic church were destroyed during the Revolution in 1797.

At number 51 you should note the Lapérouse restaurant, which dates from the end of the 18th century.

Continue down to place St-Michel and:

7. Pont St-Michel, which was named for the no longer extant Palace Chapel (dedicated to the Archangel Michel) in which Philippe Auguste was baptized in 1165.

If you look from the bridge to the right as you walk along the river, across the place St-Michel, you'll see a fountain that depicts Saint Michel slaying the dragon, designed by Gabriel Davioud between 1856 and 1860. The fountain is 75 feet high and 15 feet wide.

Continue along and you'll be headed onto:

8. Quai St-Michel. Built between 1812 and 1816, the quai St-Michel supplanted some row houses that used to overhang the river. Matisse had his studio at number 19 quai St-Michel, and it was from his window in 1914 that he painted several times the famous view that includes Notre Dame, the Petit-Pont, and the top of the Sainte-Chapelle.

Just a bit farther along the quai St-Michel, on the right, is the alley rue du Chat-qui-Pêche. There's nothing to see here, except for some garbage cans, but it does happen to be the narrowest street in Paris, and it existed even before the quay was built. Legend has it that before the quay was built the Seine would sometimes rise above its banks, flooding the cellars of the buildings that used to be here, and an enterprising neighborhood cat would take advantage of its good fortune and go fishing within the confines of the cellars—hence the street's name.

Continue to the end of quai St-Michel and you'll be at:

9. Petit-Pont, aptly named because at 131 feet it is the shortest bridge in Paris. Built under the direction of Bishop Maurice de Sully in 1186, the Petit-Pont was destroyed 11 times by fire and flood; the present bridge has been standing since the 19th century.

After you pass the Petit-Pont you'll be on the:

10. Quai de Montebello, built between 1811 and 1813 to commemorate Maréchal Lannes, duc de Montebello, who was killed at Essling, Austria, in 1809.

As you walk, look to your right, and you'll see the current Shakespeare & Company, which carries on the legacy of Sylvia Beach's original Shakespeare & Company (more about Shakespeare & Company in Walking Tour 4, stop 25). Inside this cramped bookstore you'll find a wide selection of books in English and (up a very steep, very narrow flight of stairs) part of Sylvia Beach's personal library. You're welcome to sit up there on the makeshift sofas and browse for as long as you like.

Turn right when exiting Shakespeare & Company, and a few steps down on your right you'll see St-Julien-le-Pauvre, one of the oldest churches in Paris. Next door to that is the square René-Viviani in which there's a false acacia that's supposedly the oldest tree in Paris (you'll know it by the concrete blocks that are holding it up).

Just beyond the square René-Viviani is:

11. Pont au Double, so named because of the double toll that was once imposed on those visiting the sick wards of the Hôtel Dieu, which occupied part of the bridge—one toll as they entered, and another as they departed. As you can imagine, back then the river was a convenient spot in which to dump hospital waste. Thankfully, the hospital sick wards were gone by 1835. The present bridge dates from 1882 and is made of cast iron.

Continue on quai de Montebello where you'll see some of the:

12. Bouquinistes, or booksellers. Situated right on the banks of the Seine these green bookstalls represent one of Paris's oldest markets. (They were originally located on the Pont Neuf but were evicted in 1650.) Here you'll find everything from postcards to the works of Balzac. Most of the bouquinistes sell the things they like, which means that they're generally very knowledgeable about their stock—some even have a specialty, although many lament that the bouquinistes are not what they used to be.

Even so, a host of famous writers and artists have haunted the stalls of the bouquinistes; imagine them wandering along checking out the books. Hemingway was spotted here on many occasions—it was one of his favorite spots in the whole city.

Note that the bouquinistes don't usually open until after 11am and close before 7pm, so if they're closed, try to stop back later in the day or another day because the quay is a lot more active and exciting when they are open.

As you continue along you'll come to pont de l'Archevêché, which provides one of the best, if not the best, view of Notre Dame. After passing the Pont de l'Archevêché you will find yourself on:

13. Quai de la Tournelle. Built in 1554 as the quai des Bernaldins, it became quai de la Tournelle in 1750, named after the tower that was part of Philippe Auguste's wall in the Middle Ages.

On your right at number 47 is the Musée de l'Assistance Publique (Museum of Public Health and Welfare). Housed in a 17th-century mansion, it was once used as the central pharmacy for all Parisian hospitals. In 1934 the museum was established; it holds an interesting collection of old pharmaceutical containers and implements, including such items as apothecary jars and surgery kits (the surgical kit of Dupuytren among them). Its displays of historical documents and various paintings will give you a good idea of how hospitals developed and how they were run. It will probably make you grateful for modern medicine!

Head along to:

14. Pont de la Tournelle, which like many of the city's bridges was originally built of wood. When it was washed away by the rising waters of the Seine, a new plan for a stone bridge that aligned with the Pont Marie was implemented, in 1656. It was later widened, and in 1928 the tower with the statue of Sainte Geneviève (Paris's patron saint) was erected.

On your right at 15 quai de la Tournelle, just past the bridge, is the famous 16th-century restaurant,

15. La Tour d'Argent. Opened during the reign of Henry III in 1582 named after the tower of the Conciergerie on the Ile de la Cité across the river, La Tour d'Argent is still one of Paris's most prestigious restaurants. The wine cellars here are legendary, and so are the prices ($120 for a slice of pâté de foie gras).

Since the Tour d'Argent has been open for 400 years, it's only fitting that it has opened a gastronomic museum, located on the ground floor.

Continue along the quai de la Tournelle to:

16. Pont de Sully. The most interesting thing about the Pont de Sully, named for Maximilien de Béthune, duc de Sully, is that it is actually two separate metal bridges that rest on the tip of the Ile St-Louis, and it's the only one constructed in that way. (*Note:* If you're a fan of modern sculpture, I would suggest continuing on a little farther to the Musée de Sculpture en Plein Air (Open-Air Sculpture Museum) before crossing the Pont de Sully.)

Note on your right before you cross the bridge, the building that houses the Institut du Monde Arabe—one of very few examples of modern architecture in Paris.

Cross pont de Sully. When you reach the other side of the bridge, note the small park on your right:

17. Square Barye, named for Antoine-Louis Barye (1796–1875), who is best known for his animal sculptures. He acquired most of his knowledge of animals while employed by a goldsmith who required him to make models of animals at the Jardin des Plantes between 1823 and 1831. Barye particularly enjoyed sculpting animals in an aggressive, violent, or tense posture—a tradition of the Romantic movement.

Go left after crossing the bridge around square Henri-Galli, onto:

18. Quai des Célestins, built in the latter half of the 14th century, under Charles V. Its original name was quai des Ourmetiaux, but it was renamed in 1868 for the Célestin convent which was destroyed during the Revolution.

On the corner of rue du Petit-Musc is Hôtel Fieubet (now l'École Masillion), an extraordinary building guarded by the first sphinxes ever seen in Paris. A bit farther on is number 4, where Antoine-Louis Barye died in 1875.

Continue walking along quai des Célestins. At rue St-Paul there is an interesting garden shop that sells outdoor sculpture and furniture, among other things. Stop in and take a look.

When you get to rue du Fauconnier go right and head up to rue du Figuier. Go left to number 1, rue du Figuier, the:

19. Hôtel de Sens, a prime example of medieval Parisian civic architecture, built between 1474 and 1475 as a "fortified mansion." Originally used as a stronghold for La Ligue (a group that unified the Catholics against the Calvinists), then owned by the bishops of Sens, it was later rented to art students and jam makers who practically destroyed the interior. In 1916 the city took it over, and finally in 1936, after much controversy, a restoration project was begun that took 26 years to complete. Presently the Hôtel de Sens houses the Bibliothèque Forney. Open Tuesday through Saturday, the library specializes in the fine arts, including decorative arts, crafts, and architecture. Exhibitions featuring the library's own collection are held frequently. Even if you're not interested in looking at the books in the library, do enter the gate into the courtyard and have a look at the ornate stone decoration within.

Go back the way you came to quai des Célestins. Turn right and walk past:

20. Pont Marie, a humpback bridge with five arches. Originally the bridge had some houses built along the sides of it, but in 1658 two of the arches collapsed and 22 houses disappeared into the river with them. Since 1788 there have been very few changes to the bridge.

After you pass pont Marie you'll be on the quai de l'Hôtel-de-Ville. On your left note the:

21. Pont d'Arcole, named for a young man who was killed in 1830 during a protest outside the Hôtel de Ville (see below). As he was dying he begged, "Remember that my name is d'Arcole." Well, somebody remembered, but it wasn't until 68 years later that the bridge was renamed. Originally built as a pedestrian suspension toll bridge in 1828, it was replaced by an iron footbridge in 1954.

To your right is the place de l'Hôtel-de-Ville. Head into the place de l'Hôtel-de-Ville and you'll be in front of the:

22. Hôtel de Ville, Paris's grand city hall. The place de l'Hôtel-de-Ville (originally place de Grève) was a prime site for many of the executions that were carried out from 1313 to 1830. Catherine de Médicis, apparently not satisfied with the thousands already killed in the St. Bartholomew's Day Massacre, had two Huguenot leaders hanged here. This was also the place where Henry IV's murderer Ravaillac was executed, and where witches were burned alive. Throughout history, it has seen all kinds of celebrations, rebellions, and strikes.

After coming back out of the Hôtel de Ville, continue around the quays on quai de Gesvres (which used to be the place where butchers came to slaughter their animals) along to:

23. Pont Notre Dame, which was once Paris's most fashionable bridge. The reason? There were two. First, it was here that Paris made its first attempt at a numbering system and, as a result, all of the houses on the bridge were stylishly numbered in gold. Second, it was the royal entryway into Paris.

Continue along to:

24. Pont au Change, so named because it was rebuilt in 1141 by the city's money changers and goldsmiths, at the orders of Louis VII. It was originally known as the King's Bridge because it was the royal route to Notre Dame, and when the king crossed the bridge the bird sellers from the nearby bird and flower market would release thousands of birds to honor his presence.

At the pont au Change the quai de Gesvres turns into the:

25. Quai de la Mégisserie. For 500 years, city tanners came here to cure their leather. There are still bird and flower markets here, and as you walk you can busy yourself by checking out the different types of birds, from chickens to doves, and the garden and flower shops—perhaps you'd like to purchase some tulip bulbs direct from Holland at one of them.

At the end of quai de la Mégisserie you'll come to the:

26. Pont Neuf, the oldest and most famous bridge in Paris. Henry III laid the first stone on May 31, 1578, but was long gone by the time it was finished and officially opened 29 years later—by Henry IV in 1607. It was the first stone bridge built that wasn't lined with houses. With a total of 12 arches, the pont Neuf is actually two bridges (that don't quite line up)—one stretching from the Right Bank to the Ile de la Cité, the other stretching from the Left Bank. Originally it served as a lively social center where Parisians went to do their banking, be entertained by jokers and street performers, and even have their teeth pulled.

We're almost to the end of the tour now and you're probably ready for a break, so you might want to make a stop.

REFRESHMENT STOP Stop in at **Taverne Henri IV,** 13 place du Pont-Neuf, a 17th-century building that houses one of Paris's most famous wine bars. Named after the statue of Henri IV you can see in the middle of Pont Neuf, it serves bistro-style food at moderate prices, as well as a full selection of wines.

To get to the restaurant, go left to the middle of the Pont Neuf. It will be on your left.

From the tavern go back across the bridge to the quai de la Mégisserie. Go left, and you'll see:

27. La Samaritaine, the biggest department store in Paris. It was named after the Pont Neuf water pump that used to carry water to the Jardin des Tuileries (the pump was named and decorated in honor of the woman of Samaria who offered Jesus a drink of water). La Samaritaine has everything and anything you might be looking for, from hats to belts and kitchen to bath.

The architectural history of the buildings that comprise the store spans about 30 years (from 1900 to 1930), but the real attraction in the glass- and iron-front main store is the art nouveau ironwork staircase. If you head up to the ninth floor you'll be treated to a spectacular panoramic view of the city.

When you're finished shopping come out of the department store, and you can either go right back to where we started this tour or head over the pont Neuf and begin the next walking tour, which is a tour of the Islands.

WALKING TOUR 2

Ile de la Cité & Ile St-Louis

Start: Métro station at the Pont Neuf.
Finish: Square Barye.
Time: About three hours.
Best Time: Any time during the day.

As you begin your walk on the Ile de la Cité you'll be following in the footsteps of the men and women who are responsible for the city's very beginnings. This is the place where the Romans put down their roots, and this is the place out of which the wonderful city of Paris exploded.

Tourists love the Ile de la Cité because it's where the spires of two of the world's most incredible churches, the Sainte-Chapelle and Notre Dame, soar to the sky. You can visit the former royal prisons and today's courts of law, walk through a huge flower and bird market, and stand on the spot that marks the very center of Paris.

As you cross from Ile de la Cité to Ile St-Louis you'll pass by the flying buttresses of Notre Dame, and you'll be able to visit one of the most moving monuments to the victims of the Holocaust that you'll ever encounter.

Once on the Ile St-Louis, you'll be transported back to a time when Paris was more quiet and residential. You'll walk by some of the most sought-after pieces of real estate in all of Paris and you'll come across current residents who rarely even step off the island. Here you'll find the places where Baudelaire's hashish club met, where Chopin played, and where the writer James Jones once lived.

Hopefully, when you finish this tour you will feel like you've gained an idea of the way Paris once was, and you'll be thankful to know that on these small islands a good deal of the distant past still remains intact.

From the Métro station walk about halfway out on the Pont Neuf. Go left down the stairs behind the statue of Henri IV (which was erected by Louis XVIII using bronze melted down from a statue of Napoléon that originally stood atop the column in the place Vendôme) into the:

1. Square du Vert-Galant. *Vert Galant,* or "Gay Blade," was Henri IV's nickname. This is a great place to sit and have a picnic—you'll be just about as close to the river as you can get without actually being in it. A baguette, some cheese, something from a trip to the charcuterie, and a bottle of wine in this shady, secluded park—what could be better. On summer weekend afternoons crowds can fill the park, but for the most part you'll find yourself with enough privacy here. Absorb the view of the Louvre and the Hôtel de la Monnaie (see Walking Tour 1, stop 4 for more information about the latter). Tourist boats that will take you on a trip along the Seine also depart from here.

Come back up the stairs and cross the Pont Neuf. Go between the buildings and you'll be in:

2. Place Dauphine, which many believe to be the most quaint square in Paris. Originally the Ile de la Cité was three separate islands. In 1607 when the islands were joined, the result was the place Dauphine. Have a little walk around the square—you won't find a quieter one in all the city. Note that Ludovic Halévy, the French author who was the librettist of *Carmen,* died at number 26 in 1908. Imagine yourself here in 1660, when Louis XIV and Marie Thérèse visited the Ile de la Cité and a gateway made entirely of sugar was placed in the place Dauphine, along with a carousel, specifically to honor their visit.

Another significant event that occurred here was in 1728, when Jean-Baptiste-Siméon Chardin (1699–1779), one of the greatest French masters of still-life painting, first showed the painting *La Raie* (The Rayfish, now at the Louvre).

Ahead of you is the Palais de Justice. Go left on rue de Harlay to quai de l'Horloge. Go right. Look up at the various towers on the side of the:

3. Palais de Justice and the **Conciergerie,** on the right side of the street as you walk.

The Palais de Justice, originally the Palais de la Cité (or the royal palace, erected in the Middle Ages) served as home to France's medieval kings. Philippe Auguste was born here, and Philippe le Bel enlarged the palace. By the mid-14th century, the king chose to spend less time here and more time at the Louvre; the move was made permanent when in 1358 Charles V saw his entire staff killed by a mob led by Etienne Marcel. After Charles V fled, the buildings were used as the royal prison and court. In 1618 and 1776 the buildings were ravaged by fire; the only remaining medieval structure is the Sainte-Chapelle (see below).

The first tower that you'll see on your right is the Tour de Bonbec, known as the "babbler" because the torture inflicted here was so intense. Prisoners were subjected to having their legs squeezed between two planks, or having ropes tied progressively tighter and tighter around different parts of their bodies until they cut into the skin. The oldest form of torture used here was a trap door in the floor that opened into a pit of razor-sharp spikes.

The next tower, the Tour d'Argent, is also where the crown jewels were stored at one time. The third tower, the Tour de César, is where Ravaillac, assassin of Henry IV, was held—and presumably tortured—while awaiting his execution.

During the Revolution, the prisons of this building, now called the Conciergerie, were used as holding cells during the tribunals. Marie Antoinette was held here before her execution. Others held here prior to execution included Robespierre and Danton. You can go into the Conciergerie and see the old prisons. The entrance is at 1 quai de l'Horloge.

On the corner of quai de l'Horloge and boulevard du Palais you will also see the Tour de l'Horloge, the site of Paris's first public clock. (The one you see today is not the original, and it is nonworking.) The Tour de l'Horloge is also the tower from which the signal for the St. Bartholomew's Day Massacre was given. Bells sounded, and at the alarm, the Catholics ran through the streets, killing several thousand Protestants.

Go right at the corner here to the entrance of the Palais de Justice—the site of Paris's present-day courts of law. Go right into the Cour du Mai (the May Courtyard), which is named for the trees from the royal forest that were planted here (they're long gone by now). This is the exact spot where prisoners such as Marie Antoinette and Robespierre had to wait before being led to the place de la Concorde for their executions. Visitors are allowed to enter the present courtrooms in the Palais de Justice.

To your left you'll see the:

4. Sainte-Chapelle. The Sainte-Chapelle is the oldest part of the Palais de Justice complex and was built by Saint Louis to house two significant religious artifacts, a piece of Christ's original cross and the Crown of Thorns (which have since been moved to Notre Dame and are only on view on Good Friday). Most of what you see today does not date back to the church's completion 700 years ago, but there are tombstones set in the floor that date from the 14th and 15th centuries; much of the sculpture, spire, doors, and paintings date from the 19th century. However, the real reason to visit the Sainte-Chapelle (and, yes, it is worth standing in the long line that always forms in front of the church) is to see the 15 astonishing, immense (50 feet high by 14 feet wide) stained glass windows. About half of the glass in the windows dates back to the 13th century; the rest is an extremely careful 19th-century restoration. The windows actually illustrate the Bible, from Genesis to the crucifixion of Christ. To "read" the windows chronologically would likely take several years, but if you do try to read them, you should start to the left of the entrance and read clockwise around the church, reading each window from the bottom to the top. Some of the windows show the construction of the church, and the great Rose Window is meant to depict the Apocalypse. There are 1,134 scenes in the windows, and they are stunning.

As you come out of the Sainte-Chapelle, cross boulevard du Palais diagonally to your left and you'll be at rue de Lutèce. Turn right on rue de Lutèce and walk to the:

5. Cité Métro station, which will be on your left. This original Art Nouveau dragonfly "Métropolitain" station, which looks sort of like the entrance to the Bat Cave, dates back to 1900. Designed by Hector Guimard (1867–1942), the plantlike forms are made of cast iron and are considered to be Guimard's most inspired works. There are only a few originals left.

Located just beyond the Métro station is:

6. Place Louis-Lépine, where every day (except Sunday) a flower market is held. On Sunday the flower market becomes a bird market, carrying on the long tradition of bird sellers in Paris. Take a leisurely stroll through here, whether it's bird day or flower day.

After you've gone through the market you should end up on rue de la Cité. Go right and on your left you'll see the:

7. Hôtel Dieu. Built from 1866 to 1878 in neo-Florentine style by Diet, the Hôtel Dieu is the main hospital for the center of Paris. The site was previously occupied by an orphanage.

As you continue along, on your right you'll see the:

8. Préfecture de Police. Here in the old barracks of the Palais de la Cité, the police joined in the resistance against the Nazis in 1944 by twice locking themselves inside—once on August 19, and the second time on August 26. Almost 300 were killed.

When you get to the corner, go left into another square and you'll see the entrance (to your right if you're facing Notre Dame) of the:

9. Crypte du Parvis Notre Dame. If you're interested in archaeology, you will want to stop and visit the excavations of what used to be the central square of the Ile de la Cité (discovered during excavations for an underground parking lot), which include Roman walls dating from approximately A.D. 300.

To help you visualize what kinds of buildings once stood here, there are some scale models that show how the city of Paris grew from a small settlement to a Roman city.

Emerge from the Crypte and head toward Notre Dame. You are in the:

10. Place du Parvis-Notre-Dame. To your right is a statue of Charlemagne that dates from approximately 1882.

In 1768 it was announced that a spot at the far end of the place du Parvis, just in front of Notre Dame, would be the starting point of all national highways that connect Paris to other points in the country. As a result, it has since been called *kilomètre zéro.* You are literally standing at the center of Paris.

Continue through the square up to:

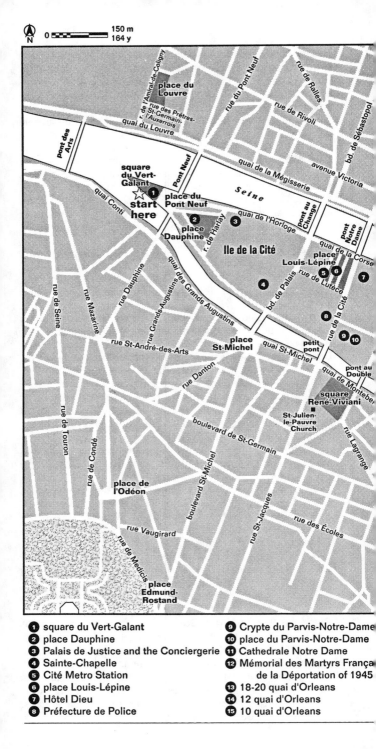

0 — 150 m / 164 y

1 square du Vert-Galant
2 place Dauphine
3 Palais de Justice and the Conciergerie
4 Sainte-Chapelle
5 Cité Metro Station
6 place Louis-Lépine
7 Hôtel Dieu
8 Préfecture de Police
9 Crypte du Parvis-Notre-Dame
10 place du Parvis-Notre-Dame
11 Cathedrale Notre Dame
12 Mémorial des Martyrs Françai de la Déportation of 1945
13 18-20 quai d'Orleans
14 12 quai d'Orleans
15 10 quai d'Orleans

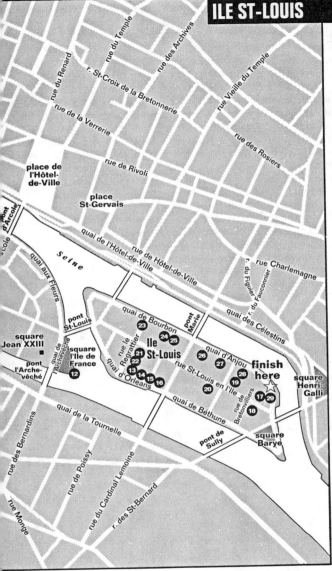

ILE DE LA CITE & ILE ST-LOUIS

16 Musée Adam Mickiewicz
17 Hôtel Lambert
18 5 rue St-Louis-en-l'Ile
19 Librairie Libella
20 St-Louis-en-l'Ile
21 6 rue Le Regrattier
22 2 rue Le Regrattier
23 headless statue

24 plaque commemorating
   Camille Claudel
25 15 quai de Bourbon
26 37 quai d'Anjou
27 29 quai d'Anjou
28 Hôtel Lauzun
29 9 quai d'Anjou

11. Cathédrale Notre Dame. In 1160, Maurice de Sully, then the bishop of Paris, had an idea to build one immense, incredible church to replace two—old Notre Dame as well as Saint-Etienne. Three years later the work began on the cathedral you see today. You can probably appreciate the fact that it took almost 200 years to complete—construction ended in 1359.

Unfortunately, little of the interior furnishings of the church remain, because Notre Dame was badly damaged and stripped of valuables during the Revolution. It was some time during this period in history that all the stained glass windows were removed and replaced with clear glass, and the walls were whitewashed. It wasn't until the 1830s and 1840s that anyone bothered to do anything to restore the church. Victor Hugo's *The Hunchback of Notre Dame* (1831) played a large role in generating public interest in the church and, finally, stimulating a restoration project. In 1844 Louis Philippe ordered the restoration of the cathedral. (You'll notice that the exterior of Notre Dame is again being cleaned and restored).

Inside, don't miss the rose windows (some stained glass inside was salvaged and does date from the 13th century); the sculptures by Coustou and Coysevox in the choir; the Robert de Cotte choir stalls; and Cliquot's organ, which dates from 1730. In the Treasury of Notre Dame the gold, enamel, and jeweled relics brought back by Saint Louis from the Crusades can be viewed for a small fee. You should also go upstairs and take in Paris from aloft—the view is unparalleled.

Throughout the ages Notre Dame has served as a central meeting place for all of Paris. Wonderfully extravagant banquets were often held inside; the church's doors were always open to weary travelers who needed a place to stay. Philippe le Bel once even rode into the church on horseback, and it was here in 1431 that Henri VI was crowned king. In 1779, Louis XIV dowered 100 young women and married them off here en masse. In 1793, during a particularly impious period in Paris history, a belly dancer was placed on the high altar and the saints in the niches were replaced by statues of the likes of Voltaire and Rousseau. And let us not forget that it was here in 1804 that Napoléon Bonaparte, in the presence of Pope Pius VII, crowned himself emperor and his wife, Josephine, empress.

The sheer beauty and force of the building, with its sculpture-encrusted facade, gargoyles, and flying buttresses (erected in the 14th century) at the back have brought many a wayward Catholic back to his or her religion. The sense of awe felt all over the world for this great Gothic work of art crosses all religious lines.

Come back out of Notre Dame and, facing away from the cathedral, go left. You'll pass several street portraitists and caricaturists. Go left through the gate into square Jean XXIII and around the back of the cathedral, where you can view the flying buttresses up close. At the end of square Jean XXIII is quai de l'Archevêché (you'll more than likely know it from the rows of tour buses that are parked along it). Cross quai de l'Archevêché and head into square de l'Ile de France, which is actually a park on the tip of Ile de la Cité. Go through Square de l'Ile de France to the:

12. Memorial de les Martyrs Français de la Déportation de 1945. To reach the actual memorial, go down the stairs (you'll see the iron spikes that block the opening at the very tip of the island), then turn left at the bottom and go through the narrow opening. Inside you will find an eternal flame, dedicated to the 200,000 French who died in Nazi concentration camps during World War II.

Designed by G. H. Pingusson in 1962, the memorial is constructed around 200,000 quartz pebbles. The pebbles are symbolic because in the Jewish religion it is traditional to place a stone or pebble upon a grave. There is one pebble for each person who died. Also inside are several other small tombs that hold bits of soil from each of the concentration camps.

You don't have to do too much meditating in here to be moved by this memorial. The iron spikes and prison bars coupled with the red scrawl on the walls and the small rooms give you the feeling that you're imprisoned. It's one of the city's most moving monuments.

When you've finished paying your respects, come back up to the square de l'Ile de France and, for the sake of variety, go up the stairs on the other side (the ones you didn't come down). Go through the gate, exiting the small park, and cross the pont St-Louis onto the Ile St-Louis. After crossing the bridge, go right on quai d'Orléans to:

13. Number 18–20 quai d'Orléans, on the left side. Walter Lippmann (1889–1974) lived here with his wife for a short time in 1938. A journalist and editor who worked for the *New Republic,* the *Washington Post,* and the *New York Herald Tribune,* Lippmann was a Pulitzer Prize recipient in 1958.

Continue to:

14. Number 12, where Harry and Caresse Crosby (Caresse's real name was Mary Phelps Jacob—Caresse was a nickname that stuck) spent the summer of 1923. The Crosbys were the founders of Black Sun Press, and they spent a good deal of time and money publishing their own poems and books of letters by well-known writers (such as Proust, Henry James, and D. H. Lawrence). Basically, they were a couple of Americans who had joined the rest of the crew in Paris and were enjoying themselves more than they ever thought possible. The publishing company was no more than a way for them to gain access to the literary and artistic circles in Paris at the time.

While living here Harry was known to keep a rowboat tied up on the Seine near his apartment building so that he could row across the river and then walk to work.

Continue along to:

15. Number 10 quai d'Orléans, where James Jones lived from 1958 to 1975. Jones, the author of *From Here to Eternity* (1951) played host to a constant parade of famous names. His many friends included Mary McCarthy, James Baldwin, Sylvia Beach, the ever-present-for-a-free-drink-or-meal Henry Miller, Man Ray, Gene Kelly, Art Buchwald, Arthur Miller, Alice B. Toklas, and Thornton Wilder, to name a few. Jones appreciated his friends, and after the publication of *From Here to Eternity*, it is said that he carried around a pile of envelopes, each of which contained 67 cents. Every time he found out that a friend had purchased a copy of his book he would give him or her an envelope and say, "That's my royalty on each copy. I don't want to make money on my friends."

Next at number 6 quai d'Orléans you'll find yourself in front of the:

16. Musée Adam Mickiewicz, the main attraction on this quay. The museum is dedicated to the exiled poet who was known as the "Byron of Poland." The second-floor museum houses mementos as well as a library. There is an entire room dedicated to Chopin, the composer, on the ground floor—it even holds his old armchair. Unfortunately the museum has very limited hours (3 to 6pm daily) and is closed from mid-July to mid-September, but if you happen to get there when it's open, you should definitely go in and have a look around.

Continue along, straight onto quai de Béthune. At number 24 you'll pass the apartment building in which Helena Rubinstein resided while in Paris.

Go left on rue Bretonvilliers and under the archway to rue St-Louis-en-l'Ile. Go right to number 2 rue St-Louis-en-l'Ile, the:

17. Hôtel Lambert. This 17th-century residence was the masterpiece of Louis Le Vau, built in 1645 for Nicolas Lambert de Thorigny, the president of the Chambre des Comptes. For a century the hotel was the home of the royal family of Poland, the Czartoryskis, who were lucky enough to have entertained Chopin (or rather, were lucky enough to have been entertained by Chopin).

At one time, Voltaire was a resident of Hôtel Lambert with his mistress Emilie de Breteuil, the marquise de Châtelet. They had such raucous fights that they were talked about all over Europe.

Unfortunately, this magnificent home is rarely open to the public.

Across the street at:

18. Number 5 lived literary agent William Aspenwall Bradley, who represented Katherine Anne Porter, Edith Wharton, Gertrude Stein, and John Dos Passos. He and Alfred Knopf encouraged Sylvia Beach to write her memoirs, but incredibly, they wanted her to leave out all mention of James Joyce, the French, and Gertrude Stein. It wasn't until many years later that Beach wrote her memoirs, and naturally, she did write about her friends in Paris, including Gertrude Stein and James Joyce.

Retrace your steps, crossing rue Bretonvilliers. Along the way you'll pass:

LOUIS LE VAU

Louis Le Vau (1612–70) was the chief architect on some of the most significant building projects commissioned by Louis XIV. He made the Ile St-Louis his home, and on it he built the Hôtel Lambert and the Hôtel Lauzun. In 1655 he became the head architect for the Louvre, and he designed the palace at Versailles (in collaboration with Charles Le Brun).

19. **Librairie Libella** (12 rue St-Louis-en-l'Ile), a Polish bookstore and gallery. If you're interested in Poland (or just interested in books in general), stop in. The bookstore's claim to fame is that its owners secretly got their hands on and published the sermons of Polish dissident Jerzy Popieluszko in 1984. The gallery shows the works of contemporary Polish and Eastern European artists.

    A bit farther on at 19 bis rue St-Louis-en-l'Ile is the church:

20. **St-Louis-en-l'Ile.** Built between 1664 and 1726, in Jesuit Baroque style, according to the original designs of Louis Le Vau, this church is and has been the site of many Parisian weddings. Inside you'll find a wonderful glazed terra-cotta statue of Saint Louis, as well as a 1926 plaque that reads, "In grateful memory of St. Louis in whose honor the city of St. Louis, Missouri, USA, is named." Note the iron spire, which dates from 1765.

REFRESHMENT STOP On your left at number 31 rue St-Louis-en-l'Ile is **Berthillon.** It is said to be the best ice cream and sorbet parlor in all of Europe, so you simply must stop in here for a snack. The ice cream flavors range all the way from your standard chocolate and vanilla to Grand Marnier and mocha; the sorbets range from lime to rhubarb.

Note: Berthillon is closed from the end of July to the beginning of September (which is a testament to how good the product here is: an ice cream business that can support itself without the summer rush—unheard of!).

Continue along and when you get to rue Le Regrattier walk to:

21. **Number 6 rue Le Regrattier.** This is where Baudelaire's mistress Jeanne Duval, (the "Black Venus,") lived.

    Continue along to:

22. **Number 2 rue Le Regrattier,** which is where Nancy Cunard lived. Cunard was a poet and the daughter of Lady Cunard, who was described by Janet Flanner (writing under her famous pen name, Genet) as being "one of London's greatest American hostesses." Nancy Cunard was a serious collector of art and

managed to put together a wonderful collection of African pieces. In 1929 she set up Hours Press, which published new, rare, and limited editions (signed by the authors) on an 18th-century Belgian handpress.

When you get to the end of rue Le Regrattier you will be back on quai d'Orléans. Go right. This is a more interesting way to walk along the quay because it affords you a spectacular view of the back of Notre Dame.

Follow quai d'Orléans to rue Jean-du-Bellay. Go right on rue Jean-du-Bellay to the quai de Bourbon. Go right on quai de Bourbon to the intersection of rue Le Regrattier and quai de Bourbon, where you will see a:

23. Headless statue. It gave rue Le Regrattier its original name, "rue de la Femme Sans Teste," or "street of the Headless Woman." In actuality, the statue is thought not to be a woman at all, but a statue of Saint Nicolas, the patron saint of boatmen.

Continue along, and at number 19 you will see:

24. A plaque commemorating Camille Claudel, sculptor, who lived and worked in the ground-floor apartment that faces out to the courtyard from 1899 to 1913.

Unfortunately, Claudel is one of those very talented woman artists who was lost to history for many years. In a recent resurrection aided by the film *Camille Claudel* (in French with English subtitles), she has been rediscovered—not just because she was the student and lover of Auguste Rodin (who was many years her senior), but also because she herself was an incredible sculptor. Some of her work, including my favorite, *La Petite Châtelaine,* can be viewed at the Musée Rodin. The Musée d'Orsay has a couple of pieces, including a remarkable sculpture of an old woman, *Clotho.* Regrettably, Claudel destroyed much of her own work when she had a mental breakdown, which was caused by the breakup of her relationship with Rodin and her paranoia that he was trying to destroy her career as a sculptor. She was able to spend only half of her life sculpting—the other half was spent in a mental asylum, where, sadly, she did no sculpting and eventually died.

Just a couple of doors down at:

25. Number 15 quai de Bourbon is where Emile Bernard (1868–1941), French painter and writer, lived. A contemporary of van Gogh's and Toulouse-Lautrec's, he helped develop (along with Louis Anguetin) the technique of "Cloisonnism," an emulation on canvas of cloissonné enamel. From 1888 to 1891 he worked closely with Gauguin at Pont Avon and in Paris, but shortly thereafter his writing took precedence.

Continue along quai de Bourbon onto quai d'Anjou, where:

26. Number 37 was home to John Dos Passos in 1921, about the time his novel *Three Soldiers* was published. Very popular with the French, Dos Passos was considered the most "American" of the expatriates living in Paris at that time.

A couple of buildings down is number 33 quai d'Anjou, the former location of Le Rendezvous des Mariners, a favorite dining spot of John Dos Passos. He often met Hemingway here for meals.

Still farther along is:

27. Number 29 quai d'Anjou, where in 1922 William Bird established Three Mountains Press. Hemingway met Bird in 1922 at the Genoa Economic Conference, where they were both working as journalists, and not long after that Bird suggested that Hemingway do some writing for him. In 1924 Bird was able to publish Hemingway's experimental work. Ezra Pound worked as Bird's editor, and in 1923 Pound's was the first title published by Three Mountains Press. Unfortunately the books Bird published were not profitable, and the whole operation, in spite of the beautiful hand-built 17th-century printing press he used, folded by 1929.

Continue ahead to number 17 quai d'Anjou, the:

28. Hôtel Lauzun, another one of Louis Le Vau's masterpieces. The exterior doesn't look like much, but the interior is a splendid amalgamation of the plans of a group of architects, including Le Vau, Le Brun, Lepautre, and Sebastien Bourdon. The painted ceilings and intricately carved wood paneling (or *boiserie*) have been preserved, along with some statues, tapestries, and paintings. It is possible to visit the interior of the house, but you have to make arrangements well in advance of your visit.

The mansion was built in 1656–1657 for Charles Gruyn des Bordes. In 1682 it was sold to the duc de Lauzun, who only resided here for three years. After that it had several other famous tenants, among them Baudelaire and Théophile Gautier. In fact, Baudelaire and his hashish club did the research for *Les Paradis Artificiels,* or rather, drug-induced states of fantasy, here in 1834.

Lauzun was the brother-in-law of Louis de Rouvroy, duc de Saint-Simon, who described Lauzan in his famous diary as being the kind of person who was never happy, who was bad natured, and who enjoyed spending most of his time alone. However, history shows that he had a mischievous side as well. Once he hid under the bed in which Louis XIV and Madame de Montespan were making love and later reported to her exactly, word for word, what he had heard while in his most extraordinary hiding place. (One has to wonder, however, how he fit under that bed at all because he was also described as having a gluttonous appetite.)

Be sure to note the wrought-iron balcony and the fish pipes on the exterior facade.

Just a little farther down is:

29. Number 9 quai d'Anjou, where the sculptor, painter, and caricaturist Honoré Daumier once lived. (See Walking Tour 11: stop 29 for more information about Daumier.)

As you follow the quay to the end, you'll be at pont de Sully. Go right to the square Barye for a rest before heading out on your next walk. You're standing (or sitting) in what was once part of the terraced gardens of the duc de Bretonvilliers.

WALKING TOUR 3

Montparnasse

Start: Gare Montparnasse.
Finish: Intersection of boulevard Raspail and boulevard Edgar-Quinet.
Time: Three to four hours.
Best Time: Between 10am and 4pm, Tuesday through Sunday, when the Musée Bourdelle is open.

Originally nicknamed Mount Parnassus by a group of students, the "mount" was flattened and the boulevard du Montparnasse was laid. Not long after, with the openings of cafés and cabarets, the boulevard began to grow.

By the 1920s Montparnasse had become the Left Bank home of the Lost Generation. Stein, Hemingway, Duncan, and many other American expatriates gathered in this bohemian paradise to drink, philosophize, and dance in the 1920s. They mixed and mingled here with Simone de Beauvoir and Jean-Paul Sartre, as well as Russian political exiles like Trotsky and Stravinsky.

Today, after a massive redevelopment project, Montparnasse has lost a lot of its old-world charm, but if you overlook the neon, movie theaters, and modern nightclubs you can imagine what it was like for Modigliani and Malvina Hoffman to live and work here. Perhaps you can conjure the old Montparnasse and see Hemingway sitting under a lilac bush at the Closerie des Lilas with his friend John Dos Passos, or James Joyce sitting in his favorite restaurant singing an old Irish ballad with his friends.

Begin your tour in the:

1. Gare Montparnasse. Opened in 1974, this rail station is the Paris terminal that serves Brittany, Mayenne, and Basse-Normandie. There is even a chapel located within (St-Bernard), that was made from a railway sleeper car.

Come out of the station into place R. Dautry and you'll be facing:

2. Tour Montparnasse, a 688-foot-high tower. It dwarfs the surrounding buildings because it's the highest structure around; however, it was built in a curved shape to "soften" its otherwise harsh architectural shape. Many consider it an eyesore. Saul Bellow described it as "something that had strayed away from Chicago and had come to rest on a Parisian street corner." On the 56th floor is an observatory with a bar and restaurant, and on a clear day you can see for approximately 30 miles.

Go left out of the plaza and cross boulevard Vaugirard onto avenue du Maine. Follow avenue du Maine through place Bienvenüe and go left onto rue Antoine-Bourdelle. Continue to the:

3. Musée Bourdelle, located on the right side of the street. Considered a small treasure by avid art lovers, Musée Bourdelle is actually the former home, garden, and working studio of French sculptor Emile Antoine Bourdelle (1861–1929).

Born at Montauban, Bourdelle learned his first sculpting skills by helping out in the workshop of his father, who was a cabinetmaker. In 1876 he studied at l'Ecole des Beaux Arts at Toulouse, and eventually won a scholarship to attend l'Ecole des Beaux-Arts in Paris in 1884. Not long afterward he became Rodin's head assistant, but his work was frequently ignored because it was overshadowed by the work of the "Master." Later he became a teacher and started an atelier, or studio, that thereafter became a school known as La Grande Chaumière.

Bourdelle did the sculptures of Isadora Duncan on the facade of the Théâtre des Champs-Elysées in 1912, and they are some of his finest work. Some of the most interesting pieces in the museum are his busts of Rodin and the many portraits and studies of Beethoven.

Go back out to rue Antoine-Bourdelle and go left to avenue du Maine. Go left on avenue du Maine and go right on rue d'Alençon. Turn right on boulevard du Montparnasse and look across the street for:

4. Number 60. Alexander Calder (1898–1976), the American sculptor and painter who invented the mobile, stayed here for several months in 1926. According to Calder, his interest in art began in 1922 as a result of his study in mechanical engineering, rather than through the work of his father and grandfather, who were both sculptors in their own right.

In 1923, Calder attended the Art Students League in New York City, where he used to sit outside and make rapid drawings of passersby. This drawing method helped develop his skill at showing movement with one unbroken line. Wire sculptures were a logical next step, and in 1927 he began working for the Gould Manufacturing Company, making toys. His abstract works became extremely popular in both the United States and Paris, and he has since been acknowledged as a pioneer in the field of kinetic art.

Continue along to:

5. Place du 18 Juin 1940. James Joyce's favorite eatery, Restaurant Trianon, was located at number 5. One of his favorite dinner companions was John Dos Passos.

As you head back along boulevard du Montparnasse, look on your left for:

6. Number 81, the former atelier of Carolus-Duran. He opened a school here in 1872 to teach painting, not the basics of anatomy and life drawing. Because it departed from traditional art instruction his school was thought of as "cutting edge," but unfortunately if you didn't already have drawing skills it was difficult to produce work of any significance here.

John Singer Sargent (1856–1925), an American born in Florence, Italy, came to work here at the age of 18 in 1874. Sargent was already highly skilled in life drawing, so he was able to jump to the head of the class shortly after he joined, and as a result spent some time working as Duran's assistant. By 1878 Sargent was out working on his own.

Sargent had the privilege of growing up internationally schooled and influenced. William Starkweather once described him as "An American born in Italy, educated in France, who looks like a German, speaks like an Englishman, and paints like a Spaniard." It will come as no surprise then that he was a great lover of Velázquez's work.

On the left-hand corner of rue du Montparnasse and boulevard du Montparnasse you'll pass the church of Notre-Dames-des-Champs. Continue along boulevard du Montparnasse to the corner of rue Vavin, where you'll find:

7. Le Sélect, at number 99 boulevard du Montparnasse. This cáfe was one of the most popular in Paris in the 1920s and it was frequented by, among others, Ernest Hemingway and Joan Miró (1893–1983).

Here too Isadora Duncan held an impromptu "demonstration" in support of the anarchists Sacco and Vanzetti, who were convicted of murder. A fight with another one of Le Sélect's patrons, journalist Floyd Gibbons, over whether or not Sacco's and Vanzetti's lives should be spared prompted her to lead a small march to the American embassy to protest their impending executions.

Continue along and on your left you'll see:

8. La Rotonde, at 103–105 boulevard du Montparnasse, a café that was originally housed at number 105 when it opened in 1911. It was more than just a café. Stanton MacDonald Wright, an American painter who frequented La Rotonde, described it as

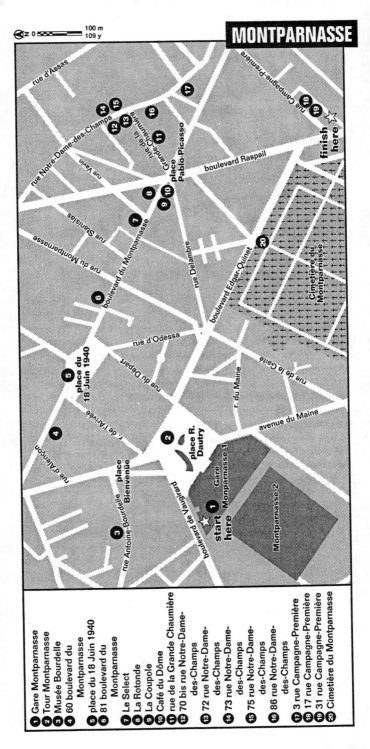

MONTPARNASSE

100 m
109 y

1 Gare Montparnasse
2 Tour Montparnasse
3 Musée Bourdelle
4 60 boulevard du Montparnasse
5 place du 18 Juin 1940
6 81 boulevard du Montparnasse
7 Le Select
8 La Rotonde
9 La Coupole
10 Café du Dôme
11 rue de la Grande Chaumière
12 70 bis rue Notre-Dame-des-Champs
13 72 rue Notre-Dame-des-Champs
14 73 rue Notre-Dame-des-Champs
15 75 rue Notre-Dame-des-Champs
16 86 rue Notre-Dame-des-Champs
17 3 rue Campagne-Première
18 17 rue Campagne-Première
19 31 rue Campagne-Première
20 Cimetière du Montparnasse

"a gathering place of most American and German artists; André, the waiter there, lent the boys [the artists] money and treated many as a father would." He also said that the café was at that time "a small zinc bar in a long narrow room with a terrace where [they] drank and warmed [themselves] at great porcelain stoves."

Around 1924 La Rotonde had become popular enough to warrant taking over the space next door at number 103. Apollinaire, Max Jacob, Picasso, and Modigliani enjoyed spending time in the café and nightclub. There was an artists' gallery located on the premises as well. Edna St. Vincent Millay, the American romantic poet, liked spending time here during her visit in the spring of 1922.

Note at the intersection of boulevard du Montparnasse and boulevard Raspail the controversial bust of Balzac by Auguste Rodin. Before continuing, look across boulevard du Montparnasse to:

9. La Coupole, at number 102 boulevard du Montparnasse, opened in December of 1927 and a favorite spot of Russian exiles and emigrées before and after the Bolshevik Revolution (including Leon Trotsky and Igor Stravinsky). It also played host to the area's artistic community, including Josephine Baker, Matisse, and Kiki and her lover, the photographer Man Ray.

The 12 columns inside were painted (in exchange for a meal) by, among others Brancusi, Gris, Léger, Chagall, Soutine, and Delaunay, and are registered as an historic monument.

On the same side of boulevard du Montparnasse, a couple of doors down at number 108 is:

10. Café du Dôme, which opened in 1897. Like the others, it was very popular with Americans and various other expatriates in the 1920s. Hemingway and Sinclair Lewis both frequented the Dôme.

EDNA ST. VINCENT MILLAY

A graduate of Vassar College, Edna St. Vincent Millay (1892–1950) was born in Rockland, Maine. Around the time she was born her uncle survived a life-threatening stay at New York's St. Vincent Hospital, and so her mother gave her the middle name St. Vincent. Not long after her college graduation, Millay headed for New York City and set up home in Greenwich Village. For a while, to support herself, she wrote articles for *Vanity Fair* magazine under the pseudonym Nancy Boyd.

As her poetic career flourished, she came to be well respected by her contemporaries, and well liked by her popular audience. In 1922 she won a Pulitzer Prize for her poem "The Ballad of the Harp Weaver."

KIKI OF MONTPARNASSE

Born an illegitimate child and raised by her grandmother in Burgundy, Kiki (?–1953) was called to Paris by her mother, who put her to work—first in a printing shop, then in a shoe factory, and finally in a florist's shop on the rue Mouffetard, where she was discovered by a sculptor. So began her career as an artists' model. She later became a nightclub dancer at the Jockey-Bar (the first nightclub in Montparnasse) after her mother disowned her at age 14.

She was voluptuous, seductive, and nonconformist and would bare her breasts to anyone who would pay her three francs. Kiki is most closely associated with Montparnasse because she spent 20 years hanging around at the Dôme, Le Sélect, and La Rotonde.

As she got older her quality of life deteriorated and she began abusing drugs and alcohol. She died in 1953.

Go left up the:

11. Rue de la Grande-Chaumière. As you walk, check out the sculpture in the window of the Art et Buffet Restaurant. At number 14 bis, on your left, is the Académie de la Grande-Chaumière, the art school begun by Antoine Bourdelle. Number 9, across the street on the right side (now Best Western Villa des Artistes) was once the Hôtel Liberia, the haunt of many an artist and writer. Among them was Nathanael West (1903–40), who moved here in 1926 and lived in Paris for two years. An American novelist whose birth name was Nathan Weinstein, West was fascinated with the idea of the American dream. His best-known work is probably *Miss Lonelyhearts,* published in 1933. During his lifetime he worked as an editor for several magazines, and two years after the publication of *Miss Lonelyhearts* he moved to Hollywood to become a scriptwriter.

The sculptor Malvina Hoffman (1887–1966; see stop 13 below) also took furnished rooms somewhere on this street, which was fondly referred to as the "rabbit hutch" around 1920. Hoffman described the sounds of rue de la Grande-Chaumière as a veritable cacophony of "the calls of the knife sharpeners and mattress makers, the pan pipes of vendors of goats while leading their bleating flocks."

At number 8, on your left, is the old studio of Amedeo Modigliani (for more about Modigliani, see Walking Tour 11, stop 15).

Take a quick detour to the left on rue Notre-Dame-des-Champs to:

12. Number 70 bis, on the left, where Ezra Pound and his wife Dorothy moved into an apartment in 1921. The apartment overlooked the courtyard and garden, and even though all his furniture was homemade (out of boxes and various other discarded items), the apartment was rather charming. It didn't matter to him that he was completely poverty-stricken, he loved to throw parties, and just about everybody who was anybody during the time he lived here visited this apartment. Hemingway often spent time here boxing and writing with Pound.

Katherine Anne Porter (1890–1980) lived in the very same apartment in 1934. She came to Europe on a Guggenheim grant and joined Sylvia Beach's Shakespeare and Company Library in 1933. She remained in Paris until 1936 and is acclaimed for her collection of short stories, *Flowering Judas* (1930), and her most famous novel, *Ship of Fools* (1962).

Look for:

13. Number 72, also on your left. A second-floor apartment in this building was Malvina Hoffman's first studio, and its only running water was from a tap down the hall.

This is where she worked on her first commission—a bust of the American ambassador to France Robert Bacon. While living here she met Rodin. She went to his studio, and he asked her to pick out one of the sculptures that were on display and study it carefully until he came back. She knew that this was a test and intensely studied the one she had chosen. He returned about 20 minutes later and took her to another room. Before he left her again, he gave her some clay and instructed her to sculpt the head she had just studied from memory. He walked out and locked the door behind him. When he came back he found that she had done an excellent job and took her to lunch. This is how she was accepted as a student of Rodin's.

Only five years after she began working with Rodin, Hoffman achieved national recognition for her *Pavlova La Gavotte* and *Bacchanale Russe*. She is also responsible for the creation of the Hall of Man at the Field Museum of Chicago.

Across the street on your right is:

14. Number 73, where John Singer Sargent once shared a studio with Carroll Beckwith. Here he completed his first major commission—a portrait of the French playwright Edouard Pailleron.

Also look for:

15. Number 75, the home of Alice B. Toklas and Harriet Levy. When Alice B. Toklas first came to Paris, she traveled with her friend and fellow San Franciscan Harriet Levy, and they moved into an apartment here. In 1912 Levy moved back to the United States, but Toklas decided to stay and moved in with Gertrude and Leo Stein (she had been typing manuscript pages for Gertrude since she moved to Paris). When Leo moved to Italy in 1914, Toklas stayed and stayed and stayed, for the next 32 years.

Continue along, crossing the intersection of rue de la Grande-Chaumière, following along rue Notre-Dame-des-Champs to:

16. Number 86, James Abbott McNeill Whistler's studio. A painter and graphic artist, Whistler (1834–1903) was active mainly in England. He began his training as an artist after he left West Point Academy. In 1855 he moved to Paris and, like many before and after him, spent a great deal of time making copies in the Louvre. Four years later he decided to settle in London, but he returned to France often. He was a great friend of Oscar Wilde's and, like him, was a believer in art for art's sake. He particularly enjoyed describing his works in musical terms and often gave his pieces musical titles. From his studio window here, he had a lovely view of the Luxembourg Gardens.

Follow rue Notre-Dame-des-Champs to the end. Go right at the corner.

REFRESHMENT STOP At number 171 boulevard du Montparnasse is **Closerie des Lilas,** a nice place to stop for a drink. Closerie des Lilas was Hemingway's favorite neighborhood hangout. Every morning he would come here and write—in fact, he did some rewriting of *The Sun Also Rises* here. Often he could be found contemplating the statue of Marshal Ney (the marshal of France under Napoleon I who was shot for treason) which stands outside on the very spot where Ney was killed. He often came with John Dos Passos, and the two would sit outside under the lilac bushes and read the New Testament to each other.

Go right as you come out of Closerie des Lilas on boulevard du Montparnasse to rue Campagne-Première. Go left on rue Campagne-Première to:

17. Number 3, a new building standing on the site of the building in which Whistler stayed while studying under Charles Gabriel Gleyre (1808–74), a Swiss painter. In 1843, when Paul Delaroche (a French historical painter) closed his studio, a number of his students went to work with Gleyre, who encouraged outdoor painting. Whistler wasn't the only well-known student of Gleyre's; others included Sisley, Monet, and Renoir. His studio closed in 1864.

Continue to:

18. Number 17, the building in which Eugène Atget had a studio from 1898 to 1927. One of France's most famous photographers, Atget began his life as a seaman and then moved to a career in acting. It wasn't until his 42nd year that he became a photographer.

At first he made money by selling some of his photographs to painters for use as source material, and others to the city of Paris for use as historical records. Not long after he began, his documentary work crossed the line and became artwork, and he started producing his famed poetic images.

Continue to:

19. Number 31 bis rue Campagne-Première. Man Ray

(1890–1977) lived here in July of 1922. The model Kiki became his mistress while he was living here and stayed with him for the next six years.

One of the most important photographers of his time, he was a prominent figure in the dadaist and surrealist movements, and a friend of Marcel Duchamp's. In the 1930s he invented the rayograph (or what is known today as a photogram), made by strategically placing objects on photographic paper and then exposing it to light to create an image. This technique is often utilized today as one of the first exercises in photography classes to demonstrate the effects of light on photographic paper.

Cross boulevard Raspail at the end of rue Campagne-Première and go left onto boulevard Edgar-Quinet. Not far along is the main entrance to the:

20. Cimetière du Montparnasse. Be sure you go in the main entrance.

I'm going to take you on a brief tour of the cemetery, with directions for the general locations of grave sites you might be interested in visiting.

First, as you enter the cemetery, go right to the graves of **Jean-Paul Sartre** (1905–80) and **Simone de Beauvoir** (1908–86) on the right side of the roadway. Sartre was an existentialist playwright, philosopher, and novelist. During World War II he was taken prisoner, but he escaped and became a Resistance leader. During the Occupation he wrote *Being and Nothingness* (1943) and *No Exit* (1944). He declined the Nobel Prize in 1964. Simone de Beauvoir, Sartre's intimate friend and occasional lover, was also an existentialist novelist and a teacher of philosophy, but she is probably best known for her analysis of women in her book *The Second Sex* (1949–50). Towards the end of her life she wrote another book, about the way different cultures treat and respond to the elderly, entitled *The Coming of Age* (1970).

Continue along, and at avenue de l'Ouest go left, and on your left you'll find the grave of **Chaim Soutine** (1894–1943). Born in Lithuania, Soutine arrived in France in 1913 and became one of the greatest contributors to L'Ecole de Paris (a loose term combining those artists who participated in the dadaist, cubist, and surrealist movements). He isn't particularly well known because he suffered from depression and a lack of self-confidence that led him to refrain from showing his work in public, but many believe Soutine was a man of great genius. It is said that he often destroyed his paintings. He preferred the work of the old masters to his contemporaries and particularly admired Rembrandt's *Flayed Ox*. Soutine's own *Side of Beef* (c. 1925) was inspired by the old masters. He was a frequent visitor to the slaughterhouses and once brought a carcass home to paint. When his neighbors called the police to complain about the smell, Soutine confronted them with a discourse on the importance of art over sanitation!

Keep going, and after you cross avenue du Nord you'll find,

also on your left, the grave of **Charles Baudelaire** (1821–67), French symbolist poet and critic. Only one volume of Baudelaire's major work, *Les Fleurs du Mal* (1857), was published in his lifetime, and it was met with great animosity. Once considered obscene, *Les Fleurs du Mal* is now regarded a masterpiece.

Continue ahead, crossing avenue Transversale, and on your right you'll find the grave of **Tristan Tzara** (see Walking Tour 10, stop 16 for more information). Still farther ahead, across allée Raffet, on your right, is the grave of **Antoine Bourdelle** (see stop 3 for more information).

Turn around and head back to allée Raffet and go right on allée Raffet to avenue Principale. Follow avenue Principale around the circle to the left and straight through to avenue du Nord. Turn right to the grave of **Charles-Camille Saint-Saëns** (1835–1921), a French composer and child prodigy who made his debut as a pianist at the age of 10. Only three years later, he entered the Paris Conservatory, and for 20 years he was the organist at the Madeleine Church (see Walking Tour 8, stop 13 for more about the Madeleine). He disliked modern music, and his most famous work was the romantic opera *Samson and Dalila,* composed in 1877.

Located diagonally across the street to the left is the grave of **Constantin Brancusi** (1876–1957). A Romanian sculptor, Brancusi decided to come to Paris to work, and soon after his arrival he was invited by Rodin to work in his studio. Brancusi did the unthinkable—he declined Rodin's offer, saying wisely, "Nothing grows well in the shade of a big tree." An abstract sculptor, Brancusi was unafraid of controversy. He believed in the absolute simplification of form and liked working in metal, stone, and wood. His most famous sculpture is *The Kiss* (1908), which you'll find if you continue on avenue du Nord to rue Emile-Richard and turn left to the first intersection.

Exit the cemetery by continuing straight ahead and go right to the Raspail Métro station.

WALKING TOUR 4

St-Germain-des-Prés

Start: The intersection of rue de Bellechasse and rue de Lille. (Métro: Get off at Solferino and walk two blocks up to rue de Lille.)
Finish: The intersection of rue de Fleurus and rue Raspail.
Time: Four to six hours.
Best Time: Start at about 10am from Wednesday to Saturday.
Worst Time: Monday and Tuesday, when museums are closed.

Originally the site of a large abbey in the 8th century, the Left Bank neighborhood St-Germain-des-Prés is where 18th-century Parisian aristocrats built elegant mansions or *hôtels particuliers*. It quickly developed into one of the most chic areas of Paris, attracting residents like the queen of the Netherlands, Chateaubriand, and André Gide.

Activity in the neighborhood often centered around the St-Germain-des-Prés church and the cafés (Café de Flore and Café des Deux Magots) that grew up around it. Because of the presence of the Ecole des Beaux-Arts here, the neighborhood also attracted a great number of artists, including Picasso.

Presently the neighborhood is home to some of the most exclusive antique shops and boutiques, as well as street markets and bookshops. On this walk you'll have the opportunity to visit the world's greatest collection of Impressionist art at the Musée d'Orsay, the rue de Buci Market, and the place where Natalie Barney held her famous salon that attracted the likes of Marcel Proust. Spend some time at the Delacroix Museum and visit the original location of Sylvia Beach's Shakespeare & Company.

It's a long walk, so you should make plans about where you want to spend time before you leave.

1. Musée d'Orsay. Constructed within the old Gare d'Orsay (designed by Victor Laloux), this museum houses one of the greatest collections of art from the second half of the 19th century. A visit here could take anywhere from two hours to all day, so if you want to finish this tour, plan accordingly—perhaps you can plan to come back another day if you want to spend more time.

The display areas are flooded with natural light that comes in through the glass ceilings and enormous windows, which makes the impact of the central sculpture gallery inspiring. The collections came mainly from the Louvre, but the museum also holds the collection of Impressionist work that was squeezed into the Jeu de Paume for so many years. You'll see sculptures by Claudel, Maillol, and Rodin (to name a few), as well as a large collection of caricatures by Daumier. There's a fantastic decorative arts display, including several rooms devoted to Art Nouveau furnishings. You also shouldn't miss the stunning collection of Toulouse-Lautrec's pastel drawings.

It would be simply too difficult to tell you what you can skip here because everything in the museum is worth seeing. It's easy to find your way around, and if you purchase the museum guidebook you can't go wrong.

There's a restaurant and café on the upper level, and there's also a fantastic bookstore and poster shop—don't miss them.

Across the street from the Musée d'Orsay on the rue de Bellechasse is the:

2. Palais de la Légion d'Honneur. Originally the Hotel de Salm-Kyrkburg, it was built in 1782 for the Prince de Salm-Kyrbourg. Napoléon acquired the building in 1804 intending to house the Legion d'Honneur, which was to employ those "who by their talents contribute to the safety and prosperity of the nation." The original structure burned in 1871, and the one you see today has been heavily restored. Inside the classical structure you'll learn the history of the Legion of Honor and see busts of Henry IV and Bonaparte Lacepede, as well as medals and insignia. There's even a room dedicated to women.

Walk to the right down rue de Bellechasse to rue de l'Université and turn left, looking for:

3. Number 50, where Edna St. Vincent Millay crafted her Pulitzer Prize–winning poem, *The Ballad of the Harp Weaver.*

Go left when you get to rue de Poitiers to rue de Verneuil. Go right on rue de Verneuil. Go left on rue du Bac and right on quai Voltaire. After crossing rue de Beaune, stop at number 19 quai Voltaire, the:

4. Hôtel du Quai Voltaire. Willa Sibert Cather (1876–1947), the American novelist, stayed here for two months in 1920. At the age of nine, Cather moved with her family to the Nebraska prairie, where she eventually attended the University of Nebraska. Later, she moved to Pittsburgh and worked as a journalist and teacher. In 1904 she moved to New York City and lived in Greenwich Village while working as an editor for *McClure's Magazine*. In 1912 she left *McClure's* (after having been promoted to managing editor) so that she could devote herself entirely to her fiction writing. Author of *O Pioneers!* (1913) and *My Antonia* (1918), she won a Pulitzer Prize for her novel *One of Ours* (1922), which she worked on while she lived here at 19 quai Voltaire.

Baudelaire spent time working on *Les Fleurs du Mal* while he stayed here from 1856 to 1858. Richard Wagner and Oscar Wilde were also guests here for a brief period.

Just a bit farther on is:

5. **Number 17,** where Virgil Thomson (1896–1989), the American composer and organist, lived from 1927 to 1940. During his stay in Paris he was inspired to write two operas for librettos written by Gertrude Stein, *Four Saints in Three Acts* (1928) and *The Mother of us All* (1947). Aside from those operas, he composed works for organ, piano, and chamber ensembles, and he worked as a music critic for the *New York Herald Tribune* for 14 years (1940–54).

Backtrack to rue de Beaune and go left. Henry James met Ralph Waldo Emerson for the first time at number 7 in 1872 while on assignment to write letters on Parisian life for the *New York Tribune*. And Ezra Pound lived next door at number 9 in July of 1920. Continue down rue de Beaune to rue de l'Université and go left. At the corner, just before rue de l'Université becomes rue Jacob, on the right, is:

6. **Number 2–4 rue de l'Université.** Benjamin Franklin lived here in 1776 while trying to get support from the French for the American Revolution. Being a devotee of the good life, Ben loved Paris, and the French returned the affection. In fact, when he was scheduled to board ship to go back to the United States, the queen herself sent her personal litter and two mules to take him to the ship.

Turn right and walk down rue des Sts-Pères.

REFRESHMENT STOP   Debauve and Gallais, on your right at 30 rue des Sts-Pères, is a good place to stop for a quick snack. It's a chocolate shop, so don't go in looking for lunch—this is simply a stop to raise your caloric level. Many years ago it was a pharmacy that distributed "medicinal chocolate." It is open Tuesday through Saturday.

When you reach boulevard St-Germain, cross to the other side and then go left to rue du Dragon. Incidentally, rue du

Dragon used to be named rue du Sépulchre, but its name was changed in the 18th century because the residents preferred the name Dragon—after the huge gateway of the Cour du Dragon (you can see a copy of the gateway at number 44 if you choose to continue walking down after the next stop). Go right down rue du Dragon (a quaint little shopping street) to number 31, the:

7. **Académie Jullian,** on the left side of the street. Many artists who couldn't gain entrance to the Ecole des Beaux-Arts attended this school, which opened in 1868 but didn't move to rue du Dragon until 1890. In the tradition of French teaching, it was a conservative, traditional school, but it was considered inferior to Beaux-Arts. Among the many Americans who studied here were Maurice B. Prendergast from 1891 to 1893, Max Weber in 1905 and Jacques Lipchitz in 1910. George Biddle described the place in 1911 as "a cold, filthy, uninviting firetrap"; when he arrived, he found this scene: "Three nude girls were posing downstairs. The acrid smell of their bodies and the smell of the students mingled with that of turpentine and oil paint in the overheated, tobacco-laden air." He also said that while the artists "worked there was a pandemonium of songs, catcalls, whistling and recitations of a highly salacious and bawdy nature." Not the prettiest of pictures, but probably very accurate.

Turn around and head back up rue du Dragon to boulevard St-Germain. Go right to:

8. **Brasserie Lipp,** at 151 boulevard St-Germain, on your right. Frequented by Ernest Hemingway, Brasserie Lipp has been a particular favorite of the literati since the 1920s. The best reason to go inside (because the Alsatian food isn't), is to see the painted ceilings and the Art Nouveau ceramics.

9. **Café de Flore** is across the boulevard St-Germain on your left. Pablo Picasso used to hang out at the Café de Flore after 1945. As Janet Flanner describes, "He always sat at the second table in front of the main door, with Spanish friends. . . . He never did anything except sip his one small bottle of mineral water, speak with his Spanish friends, and look at all the people who were not looking directly at him. When he had finished his libation, he left for home, invariably before eleven." Jean-Paul Sartre and Simone de Beauvoir also rendezvoused here in the early 1940s and worked on their writing.

Cross the street at the place St-Germain-des-Prés, and on your left, across from the church, will be:

10. **Café des Deux Magots.** It is named after sculptures attached to the column, of two Chinese dignitaries (or *magots*) who sit on boxes of money. Deux Magots was another of Hemingway's hangouts. Janet Flanner, a close friend of Hemingway's and the writer who (under the pen name Genet), vividly captured Paris's café and salon scene in the twenties, described Hemingway's habit of coming here to have "serious talk" and read works out

1 Musée d'Orsay
2 Palais de la Légion d'Honneur
3 50 rue de l'Université
4 Hôtel du quai Voltaire
5 17 quai Voltaire
6 2-4 rue de l'Université
7 Académie Jullian
8 Brasserie Lipp
9 Café de Flore
10 Café des Deux Magots
11 St-Germain-des-Prés
12 place de Furstemberg
13 Musée Eugène Delacroix
14 20 rue Jacob
15 rue Visconti
16 École des Beaux-Arts
17 Buci Market
18 15 rue Christine
19 7 rue des Grands-Augustins
20 28 rue St-Andre-des-Arts
21 Cour du Commerce St-Andre
22 Le Procope
23 carrefour de l'Odéon
24 Galerie Regine Lussan
25 12 rue de l'Odéon
26 Hôtel Michelet Odéon
27 Théâtre de l'Odéon
28 55 rue Monsieur-le-Prince
29 22 rue Monsieur-le-Prince
30 14 rue Monsieur-le-Prince
31 Marché St-Germain
32 St-Sulpice
33 rue Férou
34 42 rue de Vaugirard
35 Palais du Luxembourg
36 Jardin du Luxembourg
37 27 rue de Fleurus

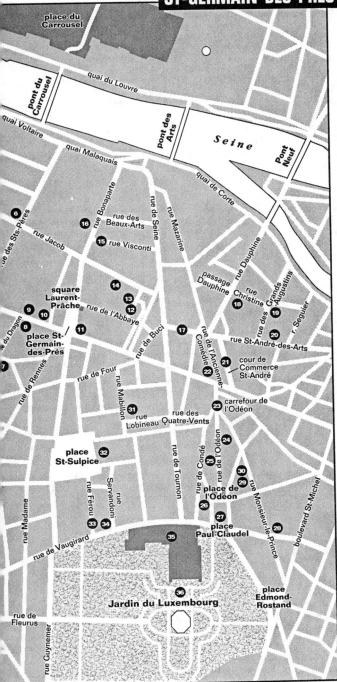

ST-GERMAIN-DES-PRES

place du Carrousel

pont du Carrousel

quai du Louvre

quai Voltaire

pont des Arts

quai Malaquais

Seine

Pont Neuf

quai de Corte

rue des Sts-Pères

rue Jacob

rue Bonaparte

rue des Beaux-Arts

rue de Seine

rue Visconti

rue Mazarine

rue Dauphine

passage Dauphine

rue Christine

rue des Grands-Augustins

r. Seguier

square Laurent-Prâche

rue de l'Abbaye

rue du Dragon

place St-Germain-des-Prés

rue de Buci

rue de l'Ancienne-Comédie

rue St-André-des-Arts

cour de Commerce St-André

rue de Rennes

rue de Four

rue Mabillon

carrefour de l'Odéon

rue Lobineau

rue des Quatre-Vents

rue de l'Odéon

place St-Sulpice

rue de Tournon

rue de Condé

place de l'Odéon

rue Monsieur-le-Prince

boulevard St-Michel

rue Férou

rue Servandoni

rue Madame

place Paul-Claudel

rue de Vaugirard

Jardin du Luxembourg

place Edmond-Rostand

rue de Fleurus

rue Guynemer

loud. His love for Deux Magots can be seen in several passages of *The Sun also Rises,* particularly the one in which Jake Barnes and Lady Brett meet.

Head across the place St-Germain-des-Prés to:

11. St-Germain-des-Prés, the oldest of Paris's large churches, which is built on the site of a former temple to the Egyptian goddess Isis. In Roman times, this area was just an open field, or *prés.* The original church was built here in 452 by the Merovingian king Childebert; however, it was continually built, destroyed by the Normans, and rebuilt. Eventually, in 1163, it was rebuilt for the last time.

Much later, near the end of the 18th century, French revolutionaries took over the abbey that was here and filled it with prisoners. Later they held tribunals, or very quick trials, which led to the massacre of over 200 people, including a few of Louis XVI's ministers and his father confessor, in the abbey's courtyard (right here on the corner of rue Bonaparte and boulevard St-Germain). After the massacre, while the bodies still lay in piles, there was an auction of the victims' personal belongings.

On a much less horrifying note, it was also here that a fairground sprang up, and it hosted many a juggler and dancing bear, not to mention performing artists of all kinds. You'll still find street performers in front of the church today, especially if it's warm outside.

In the nave are murals by Hippolyte Flandrin (1809–64), one of Ingres's favorite students and winner of the Prix de Rome (1830). While in Italy, Flandrin was greatly impressed by the "monumental" work that was being done, and when he returned to Paris in 1838 he became the leading muralist of his time. The murals he executed here in St-Germain-des-Prés were done over a period of five years, from 1856 to 1861.

Within the church you'll also find a memorial to René Descartes, the 17th-century philosopher and mathematician, whose skull is buried here; and a bust of Jean Mabillon (1623–1707), a French scholar and Benedictine monk who developed a technique for determining the authenticity of documents.

When you come out of the church, go around the front to rue de l'Abbaye. In the square Laurent-Prâche, a tiny, quiet park at the back of the church, you will find a bronze bust of a woman, sculpted by Picasso and dedicated to Guillaume Apollinaire. Picasso and Apollinaire were great friends, and the bust was dedicated 41 years after Apollinaire's death.

Continue to the right (if you're facing away from the square Laurent-Prâche), along rue de l'Abbaye. On your left look for the rue de Furstemberg. Go left into rue de Furstemberg where you'll find:

12. Place de Furstemberg, named for Cardinal Egon von Furstemberg, abbot of St-Germain-des-Prés in the late 17th century. This is a wonderful little out-of-the-way spot—in fact, it was one of Henry Miller's favorites. Sometimes, if you're lucky, you might find a group of musicians giving an impromptu mini-concert.

To your left, diagonally across the center of the square at number 6 rue de Furstemberg, is the:

13. **Musée Eugène Delacroix,** the home and studio of Eugène Delacroix (1798–1863), the French Romantic painter. He lived here from December 28, 1857, to August 13, 1863. Following are the entries from his journal the day he moved into this studio:

"Made a quick change to the new studio today... Decidedly, my new place is charming. After dinner, I felt a bit of melancholy over finding myself transplanted. Little by little I got reconciled and was perfectly happy when I went to bed.

Woke up the next morning and saw the most gracious sunlight on the houses opposite my window. The sight of my little garden and the smiling aspect of my studio always cause a feeling of pleasure in me."

You can look out on the garden he describes today if you go inside the museum.

Among the pieces you'll find in the museum are Delacroix's portraits of George Sand, his self-portraits, and his animal paintings. Also on view are his collections of sketches and many of his letters. Exhibits rotate, so there's no telling which part of the enormous collection you're going to see.

After exiting the museum go left up rue de Furstemberg to rue Jacob. (Note that to your left and right are some wonderful fabric shops as you approach rue Jacob). Go left on rue Jacob to:

14. **Number 20,** the former residence of Natalie Clifford Barney (1876–1972), who moved here from the United States in 1909 as a student and stayed for just over 60 years. Although Barney was virtually unknown in America, she was famous all over Paris for her literary salons. Virgil Thomson, Carl van Vechten, Sherwood Anderson, T. S. Eliot, James Joyce, and Marcel Proust were among the many who visited her salon on Friday nights. A rich,

GEORGE SAND

A popular French romance novelist, George Sand (born Amandine-Aurore-Lucie Dupin, 1804–76) wrote 80 novels in her lifetime. She was married to the Baron Dudevant, had two children by him, got a divorce, and then proceeded to have a series of affairs, first with Jules Sandeau (from whom she derived her pseudonym), then Chopin, and then with the poet and novelist Alfred de Musset. Her most famous eccentricity? She wore men's clothes.

beautiful lesbian, Barney was portrayed in many a novel, including *Lettres a l'Amazone* by Remy de Gourmont, and Radclyffe Hall's *The Well of Loneliness.* As Radclyffe Hall described her receiving her guests, Barney was "dressed all in white, and a large white fox skin was clasped round her slender and shapely shoulders. For the rest she had masses of thick fair hair, which was busily ridding itself of its hairpins." The Mata Hari once arrived at one of Barney's parties on horseback, completely naked. Barney was known to have had an affair with Dorothy Wilde, the niece of Oscar Wilde.

Continue up rue Jacob to rue Bonaparte. Go right on rue Bonaparte and make a quick right onto:

15. Rue Visconti. On your left you'll see the residence where Jean Racine (b. 1639) died on April 21, 1699. A French Classical dramatist, he played the role of court dramatist under Louis XIV. Educated at the Port-Royal abbey, he has been described as the most French of French writers. He is particularly well known for injecting his characters with a sense of psychological realism.

Just a bit farther on, in case you're interested, at number 17 is the site of Balzac's former print shop. Retrace your steps to rue Bonaparte. Go right to number 14, the:

16. Ecole des Beaux-Arts. This, the most famous of art schools, is housed in a group of buildings that date from the 17th through the 19th centuries. Originally, Beaux-Arts opened in 1648 as the Académie Royale de Peintre et de Sculpture; it became an individual institution in 1795. The Prix de Rome was bestowed by the Ecole des Beaux-Arts; its teachings remained traditional until well after World War II, and the entrance exam here was so difficult that even Auguste Rodin failed it. Among those who passed were Degas, Matisse, Monet, Renoir, and Max Weber.

Continue up rue Bonaparte and go right on rue des Beaux-Arts. Oscar Wilde died at number 13 rue des Beaux-Arts (the one with the ram's head). When you get to rue de Seine, make another right. Look for the art bookstore at number 33 rue de Seine, Fischbacher Livres d'Art, on your left. It's a wonderful store with a fine selection of books on all genres of art, in both French and English. At rue de Buci, go left to the:

17. Buci Market, which begins right at the intersection of rue de Buci and rue de Seine. It's one of the liveliest markets in the city of Paris. Here you'll find stalls selling fish, flowers, *fromage,* and fruit—the profusion of sights and smells will make you giddy. If you're in the neighborhood just before lunch, grab a picnic here—what could be better? Be aware that if you arrive at lunch time you won't find a market, because the market goes to lunch. It's best to arrive between 9am and 1pm or later in the afternoon and evening. It's also closed on Monday.

When you get to the carrefour de Buci, go left up rue Mazarine to passage Dauphine, on your right. In the passage Dauphine you'll find three sculptures by Max Ernst (all from 1938), entitled, *Sphinx et Sirene, Entrée des Fantomes,* and *Loplop Aile.* It's a great passageway, and it's the easiest way to get from rue Mazarine to rue Dauphine. Cross rue Dauphine and head directly into rue Christine. In 1938, Alice B. Toklas and Gertrude Stein moved into an apartment at:

18. **Number 15 rue Christine.** Janet Flanner reported that this apartment was formerly the apartment of Queen Christina of Sweden. In fact, it still held the queen's wall *boiseries* (panels) and her reading cabinet when Stein and Toklas moved in. On a visit to deliver a housewarming bouquet Flanner was asked to take an inventory of Stein's incredible collection of art. She found that Stein had over 130 canvases in her possession; 25 of them were Picassos.

As you continue along rue Christine, you'll find yourself on rue des Grands-Augustins. Directly across the street is:

19. **Number 7 rue des Grands-Augustins,** where Picasso lived from 1936 to 1955, very near his good friend Gertrude Stein. It was here that he painted the masterpiece *Guernica* in 1937, as is noted on the plaque.

Go right down rue des Grands-Augustins to rue St-André-des-Arts. Go left to:

20. **Number 28 rue St-André-des-Arts,** which used to be a bar called Le Gentilhomme. In 1962 Jack Kerouac spent some time here when he stopped in Paris on his way to Brittany to do some research about his family.

Retrace your steps, crossing rue des Grands-Augustins to number 46, on your right, which is where e.e. cummings lived in 1923. Continue along, and look for Bar Mazet on your left. Near the bar, go left into the:

21. **Cour du Commerce St-André.** There are many interesting shops and restaurants down here, and the passageway is associated with odd bits of history. At number 9, Dr. Guillotin perfected his invention on sheep before he decided that it was fit to use on humans. People dispute the way in which Guillotin died—some say it was by his own invention, others say it was of grief at what his invention had perpetrated. This was also the location of the printing shop to which Jean-Paul Marat (1743-93), Swiss-born French revolutionary and founder of the paper *L'Ami du Peuple,* would walk in his bathrobe every day to correct the proofs.

Exit the cour du Commerce St-André onto boulevard St-Germain. Go right to the corner of rue de l'Ancienne-Comédie, where you'll find at number 1:

22. **Le Procope** (formerly Café le Procope), founded in 1689 just after the opening of the Comédie Française (which used to be across the street) by a Sicilian named Procopio. It claims to be the world's oldest café. Indeed, Voltaire and Rousseau spent time here; later patrons included Benjamin Franklin, Victor Hugo, and Balzac. Of course, a café couldn't call itself a café (especially not the oldest one) unless Jean-Paul Sartre and Simone de Beauvoir had, at one time or another, been visitors.

The little island at the center of the boulevard is the:

23. **Carrefour de l'Odéon.** Take a look at the bronze statue of

Georges-Jacques Danton (1759–94), one of the moderate leaders of the French Revolution. A lawyer by trade, he became a leader of the Cordeliers and participated in the August 1792 storming of the Tuileries and the overthrow of the king.

After the Revolution he served as a member of the national assembly, but not for long, for he was executed by his arch-rival, Robespierre, during the Reign of Terror.

Continue across the street along into rue de l'Odéon to:

24. **Number 7,** now Galerie Regine Lussan but formerly Adrienne Monnier's bookstore La Maison des Amis des Livres, a gathering place for French writers in the 1920s. Guillaume Apollinaire, Paul Claudel, Paul Valéry (who Monnier actually published), and André Gide were all frequent visitors. Sylvia Beach's lover, Monnier committed suicide in 1955.

A bit farther along on the right is:

25. **Number 12,** where the original Shakespeare & Company was located from 1921 to 1940. Owned by Sylvia Beach, Shakespeare & Company became a favorite stopping place for expatriate Americans. Beach worked very hard nurturing James Joyce along and was the first to publish *Ulysses* (using her own funds). Later Bennet Cerf at Random House published *Ulysses* and is reported to have made at least $1 million on the book. Joyce received a $45,000 advance, but Beach was never to see any money even though she discovered, edited, and published the original. She claimed not to mind this and said that she would do anything for Joyce and his art. Joyce never returned her favors, and when her shop was threatened with closure it was André Gide, not Joyce, who came to her rescue.

Just a couple of doors down, where the Chinese import shop

SYLVIA BEACH

Born in Baltimore, Maryland, Beach (1887–1962) first came to Paris with her family as an adolescent. In 1917 she met Adrienne Monnier at her bookshop at 7 rue de l'Odéon (see stop 24) where they sat and discussed literature for hours. Monnier encouraged and inspired Beach to open an American bookshop, which she did on November 19, 1919, at 8 rue Dupuytren. The shop was furnished with flea market bargain items, and the walls were bare except for two drawings by William Blake and, later, some photographs supplied by Man Ray. In 1921 she moved the shop to rue de l'Odéon and moved in nearby with Adrienne Monnier.

During World War II Beach was safely hidden in the kitchen of an apartment on boulevard St-Michel for two years, but was later arrested and held for seven months before a high-ranking German officer was able to intervene on her behalf. She died in 1962.

Heng Seng Heng S.A. now stands, was the building in which Adrienne Monnier and Sylvia Beach had an apartment together until 1937. Go right at place de l'Odéon to number 6, now the:

26. **Hôtel Michelet Odéon.** American poet Allen Tate (1899–1979), stayed here in 1929. He too was introduced to Ernest Hemingway by Sylvia Beach.

As you continue around to the other side of place de l'Odéon you'll come to place Paul-Claudel. Here you will find the:

27. **Théâtre de l'Odéon,** built in 1782 by architects Peyre and de Wailly to house the Comédie Française. With nearly 2,000 seats, it was the biggest theater in Paris at the time. Beaumarchais's *The Marriage of Figaro* was both created and performed here in 1794. It was widely praised.

After you come out of the place Paul-Claudel go left on rue de Vaugirard to rue Monsieur-le-Prince. Go left on rue Monsieur-le-Prince to:

28. **Number 55,** on the right corner. Oliver Wendell Holmes (1809–94) lived here from 1833 to 1835 while studying medicine. A graduate of Harvard University, Holmes was a doctor, an occasional poet, and quite a wit. He came to Paris to study because during his lifetime, Paris was one of the greatest scientific and medical centers in the world. In 1857 he founded the *Atlantic Monthly* with J. R. Lowell. Dr. Holmes was easily flattered, and in his old age, he took advantage of his hearing problems and would say to his admirers, "I am a trifle deaf, you know. Do you mind repeating that a little louder?"

A bit farther up the street on the left side is:

29. **Number 22,** the building in which James Abbott McNeill Whistler had a studio on the second floor. Many of his contemporaries disliked him because he had such a high opinion of himself. In fact, a very wealthy man once visited his studio (when Whistler was still virtually unknown) and wished to know the total price of everything in the studio. Whistler quoted him a price of four million. As you can imagine, the man could hardly believe his ears. "What!" he exclaimed, to which Whistler replied, "My posthumous prices." Actually, this was probably the first time he ever underestimated himself.

Also on the left is:

30. **Number 14,** where in March 1959 Martin Luther King, Jr. visited Richard Wright in his apartment on the third floor. Sylvia Beach's bookstore was very near Wright's apartment. They became good friends and she said of him, "Of all writers I have known, he is the most unselfish and thoughtful. In fact, none of the others . . . were interested in anyone but themselves. Fellas like Hemingway appear uncouth beside Dick Wright."

Continue on, and when you get back to the place where rue de l'Odéon, rue Monsieur-le-Prince, and rue de Condé all come together to form the carrefour de l'Odéon, look for rue des Quatre-Vents to your left. Go left on rue des Quatre-Vents, crossing rue de Seine into rue Lobineau. At the corner of rue Lobineau and rue Mabillon is the:

31. Marché St-Germain. Inside this covered market you will find stalls selling fresh fruits and vegetables, fish, meats, and cheeses. If you're in the mood, wander through. If not, speed through and come out the other side of the market and go left (if for some reason you come out the way you came in, go right, and then left at the corner). Head toward:

32. St-Sulpice, one of the largest and richest churches in Paris. It also happens to be the most frequented and liveliest of the parish churches in the city.

Building actually began in 1646, but it wasn't finished until the late 18th century. The south tower never was completed. Two of the architects who worked on the church were Louis Le Vau and Jean-Baptiste Servandoni. As you enter the church note the enormous holy water stoups that are made of natural shells. The intricately carved pedestals were done by J. P. Pigalle. Go right after you enter and you will come across three of Eugène Delacroix's greatest masterpieces: *Jacob Wrestling with the Angel, Heliodorus Driven from the Temple,* and *St. Michael Vanquishing the Devil,* all of which were completed in 1881. Wander through and view the other spectacular pieces of art.

Another interesting feature of the church is the bronze meridian line that runs along the north-south transept. Somehow 19th-century scientists were able to determine that during both equinoxes and at winter solstice (at midday), sunlight would hit the line, run along the floor, climb up the obelisk to the globe on top, and light the cross.

Head across the place St-Sulpice to:

33. Rue Férou. Man Ray lived at number 2 when he came back to Paris in 1951, and Hemingway lived at number 6 while working on *A Farewell to Arms.* He had just left his wife (Hadley) and child and had moved in with Pauline Pfeiffer, his mistress. When asked why he left his wife he replied, "Because I'm a bastard."

At the end of rue Férou, go left in front of the palace to the corner of rue de Vaugirard and rue Servandoni and stop in front of:

34. 42 rue de Vaugirard. William Faulkner stayed here for several months in 1925. He particularly enjoyed going across the street to the Jardin du Luxembourg, where he could sit and write in peace. He describes the gardens in his 1931 novel *Sanctuary:*

> In the Luxembourg Gardens . . . the women sat knitting in shawls and even the men playing croquet played in coats and capes . . . the random shouts of children had that quality of autumn. . . . From beyond the circle with its spurious greek balustrade, clotted with movement, filled with a gray light of the same color and texture as the water which the fountain played into the pool, came a steady crash of music.

Located just across the street from Faulkner's old place and the Théâtre de l'Odéon is the:

35. Palais du Luxembourg, built by Marie de Médicis shortly after she was widowed by Henri IV's murder. She was never a tenant, because before it could be finished she was banished by her son, Louis XIII, for opposing Cardinal Richelieu. During the Revolution the palace was used as a prison. Currently the French Senate sits here. The palace is only open one day a month, and when it is the line is very long.

Beyond the palace is the:

36. Jardin du Luxembourg. Some people swear that Hemingway used to come here when he was broke to catch pigeons, wring their necks, and take them home for dinner. Other people believe the story is absolute nonsense. I for one wouldn't have put it past him.

As you enter the gardens, go straight until you reach the large, impressive Medici Fountain (1624), which will be on your left. This is a glorious place to sit and relax away from the crowds around the ornamental lake at the center of the gardens. Next, come around the back side of the bandstand area (near the boulevard St-Michel entrance), where you will find Rodin's portrait of Stendhal and a sculpture of George Sand (1905) by François Sicard. As you head for the other side of the gardens, look for the rose garden, the beehives, and the orchard. Also, you shouldn't miss the miniature Statue of Liberty, just off to the left of the exit at rue Guynemer.

Exit at rue Guynemer, and cross into the rue de Fleurus. At:

37. Number 27 you'll find the former home of Gertrude Stein and Alice B. Toklas—a plaque marks the spot. You're probably getting a little tired of hearing about these two at this point, but this is their most important residence, for this is the apartment in which Gertrude amassed her incredible collection of modern art, and this is where her famous salons were held. F. Scott Fitzgerald was a visitor here, and so was Hemingway. Picasso visited regularly, and so did Matisse and Gauguin. Stein helped guide the careers of more than a few of them here and took credit for many of their successes. There is no doubt that she did help the careers of many artists—the art dealers and collectors of her time watched what she and her brother Leo bought and then bought that too. She had the power to make or break almost any modern artist who walked through her front door at 27 rue de Fleurus, and in some instances, she did. Although her salons sparkled with brilliance and attracted a cast of artists, by the time she had moved to rue Christine, she had ostracized many of her literary and artistic friends.

End the tour here. If you go right at the corner of boulevard Raspail you'll reach a Métro station.

WALKING TOUR 5

The Latin Quarter Part I

Start: Place St-Michel. (Métro: Saint Michel.)
Finish: The Sorbonne.
Time: Three to five hours.
Best Time: Any time.

Since Roman times, the Quartier Latin, or Latin Quarter, has been the intellectual center of Paris. For 700 years Latin was the language of its inhabitants. Here you'll find the world-renowned Sorbonne surrounded by cafés, bookstores, and boutiques. You'll follow in the footsteps of Dante, Descartes, and Sartre, and you'll visit one of the oldest medical supply shops in the city of Paris. You'll especially enjoy the Musée de Cluny, where you can see the remains of the Roman baths and a spectacular collection of tapestries.

And as you wander pedestrian streets filled with Greek and Asian restaurants and souvenir shops, picture the streets at night, during a different time—windows lit by candles, silhouetting students bent over their desks.

1. Place St-Michel. Built by Napoléon III and famous for its fountain—the sculpture of St-Michel slaying the dragon, by Davioud (1860)—the Place St-Michel has been a center of activity for hundreds of years. Traditionally students of L'Ecole des Beaux-Arts go for a swim in the fountain after their annual ball; a less happy association is that of the students killed here by the Nazis during protests in August 1944.

From here, go down rue de la Huchette (if you're standing facing the fountain, rue de la Huchette is on your left between the yellow awnings of the bookstore Gibert Jeune, one of the few remaining truly collegiate bookstores in the Latin Quarter). At number 28 rue de la Huchette (on your left) is:

2. Hôtel Mont Blanc, the former residence of Eliot Harold Paul (1891–1958), the American author of *The Last Time I Saw Paris* (1942), a chronicle of the city in the 1920s. You'll also see a plaque commemorating Jean Albert Vouillard, who was killed here by the Gestapo at 8pm on May 17, 1944. Rue de la Huchette is almost 800 years old. It used to be home to diamond cutters and rotisseurs, who set up shop here; these days the only meat sellers you'll find are those who own the Greek restaurants that line the pedestrian alley. You'll be hard pressed to find a diamond seller.

As you walk, on your left you will pass rue du Chat-qui-Pêche, or "Street of the Fishing Cat." Continue along to the end of rue de la Huchette and go right down rue du Petit-Pont, which turns into rue St-Jacques. Go right again into rue St-Séverin. Continue past Tango du Chat Restaurant, which will be on your right. On your left will be the church of:

3. St-Séverin. Go in the side door, off rue St-Séverin. The original building here, an oratory, was built in honor of a hermit by the name of Séverin, who lived here in the sixth century. It was burned down by Norsemen in the 11th century, and a new chapel was erected in its place, which by the end of the 11th century had become the parish church of the Left Bank. The building you see today, in Flamboyant Gothic style, was begun in the early 13th century, and the work continued well into the 16th century.

The double ambulatory is what really makes St-Séverin unique among the churches of Paris. Unfortunately the organ obscures your view of the rose window, but note that the organ case was built by Dupré. Saint-Saëns was said to have played on it.

The rest of the stained glass behind the altar looks like an Impressionist painting, with its great swaths of color. Best viewed at a distance, the windows, which were designed by Jean Bazaine in 1966, depict the Seven Sacraments. You're not expected to know what they are by looking at them, there are small plaques underneath each window that tell which of the Seven Sacraments is represented.

Exit the church the way you entered, go left on rue des Prêtres-St-Séverin to the front of the church. Go along rue des Prêtres-St-Séverin to rue de la Parcheminerie. Go right to number 29 rue de la Parcheminerie, the:

4. Abbey Bookshop. A Canadian-based bookstore, the Abbey Bookshop sells books in both French and English and has a great selection of Canadian titles. The bookstore's presence here is significant because the street was in fact named after the professional letter writers, booksellers, copyists, and parchment sellers who set up shop here. At one time it was called rue des Ecrivains (or "Street of Writers").

After you've finished browsing, turn right back out onto rue de la Parcheminerie (retracing your steps). Cross rue Boutebrie and go right onto rue St-Jacques. Go left on rue Dante at this slightly confusing intersection and look on your right for number 9:

5. A L'Imagerie, a great print and poster shop. You'll find hoards of Art Deco and Art Nouveau posters, as well as any museum poster you could possibly desire. It is supposedly the oldest (not to mention biggest) shop of its kind in the city.

Keep walking to number 4 on your left, the Librairie Gourmande. It's famous for its selection of cookbooks, the only problem being that they're all in French. However, if you love to cook and your French is up to snuff you might go absolutely wild here.

Eventually rue Dante turns into a small section of street called:

6. Rue du Fouarre. This is quite a famous little *rue;* beginning in the 12th century students used to sit in the street on piles or bundles of straw (hence the name, derived from the word *feure,* meaning straw) listening to teachers lecture. Dante himself is believed to have heard some lectures here in 1304. While you're here, you might want to stop in at the bookstore and *salon de thé* (tearoom) on your left.

Backtrack and turn right onto rue Galande (the street you passed before you went onto rue du Fouarre). During Roman times rue Galande was the Lyons-Paris road. Later, during the 17th century, the street was much more attractive than it is today because it was lined with aristocratic residences. At number 42 on your right is:

7. Studio Galande. Currently a cinema (and a not-so-attractive one to boot) that's mainly famous for its nightly showing of the *Rocky Horror Picture Show,* it nevertheless features a charming 14th-century bas-relief of Saint Julien le Hospitaller (or le Pauvre) in his boat.

On your left at number 65 bis is Cybele Archaeological bookstore, which has a marvelous collection of archaeological books. At numbers 50–52 on the right is Le Chat Huant, an appealing shop that specializes in Asian merchandise, including jewelry, inks, Sumi-e kits, and a great selection of paint brushes.

At the corner of rue Galande and rue St-Julien-le-Pauvre, at number 1 bis rue St-Julien-le-Pauvre, take a little detour down the winding staircase of the Caveau des Oubliettes for a good look at a true Parisian nightclub. (This 17th-century house was built on the existing medieval foundations.)

Go right on rue St-Julien-le-Pauvre to the church of:

8. St-Julien-le-Pauvre, built some time before the ninth century and thought to be the oldest church in Paris. It began much the same way St-Séverin did—as an oratory dedicated to a Saint.

During the Revolution, the church was used to store fodder. It was so damaged during this period (and by regular wear and tear up until the Revolution) that much of it had to be rebuilt, including the facade you see today. Inside it retains one of the few rood screens extant. Since 1889 it has belonged to the Greek Orthodox church.

When you come out of the church, go right and keep an eye out for number 14 (on your left), the mansion of Isaac de Laffemas, governor of the Petit Châtelet prison. It has a wonderful portal that dates from the end of the 17th century.

REFRESHMENT STOP Also on your left is a quaint little place, **The Tea Caddy,** at number 14 rue St-Julien-le-Pauvre, where you can stop for some real English tea and scones. If you're interested in something a little more filling, light lunches are also served.

At the end of rue St-Julien-le-Pauvre, on the right, is square René-Viviani, graced with lime trees and lilac bushes. The false acacia that is held up by supports is thought to be one of the oldest trees in Paris.

If you go left at the corner of rue St-Julien-le-Pauvre you'll find:

9. **Shakespeare and Company,** located at 37 rue de la Bûcherie. Not Sylvia Beach's original Shakespeare & Company, this namesake is run by George Bates Whitman (the self-professed grandson of Walt). Whitman purchased part of Sylvia Beach's library which is housed at the top of a very treacherous flight of stairs. You're welcome to go in and browse through Beach's personal collection.

In case you're wondering if the cots located in niches all around the shop are for sitting or sleeping, they're most likely for both. I've heard that Whitman sometimes allows poor writers to spend a little time here until they can secure enough money to get a room elsewhere.

Each book you purchase will be stamped with the official Shakespeare and Company inscription, "Shakespeare and Co., Kilomètre Zéro, Paris." It's open every day from noon to midnight.

Backtrack to square René-Viviani. Go past it and at the corner make a right on rue Lagrange. Make a quick left onto the extension of rue de la Bûcherie, which got its name because barges used to load and unload shipments of wood there. Cross rue Frédéric-Sauton onto rue des Grands Degrés (it runs directly into rue de la Bûcherie). Note as you go the shop at number 6, La Route d'Alexandre, which has some great Asian pottery and jewelry. Continue out to the end and go right on quai de la Tournelle to rue de Bièvre. Go right on rue de Bièvre to:

10. **Number 22,** the home of François Mitterand, president of France. You will know you're in the right place because you'll see the guards out front (the road will also be blockaded). Mitterand still insists upon residing in his private home, rather than in the Palais de l'Elysée, the traditional home for France's presidents. Number 22 rue de Bièvre is a quaint, private home on a quiet street—can you blame him? Mitterand was a prominent figure in the Resistance during World War II, and in 1971 he founded the French Socialist party. A scholar of law and politics, he was reelected in 1988 to a second term as president.

Continue along rue de Bièvre, cross boulevard St-Germain and make a little jog off to the right onto rue Monge. If you're ready for a picnic, Rue Monge is a good place to gather your supplies. Stop at the charcuterie on the left for pâté or other delicacies; cross the street to the *fromagerie* and pick up some cheese; and a bit farther on stop at the *boulangerie/pâtisserie* for your baguette and a couple of lemon tarts. Gather all of this together and you'll find a perfect picnic spot not far ahead at square P. Langevin.

Before you go there, however, there's another interesting church along the way, on your left. It's called:

11. **St-Nicolas-du-Chardonnet** (the actual address is 30 rue St-Victor). This site was once a field of thistles (or *chardons*), and the original place of worship here was a chapel built in the 13th century. Construction of the present church began in 1656. It is thought that Charles Le Brun, a former parishioner here, designed the left side of the church.

A Catholic parish that still holds masses in Latin, St-Nicolas-du-Chardonnet is a veritable treasure trove of art, much of it the work of Charles Le Brun. Once you get inside, turn to the right to view his work *The Martyrdom of John the Baptist*. In the first chapel on the left wall as you enter is the *Baptism of Christ* by Corot. Continue around behind the altar, and as you come around to the other side you'll see the tomb of Le Brun's mother as well as a memorial to Le Brun and his wife by Antoine Coysevox (other works by this artist are pointed out in Walking Tour 8, stop 9, and Walking Tour 9, stop 4). Above the altar and on the ceiling are some fine paintings by Le Brun.

Exit to rue des Bernardins (it intersects here with rue Monge running along the side of the church) and walk to rue des Ecoles. Before you lies square P. Langevin, where you can enjoy that picnic lunch. Afterwards, return to rue des Ecoles and go left as you exit the park. On your left at number 25 bis you'll pass Librairie Presence Africaine, an African bookstore. Cross rue de la Montagne-Ste-Geneviève to rue des Carmes. At rue des Carmes turn right to number 1 bis rue des Carmes where you'll find the:

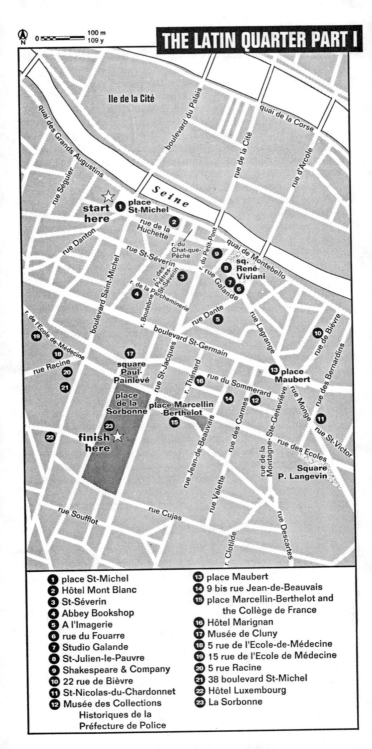

THE LATIN QUARTER PART I

0 ___ 100 m
    ___ 109 y

1. place St-Michel
2. Hôtel Mont Blanc
3. St-Séverin
4. Abbey Bookshop
5. A l'Imagerie
6. rue du Fouarre
7. Studio Galande
8. St-Julien-le-Pauvre
9. Shakespeare & Company
10. 22 rue de Bièvre
11. St-Nicolas-du-Chardonnet
12. Musée des Collections Historiques de la Préfecture de Police
13. place Maubert
14. 9 bis rue Jean-de-Beauvais
15. place Marcellin-Berthelot and the Collège de France
16. Hôtel Marignan
17. Musée de Cluny
18. 5 rue de l'Ecole-de-Médecine
19. 15 rue de l'Ecole de Médecine
20. 5 rue Racine
21. 38 boulevard St-Michel
22. Hôtel Luxembourg
23. La Sorbonne

12. **Musée des Collections Historiques de la Préfecture de Police.** This museum is located within the ugly building on your right, but don't let that deter you—it has some very interesting exhibits. For instance, the orders for the arrest of Dr. Guillotin, the bloodstained book from the assassination of President Paul Doumer (1932), and a huge collection of memorabilia from World War II's Nazi Occupation. In short, you'll find all kinds of chilling pieces of evidence, including a variety of weapons, each of which has been used to commit one crime or another.

   Continue along rue des Carmes to:

13. **Place Maubert.** Called Maubert Cesspit by Erasmus (see box below), this square was once a place of execution in which people were hanged and burned at the stake, like Etienne Dolet (b. 1509), French scholar and philosopher, who was burned here in 1546 after being convicted of heresy. Later a statue was erected as a tribute to him, but it was taken down during the Nazi invasion and was never seen again. So many Huguenots were killed here that it became a place of pilgrimage. Today the place Maubert is a well-kept, upscale shopping area—not a trace of the cesspit remains.

   Turn left on boulevard St-Germain and then left again onto rue Jean-de-Beauvais to:

14. **Number 9 bis rue Jean-de-Beauvais,** one of the Sorbonne's first college chapels. Built in 1375, its Gothic spire is the only one of its period left in the city of Paris. Since 1882 it has been used as a Romanian Orthodox church.

   Continue along and go up the stairs to rue des Ecoles. Note the interesting sculpture on your left at the top of the stairs. Turn right onto rue des Ecoles, and on your left will be:

15. **Place Marcellin-Berthelot and the Collège de France.** Rebelling against the narrow-mindedness of the teachings of the Sorbonne, François I founded the College of France in 1530.

ERASMUS

Desiderius Erasmus (1466–1536), the Dutch humanist, theologian, scholar, and writer, was an ordained priest of the Roman Catholic Church in spite of the fact that he was a reformer. He spent time studying at the University of Paris, and one of his greatest achievements was a translation of the Old Testament from its original Greek into Latin. Although a reformer, he disagreed with the ideology of Martin Luther, the father of Protestantism, and he actually attacked Luther's ideas regarding predestination with his essay, *On the Freedom of the Will*. Erasmus also said, when asked why he wasn't observing the Catholic tradition of the Lenten fast, "I have a Catholic soul, but a Lutheran stomach."

The professors at the new Collège de France were paid by the king rather than by the students, a radical change from the procedure at the Sorbonne. The school began as a trilingual institution, teaching Latin, Greek, and Hebrew—a departure from the traditional college. Not long after its founding, courses in mathematics, philosophy, surgery, medicine, law, Arabic, and astronomy were also made available. While Louis XV was king, a course in French literature was added, the first of its kind. Reflecting a tradition of nondiscriminatory policies, the inscription outside the school reads *Docet omnia,* or "All are taught here."

In place Berthelot is a bronze of Dante by Aube, as well as a statue by Eugène Guillaume of Claude Bernard, a famous 19th-century physiologist who worked in the laboratory of the Collège de France. Bernard died nearby at number 40 rue des Ecoles.

Turn right off rue des Ecoles to rue Thénard. As you walk along, look to the right down rue de Latran for a nice view of the Romanian Orthodox church you saw earlier. Continue to rue du Sommerard and go right to number 13, the:

16. Hôtel Marignan. In 1921 e.e. cummings stayed here. An American poet, cummings had a preference for lowercase letters and very little (if any) punctuation. Turn around and go back in the other direction on rue du Sommerard. At square Paul-Painlevé you'll see the:

17. Musée de Cluny, at number 6 place Paul-Painlevé. At the beginning of the third century a Gallo-Roman building, the Palais des Thermes, presumed by archaeologists to be a Roman baths, stood here. Palais des Thermes dates from between A.D. 161 and 181. The baths were thought to have been burned down several times by barbarians. About a thousand years later Pierre de Chalus, Abbot of Cluny-en-Bourgogne, bought the ruins and the neighboring land in order to build a residence for visiting abbots. The building you see today is the work of still another abbot, Jacques d'Amboise, who turned the place into something of a palace. After the Revolution the property changed hands several times and was finally purchased by Alexandre du Sommerard, an official of the state and collector of medieval art. After his death in 1842, his house and its contents were sold to the state and it opened as a museum in 1844 with Edmond Sommerard (Alexandre's son), as curator.

Today, thanks to both Sommerards, the museum houses one of the greatest collections of medieval art and artifacts in the world. The collection includes finely wrought jewelry, brilliant stained-glass windows (this is the closest you'll ever get to glass like this), and some amazing tapestries that by themselves make a visit to the museum worthwhile. Don't miss the original Abbot's Chapel, complete with an incredible vaulted ceiling.

Exit Musée de Cluny to rue du Sommerard and go to boulevard St-Michel. Cross boulevard St-Michel to rue de l'Ecole-de-Médecine and look for:

18. Number 5. This is the former location of the Brotherhood of Surgeons, founded by Saint Louis. Half barbers, half surgeons, they performed surgeries on "minor ailments" until the 17th century. Currently the building houses the Institute of Modern Languages. There's also a plaque here commemorating the birth of actress Sarah Bernhardt in this house on October 25, 1844.

Continue along rue de l'Ecole-de-Médecine, passing on your left Establissements du Docteur Anzoux S.A., which has been here since 1822. It's filled with all kinds of medical gadgets, from plastic models of the ear to scalpels and stethoscopes.

On your left at:

19. Number 15 there was once a Franciscan monastery. The first attempt at mapping the city of Paris was undertaken here by Verniquet (a geometrician) in 1785. His maps were the ones used as the basis for all later maps of Paris.

Turn around and go back to the boulevard St-Michel. Go right to rue Racine and make a right on rue Racine to:

20. Number 5 (on your left), where Henry Wadsworth Longfellow lived while he studied at the Sorbonne. In 1826 when he began his studies he lived in a *pension de famille,* or boarding house, until he began to feel imprisoned by the restrictions of curfew and mealtimes. He moved here so he could be more independent.

Go back to boulevard St-Michel. At:

21. Number 38 you'll find the apartment that Richard Wright sublet in 1946 from a professor who was on leave in Australia.

If you continue along to rue de Vaugirard to number 1 bis, you'll find the Trianon Palace Hotel, where Richard Wright took up residence when he first arrived in Paris after a long battle with the United States government for a passport.

At number 4 is the:

22. Hôtel Luxembourg (formerly the Hôtel Lisbonne) where author Will Shirer lived in September of 1925. It was a bargain at $10 a month, but Shirer reported that one had to use the bidet as a bathtub since the only bathtub in the hotel was being used as a coal bin by the owner. Further, he and other Americans who were accustomed to creature comforts had a lot of trouble learning how to use the building's Turkish toilets.

Go back to boulevard St-Michel. A side trip down the boulevard will show you the homes or studios of two more expatriates of note. Walk to number 85, where Archibald MacLeish, the American poet, lived in 1923 during his first visit to Paris. A friend of James Joyce, he originally came to Paris as a lawyer. And at number 93, now the Foyer International des Etudiantes, Sylvia Beach hid out in a kitchen on the top floor during the Nazi Occupation from 1942 to 1944.

If you're not interested in taking the long walk down boulevard St-Michel and then back up, then cross the boulevard and walk through place de la Sorbonne, built in 1634 and anchored by a statue of Auguste Comte (See Walking Tour 11, stop 11 for more details on Comte), to:

23. La Sorbonne. In 1253 Robert de Sorbon, confessor of Saint Louis, founded the Sorbonne (with the help of the king) for poor students who wished to pursue theological studies. He wanted it to be a place where they could live and go to school without having to worry about money. Since then it has seen such famous teachers as Saint Thomas Aquinas and Roger Bacon and such famous students as Dante, John Calvin, and Henry Wadsworth Longfellow. In 1469 France's first printing press was set up here, and during the Occupation the Sorbonne became the headquarters for the Resistance. The courtyard and galleries are open to the public, and in the Cour d'Honneur (the courtyard) you'll find statues of Victor Hugo and Louis Pasteur.

WALKING TOUR 6

The Latin Quarter Part II

Start: The Sorbonne. (Métro: Odéon is the closest stop.)
Finish: The intersection of rue Mouffetard and rue Daubenton.
Time: About three hours.
Best Time: Begin this one either early in the morning or late in the afternoon so you have the opportunity to visit the Mouffetard Market while it's open.

The second part of the Latin Quarter tour focuses on some major attractions, including the Panthéon (where you can visit the tombs of some of France's most notable scholars and politicians). You'll also get a chance to visit the oldest zoo in France, a mosque bedecked with some spectacular mosaics, and a fabulous food market.

Exit the Sorbonne (details in the previous tour) turn left on rue de la Sorbonne (which turns into rue Victor-Cousin), and left again onto rue Cujas. On your left you'll pass the Lycée Louis-Le-Grand, founded in 1550 and the alma mater of a long list of notables—Robespierre, Hugo, Baudelaire, Voltaire, and Pompidou are but a few. Continue along rue Cujas you'll eventually arrive at the place du Panthéon, where off to your right is the:

1. Panthéon. Located at the top of the Montagne Ste-Geneviève, it's probably one of the best-known monuments in all of Paris. There's a story behind its foundation. In 1744 Louis XV was very ill. He vowed that if he recovered he would rebuild the abbey of Ste-Geneviève in her honor. He did recover, and he entrusted the job to the marquis de Marigny, Madame de Pompadour's brother, who passed the responsibility to architect Jacques-Germain Soufflot. The original plans called for a church, but construction stopped after a round of financial difficulties and the death of Soufflot. When an important Revolution-era politician by the name of Mirabeau died, the French parliament decided that the church of Ste-Geneviève should be changed into a "Temple of Fame" to hold the remains of all the great men of France, the first of whom would be Mirabeau.

Shortly after Mirabeau's burial, the remains of Voltaire were exhumed and moved to the Panthéon, which became a "temple dedicated to all the gods." Among its denizens are Jean-Jacques Rousseau, Victor Hugo, Paul Painlevé, Louis Braille (inventor of the Braille system for the blind), Emile Zola (See Walking Tour 10, stop 19), Jean Moulin (a Resistance fighter who was tortured to death by the Germans), and Marcelin Berthelot and his wife—the only woman entombed here.

Across rue Cujas from the Panthéon stands the Bibliothèque Ste-Geneviève (1824), which houses over two million volumes. Go around to the right of the Panthéon to:

2. **St-Etienne-du-Mont,** one of the most beautiful examples of Gothic architecture in Paris. Completed and consecrated in the 17th century, the church holds a shrine to Sainte Geneviève, as well as the remains of Racine and Pascal. Walk around to the right. Notice the spiral staircases that lead up to the 16th- and 17th-century rood screen. Not far beyond the rood screen are the epitaphs of Pascal and Racine. Beyond that are the relics of Sainte Geneviève. Continue around and you'll see stained glass windows, some of which date from the 16th and 17th centuries. Here you will also see busts of Pascal and Racine.

Come out of St-Etienne-du-Mont and turn left onto rue Clovis to the:

3. **Lycée Henri IV,** which is on your right. One of the city's best-known high schools, Lycée Henri IV is housed in one of the former buildings of the abbey of Ste-Geneviève. Jean-Paul Sartre was among the teachers here. The tower that you see within the walls is Clovis tower, named for King Clovis of the Franks; he was responsible for building the original Abbaye Ste-Geneviève. The tower is all that remains of the abbey. The physicists Ampère and Arago used the tower for their experiments in the 19th century.

Continue along rue Clovis and turn right on rue Descartes to:

4. **Number 39** on the left, where poet Paul Verlaine (1844–96) died. He became a major figure in the bohemian literary world with the 1869 publication of *Fêtes galantes*. His *Romances sans paroles* distinguished him as the first symbolist poet.

When you come to the end of rue Descartes turn left onto rue Thouin. Follow rue Thouin to rue du Cardinal-Lemoine. Go right on rue du Cardinal-Lemoine to number 74, the:

5. **Salon de Thé Under Hemingway,** Hemingway's first home in Paris. In 1922 he was visited here by Gertrude Stein and Alice

SAINTE GENEVIEVE

Born at Nanterre, Sainte Geneviève (420–500) told the bishop Saint Germanus d'Auxerre when she was a small child that she wanted to devote herself to God. When she turned 15 the bishop gave her a veil that was symbolic of a virgin dedicated to God, and shortly thereafter, it is said, she performed her first miracle—she cured her mother's blindness.

Sainte Geneviève later moved to Paris. She is credited with sparing the city from an attack by Atilla the Hun by literally praying the Huns away from Paris, in 451. Virtually everyone had fled the city at the mere thought that the Huns might arrive, but Geneviève stayed and prayed. The city was delivered.

Some of her other alleged miracles included curing the sick and actually stopping a rain storm. People began to worship her even while she was alive. After her death during a terrible epidemic her relics were paraded through the streets, and the disease stopped spreading. To this day, as a consequence, her relics are paraded through the streets every year, and Sainte Geneviève is recognized as the patron saint of Paris.

B. Toklas, who told him that he needed to rewrite, from beginning to end, his first attempt at a novel.

Now, turn around and go back across rue Thouin to:

6. Number 71 rue du Cardinal-Lemoine. Irish novelist James Joyce lived here in 1921, just a year before his masterpiece *Ulysses* was published by Sylvia Beach. Other publishers considered it obscene and unpublishable.

Continue along to:

7. Number 67, where the mathematician and philosopher Blaise Pascal (1623–62) died. A child genius, Pascal invented a calculating machine at the age of 19 and was also the founder of the modern theory of probability. However, most people know Pascal for his *Pensées,* which outline a mystical faith.

A little farther down the road, across rue Monge, at number 49 you'll find the:

8. Hôtel le Brun, at which painter Jean-Antoine Watteau (1684–1721) spent the last few years of his life. One of the leading figures of Rococo art, he is famous for creating the *fête galante* (paintings of a pastoral, dreamy nature).

Go back to rue Monge and go left to rue de Navarre. Go left on rue de Navarre and follow the signs to:

9. Arènes de Lutèce, a Roman amphitheater. With its 36 rows of stone seats, it had a seating capacity of 15,000. Some of the seats actually had the names of their owners chiseled into them.

THE LATIN QUARTER PART II

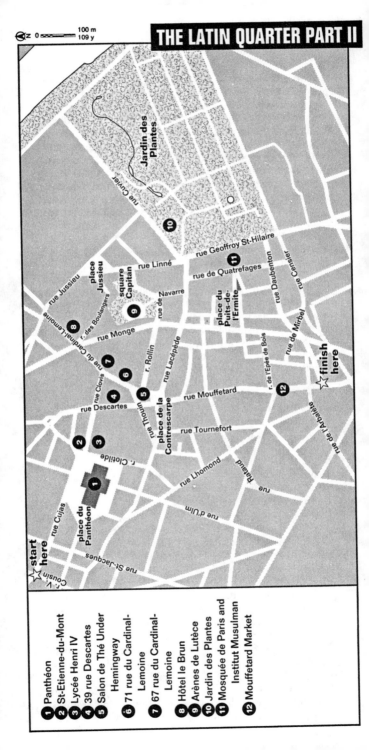

0 — 100 m / 109 y

Jardin des Plantes

rue Cuvier

rue Geoffroy St-Hilaire

rue Linné

place Jussieu

square Capitan

rue de Quatrefages

rue Jussieu

r. des Boulangers

Navarre

rue de Navarre

place du Puits-de-l'Ermite

rue Daubenton

rue Censier

rue du Cardinal-Lemoine

rue Monge

rue de Mirbel

rue Lacépède

r. Rollin

rue Clovis

rue Descartes

rue Thouin

place de la Contrescarpe

rue Mouffetard

r. de l'Epée de Bois

r. Clotilde

rue Tournefort

rue de l'Arbalète

rue Lhomond

rue Rataud

rue d'Ulm

place du Panthéon

rue Cujas

rue St-Jacques

r. V. Cousin

start here

finish here

1. Panthéon
2. St-Etienne-du-Mont
3. Lycée Henri IV
4. 39 rue Descartes
5. Salon de Thé Under Hemingway
6. 71 rue du Cardinal-Lemoine
7. 67 rue du Cardinal-Lemoine
8. Hôtel le Brun
9. Arènes de Lutèce
10. Jardin des Plantes
11. Mosquée de Paris and Institut Musulman
12. Mouffetard Market

Archaeologists believe it was built around the end of the first century A.D. At the end of the third century, when the barbarians invaded, it fell into disuse; by the fourth century people were using it as a cemetery. At the end of the 12th century it was buried when a moat was dug around Philippe Auguste's city wall. It was rediscovered in 1869 and restored. Today, it's a public garden featuring square Capitan, named for a sponsor of the restoration. You will always find a group of children playing here, accompanied by their nannies or parents; there might even be a full-fledged soccer match in progress. Retrace your steps to rue de Navarre. Go left to the corner and then right along the extension of rue de Navarre. When you come to rue Lacépède, make a left and follow it to the end. Across rue Linné and straight ahead into the rue Cuvier is the entrance to the:

10. Jardin des Plantes. In 1626 Louis XIII began to execute a plan for a medicinal botanical garden that had been conceived by Henri IV and his minister, Sully. Louis XIV's doctor, a man by the name of Fagon, traveled around the world collecting specimens and set the groundwork for the curator, Buffon, who was later able to finish Henri IV's original plans. Some of France's great naturalists worked here in the gardens, including Jussieu, Geoffroy St-Hilaire, Daubenton, Lacépède, and the famous Lamarck (who many argue was the true originator of the theory of evolution).

Today, the gardens, which include greenhouses and a maze, cover 74 acres of land; from April to October they are a riot of colors and scents.

The Ménagerie, as they call the zoo, is the oldest in France; it began as a sort of holding area for animals from Versailles that managed to survive the Revolution. The first animals weren't too thrilling, just your average zebra, hartebeest, and rhino. Elephants were brought in 1795, and by 1827 (with a couple of bears and giraffes), it was looking more like a real zoo. Unfortunately, the Ménagerie's period of growth didn't last long—many of the animals were eaten by hungry Parisians during the siege of the city in the Franco-Prussian War (1870–71). The place hasn't been quite the same since, but that doesn't matter to most of the children who visit here.

The park also contains the museum of Natural History possessing a great collection of minerals and insects.

Exit the Jardin des Plantes from the entrance and retrace your steps back to rue Lacépède. Go right on rue Lacépède and then left to rue de Quatrefages. Continue along to place du Puits-de-l'Ermite. You'll see on your left the:

11. Mosquée de Paris and Institut Musulman, at number 1 place du Puits-de-l'Ermite. These beautiful buildings were constructed between 1922 and 1926. As you enter notice the grand patio with its cedar woodwork, eucalyptus plants, and gurgling fountain. There are some lovely mosaic friezes on the walls of the mosque with quotations from the Koran, and the prayer rooms house an incredible collection of handwoven carpets, some of which date back to the 17th century. The Institut Musulman is a school that teaches Arabic and Islamic culture.

Not far from the building in which you are now standing is a Turkish bathhouse. Go outside the way you entered, and (facing away from the mosque) go left to rue Daubenton. Go left on rue Daubenton to rue Geoffroy St-Hilaire and go left again. At number 29 and 31 you'll find the bathhouse entrance. There are three steam rooms—available to men and women on different days, of course—and an Islamic art gallery is also on the premises.

REFRESHMENT STOP If you're hungry for lunch or just a snack try the Moorish café or the Arabic restaurant also located on the grounds of the mosque. They serve delicious pastries and strong, sweet Turkish coffee.

Exit the mosque, go through place du Puits-de-l'Ermite (take the roadway on the left side), and continue on rue du Puits-de-l'Ermite to rue Monge. Go left on rue Monge to rue de l'Epée-de-Bois and turn right. Follow it all the way to rue Mouffetard. Go left on rue Mouffetard to the:

12. Mouffetard Market, another of Paris's colorful outdoor food markets. The narrow street overflows with people and is lined with displays of fruits, vegetables, cheeses, and meats—sensual overstimulation indeed. Savor the experience; it may become one of your fondest memories of Paris.

If you go left from the corner of rue Daubenton and rue Mouffetard you'll find the Métro station.

WALKING TOUR 7

The Marais

Start: Place de la Bastille. (Métro: Bastille.)
Finish: Centre Pompidou.
Time: Three to eight hours, depending on how much time you spend in the museums—try to decide ahead of time which of them you'd most like to visit.
Best Time: Wednesday through Sunday, beginning at around 10am.
Worst Time: The Musée Picasso and Centre Pompidou are closed on Tuesday. The Musée Carnavalet is closed on Monday. Also, if you start late in the day, you'll never make it to more than one museum.

The Marais district, located in the 3rd and 4th arrondissements on the Right Bank, was originally a swampland that was situated outside the city walls and was set aside for grazing animals. By the 17th century, it was the seat of the Parisian aristocracy, and the nobles who lived here built incredible mansions. Unfortunately, many of these buildings were neglected until the 1960s when the minister of Cultural Affairs took an interest in restoring them. You'll see some of these *hôtels particuliers* as you walk this tour.

Presently the Marais is home to the Asian and Jewish communities of Paris. This tour will take you right into the bustling heart of the Jewish district, where homey delicatessens, patisseries, and take-out falafel shops stand beside chic boutiques. You'll also have the opportunity to visit several museums; one of them is the Musée Picasso, where you'll be able to see pieces that you've never seen before.

1. Place de la Bastille. The original fortress of the Bastille was built as a palace for Charles V. Later Cardinal Richelieu used it as a political prison for those who opposed royal power; Voltaire was twice imprisoned here. On July 14, 1789, 633 people stormed the Bastille, lynched the governor, freed the seven prisoners, and destroyed the fortress. The remains of the original fortress can be seen at number 5.

The July Column that stands at the center of the square is, however, not associated with the storming of the Bastille. Instead, it commemorates those who died in the July Revolution of 1830, which overthrew the Bourbon king Charles X and replaced him with Louis Philippe d'Orleans. The new king requested that this monument be erected in memory of the 615 people who died here for him. In 1840 the bodies of those victims were moved to the underground vaults here. The dead from the revolution of 1848 were entombed here as well.

The July Column, topped by the statue *Génie de la Liberté,* weighs 174 tons, is 154 feet tall, and if you want to reach the upper gallery you'll have to climb approximately 240 steps. The names of the victims who are entombed within are inscribed on the sides of the column.

From here, you can see the:

2. Bastille Opéra, designed by Carlos Ott, a Canadian-Uruguayan architect. A 2,700-seat venue for popular opera, it was intended to be the biggest opera house in the world.

Go out of place de la Bastille and take a left on rue St-Antoine. Follow rue St-Antoine to rue de Birague. Go right on rue de Birague to the:

3. Place des Vosges. Inaugurated on April 5, 6, and 7 in 1609, this was the first public square to be built by Henri IV. Originally called the place Royal, Henri IV intended it to be the scene of both commercial business and social festivities. During the Revolution, the square became the place de l'Invisibilité when its statue of Louis XIII was stolen (and probably melted down). At this time it was also used as a military site. Today, at the center of the square stands a replacement statue of Louis XIII.

The square enjoyed happier days after it was renamed place des Vosges (so-called because in the entire city of Paris the Vosges department was the first to pay its taxes) on September 23, 1800. When it became the center of industrialized Paris, however, it suffered. The grand buildings that surround the square were divided up into smaller rooms and apartments, and the area did not recover until recently, when it was declared an historic monument.

There are 36 pavilions around the square, and the two tall buildings facing each other at either side of the square (you came in through one of them) are known as the King and Queen's pavilions. You entered through the Pavillon du Roi. Most of the pavilions now house antique shops, bookstores, art galleries, and cafés. As you walk through you're likely to come across a whole parade of musicians playing for their dinner here—especially on weekends.

As you enter the square, go right to number 6, the:

4. Musée Victor Hugo. This museum is housed in the Hôtel de Rohan-Guéménée, where Victor Hugo lived from 1832 to 1848. (In 1848 he went into exile because he opposed Napoléon III, who had just come to power.) Inside the museum you'll find hundreds of books and drawings that were donated to the city in 1902 by Paul Meurice, Hugo's friend and the executor of his will. Because there are over 500 of his "spontaneous drawings," they are rotated on a regular basis. The museum also possesses a collection of all editions of his works.

Continue along to:

5. Number 8, the former residence of authors Théophile Gautier (see Walking Tour 10, stop 19) and Alphonse Daudet. Daudet (1840–97) literally began his career as an adolescent. Forced into a position as a "study master" at age 16 because of his father's financial problems, he came to Paris to pursue his writing career at age 17. He is most famous for his Naturalistic stories and novels, whose subjects are the lives of the French, both from a Parisian and provincial point of view. His works include *Le petit chose* (1868), and *L'Evangeliste* (1883).

As you walk around, note that at number 12 place des Vosges is the place where Henri IV's topographer, Claude de Chastillon, lived. He was, at that time, responsible for making maps, as well as reproductions of famous monuments of Paris.

Continuing around the square, take a look at the historic Pavillon de la Reine at number 28 (now one of the most fashionable hotels in this area). Farther along,

6. Number 21 was another of Alphonse Daudet's addresses, but it is more notable as the home of Cardinal Richelieu (1585–1642). Richelieu became secretary of state in 1616 with the help of the King's mother, Marie de Médicis. In 1622 he became cardinal of the Roman Catholic church, and in 1624 he was appointed prime minister under Louis XIII. Six years later, jealous of his power, Marie de Médicis turned against him, but she lacked the support of the king and was banished. Soon afterward Richelieu secured complete control over the French government.

Continue around the square, and on your right as you head back to rue de Birague (coming from the opposite direction in which you began), is the:

7. Hôtel de Sully, one of the city's most beautiful mansions. It was built in 1624 by Mesme-Gallet (a rich banker), but it was Henri IV's minister, the duc de Sully, who beautified it throughout with painted ceilings and painted and gilded pilasters. Presently, the building is home to the Caisse Nationale des Monuments Historiques et des Sites (National Historical Monuments and Sites Commission), and occasionally temporary exhibitions are held here. An interesting historical footnote— Voltaire was beaten by the servants of a nobleman under the

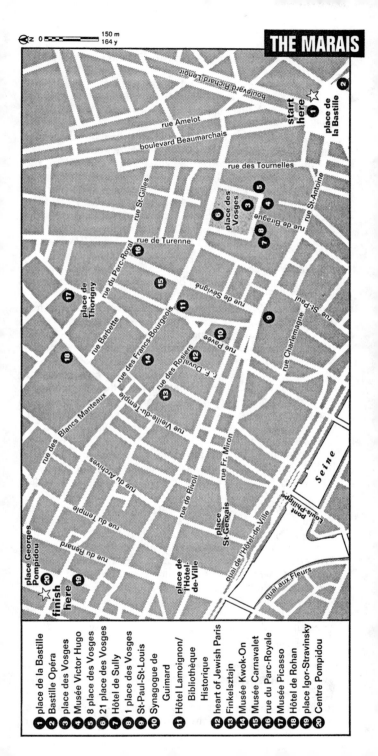

THE MARAIS

0 — 150 m / 164 y

boulevard Richard-Lenoir

rue Amelot

boulevard Beaumarchais

rue des Tournelles

rue St-Gilles

place des Vosges

rue de Birague

rue St-Antoine

start here

place de la Bastille

rue de Turenne

rue du Parc-Royal

place de Thorigny

rue de Sévigné

rue St-Paul

rue Barbette

rue des Francs-Bourgeois

rue Pavée

rue Charlemagne

rue E. Duval

rue des Rosiers

rue des Blancs Manteaux

rue Vieille-du-Temple

rue du Archives

rue Fr. Miron

rue de Rivoli

place St-Gervais

place de l'Hôtel-de-Ville

quai de l'Hôtel-de-Ville

Seine

Pont Louis-Philippe

quai aux Fleurs

rue du Temple

rue du Renard

place Georges Pompidou

finish here

1. place de la Bastille
2. Bastille Opéra
3. place des Vosges
4. Musée Victor Hugo
5. 8 place des Vosges
6. 21 place des Vosges
7. Hôtel de Sully
8. 1 place des Vosges
9. St-Paul-St-Louis
10. Synagogue de Guimard
11. Hôtel Lamoignon/ Bibliothèque Historique
12. heart of Jewish Paris
13. Finkelsztajn
14. Musée Kwok-On
15. Musée Carnavalet
16. rue du Parc-Royale
17. Musée Picasso
18. Hôtel de Rohan
19. place Igor-Stravinsky
20. Centre Pompidou

portal here. The building is open Monday through Friday after 2pm.

Come back out of the Hôtel de Sully; at:

8. **Number 1 place des Vosges** the Marquise de Sévigné, famous in French literature for the series of letters she wrote her daughter, was born on February 6, 1626.

Exit the place des Vosges the way you entered and go right onto rue St-Antoine to number 99, the church of:

9. **St-Paul-St-Louis,** constructed between 1627 and 1641 by the Jesuits. It seems that St-Paul-St-Louis was the parish church for many of the people who resided in the place des Vosges at one time or another. On May 9, 1641, Cardinal Richelieu said the first mass here. Note too that the holy water stoups on each side of the entrance were donated by Victor Hugo. It is also said that for many years the hearts of Louis XIII and Louis XIV were kept here.

When you come out of the church, turn left on rue St-Antoine to rue Pavée (it will be on your right side). Turn right on the city's first paved road to:

10. **Synagogue de Guimard,** the only synagogue ever designed (1913) by the master of Art Nouveau, Hector Guimard.

A bit farther along at number 24 rue Pavée is the:

11. **Hôtel Lamoignon/Bibliothèque Historique.** Commissioned in 1584, it was designed by Baptiste du Cerceau in 1611. Diane de France, the illegitimate daughter of Henri II (made legitimate at the age of seven by an adoption that granted her all noble rights), lived here from the time it was built until her death. Later, the hotel was rented to Guillaume de Lamoignon, the first president of the Parliament of Paris, from 1658 to 1677. In 1688 Lamoignon's son bought it.

A new building was added in the 1960s to house the Bibliothèque Historique de la Ville de Paris. You couldn't ask for a better selection of books about Paris. It's open every day except Thursday.

When you come out of the library, go left to rue des Rosiers and turn right. At number 4, you will find the Hammam, or Jewish Public Baths. As you approach the corner of rue des Rosiers and rue Ferdinand-Duval, you'll find yourself in:

12. **The heart of Jewish Paris.** Called rue des Rosiers after the rosebushes that used to grow within the walls of medieval Paris, the name hardly describes what you'll find here today. Lined with falafel shops and delis, rue des Rosiers is your best bet for a quick bite to eat. This street is always wall-to-wall people, which makes it a little difficult to get around, but take your time— there's a lot to absorb here.

REFRESHMENT STOP **Jo Goldenberg** at number 7 rue des Rosiers was founded by Albert Goldenberg. You really can't miss it because its window displays (mainly of hanging sausages) are so unusual for Paris. It will be on your left.

Head on in for some chopped liver, pastrami, or a little gefilte fish. Jo Goldenberg can be crowded, and sometimes you need to make a reservation, but there's no harm in trying to get in—if you can't, you can always stop and get a falafel at **Le Roi du Falaffel-Rosiers Alimentation** at number 34 rue des Rosiers (or any other place of its sort along the way).

Not far beyond Jo Goldenberg is:

13. Finkelsztajn, at number 27 rue des Rosiers. Established in 1851, this is one of the city's finest Jewish pastry shops. You'll have to fight the crowds to get in here, but after all this walking, you deserve a treat.

Go right when you get to the corner of rue Vieille-du-Temple. On your left at number 47 is the **Hôtel des Ambassadeurs de Hollande,** where Beaumarchais wrote *The Marriage of Figaro.* It is one of the most beautiful mansions in the Marais, and despite its name it was never occupied by anyone in the Dutch embassy. It's not open to the public. Turn right on rue Vieille-du-Temple to rue des Francs-Bourgeois. Go right on rue des Francs-Bourgeois, and continue walking until you get to the:

14. Musée Kwok-On, on your right at number 41 rue des Francs-Bourgeois, just past the trendy **Café les Enfants Gâtés** at number 43. The entrance to the museum is virtually unmarked—were it not for the small plaque near the door you'd never know it was there—so pay close attention to the numbers or you'll miss it.

Kwok-On, an Asian museum, is unique. For that reason alone, it's worth a quick visit. Inside you'll find temporary exhibitions from the collection that was donated by the Chinese collector Kwok-On. They might include costumes from the Chinese opera, masks from Indian theater, costumes from the Kabuki and Noh theaters of Japan, or an incredible collection of string and shadow puppets.

If Asian costume isn't your thing but the history of Paris is, then continue along to rue de Sévigné. Go left on rue de Sévigné to number 23, the:

15. Musée Carnavalet, which chronicles the history of Paris. Housed in the Hôtel Carnavalet (a 16th-century mansion that was occupied by Madame de Sévigné during the last 19 years of her life) and the Hôtel Le-Peletier-de-St-Fargeau (whose namesake was considered responsible for the death sentence of Louis XVI), its exhibits—which include paintings, sculptures, decorative arts, and period costumes—take you from the Middle Ages through the Renaissance and all the way up to modern-day Paris. One thing you shouldn't miss is the portrait of Madame Récamier, one of Paris's most beautiful "ladies of the evening." The painting conveys an absolutely luminous quality. A person could sit and stare at her for hours and never get bored. The museum has a good bookshop as well.

Go out of the museum and go left to the end of rue de Sévigné. As you go left onto:

16. Rue du Parc-Royal, note the series of hotels on the right side of the street, the most interesting of which are at numbers 4 and 10. At number 4 (if you make a right for a few steps), you'll find the Hôtel de Canillac, built in 17th-century style. It now houses a popular tea room, Dattes et Noix. You can order ice cream, tarts, and light lunches here. Retrace your steps, and cross rue de Sévigné. At number 10 is the Hôtel de Vigny. Although it was once scheduled to be demolished, it is now registered as an historic monument. It was saved primarily because of its beautiful painted ceilings and beams.

Continue along to place de Thorigny, where you'll find at number 5 the fantastic:

17. Musée Picasso. This museum is housed in the Hôtel Salé, which was originally built between 1656 and 1660 for Pierre Aubert de Fontenay, the salt-tax collector (hence the building's name). Ironically enough, he couldn't pay his own bills, and the house was confiscated. It has changed hands many times since, and has even housed the Ecole Arts et Métiers (which left it considerably damaged). It was eventually restored and reopened as the Musée Picasso.

Opened in September 1985, the Musée Picasso holds works from Picasso's personal collection. When he died intestate in 1973, he left behind a huge collection of his work. At one time in his life he had decided to keep a certain number of his paintings every year, and what you'll see in the museum is a large part of this collection. Picasso so liked his own work that he often even bought back his pieces from art auctions or dealers.

When the state finally decided on the collection it wanted from the works he left behind, it had chosen 203 paintings, 158 sculptures, and over 3,000 prints and drawings (not to mention reliefs, ceramics, and sketchbooks); together they track Picasso's career from beginning to end. As you walk through the museum you will see Picassos you never even knew existed, and things you would never guess were painted by Picasso. Here you will gain a new appreciation for the genius of Picasso, a man who experimented with all types of art, including traditional, cubist, surrealist, and comic. The curators have done a wonderful job arranging the collection so that visitors get a good overview of Picasso's life and work.

If you're a lover of Picasso, you won't be disappointed in this museum. There's also a great bookstore attached—you're not going to believe how many books have been published about Picasso's life.

When you exit the museum, note that Balzac once lived down the block at number 9 (to your left as you exit), and head to the right, back to the place de Thorigny. Go straight through the place onto rue Elzévir to rue Barbette. Go right on rue Barbette and follow it to the end (note the little antiquities shop at number 17, L'Eléphant Dans la Porcelaine, which has some interesting knick-knacks). At the end of rue Barbette, go right on the rue Vieille-du-Temple to the:

18. **Hôtel de Rohan.** The original occupant of the hotel, François de Rohan, was reputed to be the son of Louis XIV. The interior is open to the public only during exhibitions. The main attraction is the amusing 18th-century Salon des Singes (Monkey Room). In the courtyard (open Monday through Friday 9am to 6pm), you can see a stunning bas-relief, *The Watering of the Horses of the Sun,* which includes a nude Apollo and four horses against a background exploding with sunbursts.

Come out of the Hôtel de Rohan and go right, crossing the intersection of rue Barbette and rue Vieille-du-Temple. When you get to rue des Francs-Bourgeois, cross that intersection as well, and continue on to rue des Blancs-Manteaux. Go right on rue des Blancs-Manteaux. As you cross rue du Temple, note that rue des Blancs-Manteaux becomes rue Simon-le-Franc. Continue along, crossing rue du Renard, and you'll see the Centre Pompidou in front of you. Head along into:

19. **Place Igor-Stravinsky,** where you'll find the whimsically playful kinetic fountain *Rites of Spring,* designed by Niki de Saint-Phalle and Jean Tinguely. With its giant lips, musical notes, and all sorts of animals, it's a delight to children and adults alike. It's a great place to sit and relax for a minute before heading to your right to the huge square where you'll always find street performers of one kind or another, including jugglers, fire eaters, and acrobats in front of the:

20. **Centre Pompidou,** known as the Beaubourg. It opened in 1977, and its bold "ecoskeletal" architecture—featuring exposed pipes and infrastructure—and bright colors seemed either to attract or repulse people. More seem to have been attracted, however, because after a year, over 6 million people had visited. The main goal of the museum is to make modern art accessible to as many people as possible by making it a sort of "interactive" museum space. I still remember the first time I visited (when I was too young to know better)—I didn't remember any of the artwork I had seen, only the incredibly long escalators that allow their riders to look outside and inside at all the "inner architecture" of the museum. In some way, in spite of the fact that I was glossing over the actual paintings and sculptures, I was interacting with the building, which is a work of art in and of itself.

The entire first floor houses a library that is open to the public, and the upper levels house the Musée d'Art Moderne, which displays art from the turn of the century to the present. The collection includes works by Cézanne, Braque, Matisse, Léger, Kandinsky, Klee, Dubuffet, and Rauschenberg, among others. There is also space allocated for changing exhibitions of contemporary work.

WALKING TOUR 8

The Champs-Elysées & St-Honoré

Start: Place du Carrousel. (Métro: Palais Royal.)
Finish: Arc de Triomphe.
Time: Three or more hours.
Best Time: During the day, when shops, museums, and galleries are open. If you don't mind missing visiting the museum at the Arc de Triomphe, it's nice to schedule this tour so that you do the first half during the day and the second half after dark, so that you can see all the shops and the Champs-Elysées lit up.

This neighborhood, with the Tuileries gardens, the place de la Concorde, and the Madeleine church, is one of the most opulent in the whole city. You'll be walking through the gardens along to the Madeleine, through a flower market, past some of the city's most prestigious art galleries, and along avenue Montaigne. You'll pass Chanel, Hermès, and Gucci, and you'll rub elbows with Paris's wealthiest in the upscale "grocery store" Fauchon.

You'll discover Ben Franklin's haunts and the presidential palace, as well as the theater where Josephine Baker and Sidney Bechet made their debut in *La Revue Nègre*. You'll read as you go about the sordid history of the place de la Concorde and its guillotine, as well as the antics that went on in Paris's most exclusive, Maxim's. The walk will take you along the second half of the Champs-Elysées, and you'll end up at the magnificent Arc de Triomphe.

1. **Place du Carrousel** is situated on the west side of the Louvre between the wings of the new palace. It was here that during the Revolution the guillotine was set up from August 22, 1792, to May 10, 1793. It was moved only once during that time, for the execution of Louis XVI on January 21, 1793.

   If you look behind you, in the opposite direction of the place de la Concorde, you'll see the Louvre and its new glass pyramid entrance. The Louvre has an interesting and sometimes sordid past. Though most people think of it as the art museum it has been since 1793, we must remember that the building that holds some of the world's greatest treasures was built as a palace (and has been many other things in between, including a prison, a publishing house, a shopping mall, and an institute for advanced studies).

   The courtyard you stand in was where hundreds of Protestants were massacred on Saint Bartholomew's Day in 1572. On a lighter note, Henri IV, the "Gay Blade," turned the Louvre into something of a fairgrounds with his singing, dancing, and carrying on. While he lived here the Louvre's Grande Galerie was occupied by various commercial enterprises, including a goldsmith, a tapestry factory, and a clock maker, who reported frequent sightings of the dauphin and his pet camel walking the length of the gallery. After Henri IV's murder, the Louvre transformed itself several times over.

   Under the reign of Louis XIV, certain talented artists and scholars were given the right to live in the Grande Galerie free of rent. Later these privileges were abused and the Louvre was taken over by an assorted riffraff who looted paintings and paneling, operated a black market, cooked in the hallways, and generally brought the whole place into debauchery and disrepute. By 1773 the Louvre was in a shambles.

   After the Revolution the rebuilding of the Louvre began, but it wasn't until Napoléon took over and asked the architects Charles Percier and Pierre-François-Léonard Fontaine to restore the Louvre that it began to resemble its former condition. Napoléon and Joséphine were actually married in the Louvre after a procession along the Grande Galerie. And it was Napoléon who began to turn the place into a museum; the Musée Napoléon was to house artwork from conquered Europe, chosen and organized by Vivant Denon (for details, see box).

   Head out of the place du Carrousel straight ahead to the:

2. **Arc de Triomphe du Carrousel,** built from 1806 to 1808 by Percier and Fontaine. Leaders of the Empire style in France, they did restoration and redecoration in the Tuileries Palace similar to their work in the Louvre, but the Arc de Triomphe du Carrousel is their most notable work.

   Built in Empire style and standing 48 feet high and 64 feet wide, the arch was meant to serve as a "triumphal" entrance into the Tuileries Palace. The eight rose marble Corinthian columns that flank the arch support statues commissioned by Denon to celebrate the victories of Napoléon I. The sculptures that you see today are reproductions, not originals. The bas-reliefs on the sides also celebrate Napoléon's conquests; among them are *The Capitulation of Ulm, The Battle of Austerlitz, The Meeting of Napoléon and Alexander at Tilsit, The Entry into Munich, The Entry into Vienna,* and *The Peace of Pressburg.*

The view from under the Arc de Triomphe du Carrousel is probably one of the best known in Paris, because from here you can see all the way through the Jardin des Tuileries to the Obelisk in the place de la Concorde and beyond, up the Champs-Elysées to the Arc de Triomphe.

Go straight out of the Arc de Triomphe du Carrousel and go right along one of the garden pathways (this will be before you cross avenue du Général-Lemonnier, so if you cross it, go back). You'll be standing in front of the:

3. Musée des Arts Décoratifs. Founded in 1887, this museum houses one of the most interesting collections of decorative arts in the world, with works dating from the Middle Ages to the present. If you'd like to tour the museum, you should go around to the right to the rue de Rivoli to get to the entrance, and you should plan to spend an hour or more going through the exhibits.

Originally, the museum was established to encourage new designs in the field of decorative arts. At its inception it was thought that if people could see what decorations had been created in the past, compared to what existed in the present, they might demand more creative interior design elements, china patterns, and furnishings, thus forcing the birth of new ideas.

Today the museum displays carpets, tapestries, paintings, furniture, jewelry, porcelain, toys, and more. You can visit the room dedicated to the king of Art Nouveau, Hector Guimard,

---

BARON DOMINIQUE-VIVANT DENON

Baron Denon (1747–1825) was many things: engraver, diplomat, writer, museum official—a sort of jack-of-all-trades if you will. In 1798 he followed Napoléon on his journey to Egypt and wrote a book called *Voyage dans la basse et la haute egypte* four years later. He was appointed director of the national museums in 1804 and held the position for 11 years. Among other things, he played a large role in helping Napoléon develop the collections at the Louvre (where an entire wing is named for him). He was also responsible for commissioning the statues of the Arc de Triomphe du Carrousel.

or you might enjoy studying the gorgeous glass pieces by Lalique. There are some stunning 15th- and 16th-century tapestries, as well as a small collection of Gauguin paintings. Don't miss the 17th- and 18th-century furnishings or the collection of Restoration wallpapers.

Housed next door at number 109 rue de Rivoli is the:

4. Musée des Arts de la Mode, or the Museum of Fashion. This museum could also take up to an hour to tour, so plan accordingly—you've still got a long walk ahead of you. It holds an immense collection of costumes from the 16th century to the present, as well as a spectacular collection of material samples. Because the materials are so easily discolored or destroyed by effects of light and exposure, the collection is rotated frequently, so there's no way of knowing what you'll be able to see when you arrive. It's sure to be interesting, however.

Head back to avenue du Général-Lemonnier. Retrace your steps so that you're facing the place de la Concorde. Proceed to the place de la Concorde. You have just walked through the area that was once occupied by the:

5. Tuileries Palace, which was built on the original site of some *tuile* (tile) kilns and factories. Designed by Philibert Delorme in 1564 for Catherine de Médicis, the palace ran between the two wings of the Louvre and joined up with the Pavillon de Flore (on your left) and the Pavillon Marsan (on your right).

On August 10, 1792, the palace was attacked by a revolutionary mob and Louis XVI and his family were forced to flee. The Swiss guards who were also here at the time made an attempt to run, but two-thirds of them were slaughtered. In 1830, when Charles X was in residence, the palace was again attacked by a mob and he too fled. In 1871 the Communards set fire to the palace and caused its ultimate destruction.

Continue walking, and you'll arrive at the beginning of the:

6. Jardin des Tuileries. These gardens, now comprising 63 acres, originally had two uses: The clay soil was used at the tile factory, and other parts of the land were used as a garbage dump. François I built his stables here in 1525, and in 1564 Catherine de Médicis bought some of the land to build an Italian-style garden.

Soon afterward the Tuileries became a fashionable promenade. In 1649 the gardens were redesigned by André Le Nôtre, Louis XIV's gardener. Dotted with fine sculptures and beautifully manicured gardens, they became the favorite meeting place of the aristocracy. The Tuileries have remained a meeting place, but now they're open to everyone, and they still hold some of the world's greatest sculptures.

The first of these are directly to your right and left after you cross the avenue du Général-Lemonnier. On your immediate right is a statue of Pierre de Wissant. Across from it on your left is *Great Shadow*. A bit farther on to your right is *Jean de Frennes,* and on the left is *Meditation.* Just ahead of you is a pond that's a wonderful place to sit and relax. It's a favorite spot of tourists and Parisians alike, and if you sit long enough you're likely to see a fish jump. Continue to walk through and just past the place where they give pony rides to children you'll find a wooded area on your right. Wander around in there and have a look at the 18 bronze nudes by Aristide Maillol.

Note: You might be interested to know that a $50-million cleanup and restoration project has been scheduled for the near future.

Continue along, and just before you come upon the Octagonal Pond, take note of the four statues to the left and right that represent the four seasons. On the left you'll see *Autumn* (the one closer to you) and *Spring,* both by François Barois (1656–1726). On the right are *Winter* (closer to you) by Jean Raon (1631–1707) and *Summer* by Guillaume Coustou (1677–1746). Walk around the octagonal pond to the entrance (or exit, depending on how you look at it) of the gardens. The four statues flanking the entrance depict six rivers: *The Tiber,* by Pierre Bourdict (?–1711), is on your right, closest to you. On your left, the first one is *The Nile* by Lorenzo Ottoni (1648–1736). Just beyond on the right is *The Seine and the Marne* by Nicolas Coustou (1658–1733); to the left is *The Loire and the Loiret* by Corneille Van Cleve (1645–1732).

On your right in the distance is the:

7. **Musée de Jeu de Paume.** *Jeu de paume,* meaning literally "game of the palm," was invented by French monks in the 1400s who used to bat around a knot of rags with their hands for amusement. By the 1800s the rags had changed to balls and the hands to rackets. By then the *jeu de paume* had become the

---

ARISTIDE MAILLOL

Known primarily for his sculpture, Aristide Maillol (1861–1944) was a tapestry artist and a painter early in his career. It wasn't until 1900, at the age of 39, that he decided to devote himself entirely to his sculpture. In 1902 he had his first one-man exhibition and was praised by Rodin. Actually, Maillol was a sort of bridge for Rodin and his contemporaries from traditional, classic Greek and Roman sculpture to modern-style sculpture. He was more interested in the philosophy of expressing form, but in a way that broke from traditional Greek and Roman style: He began to look for a more simple way to express it—without mythological or literary allusion, or in connection to an architectural form. He worked at a type of sculpture that simply celebrates the form being sculpted, rather than a particular event or idea. He especially loved the nude female form and you'll be hard pressed to find other subjects in his body of work.

Rodin took Maillol's idea one step further by adding a psychological element to his sculpture.

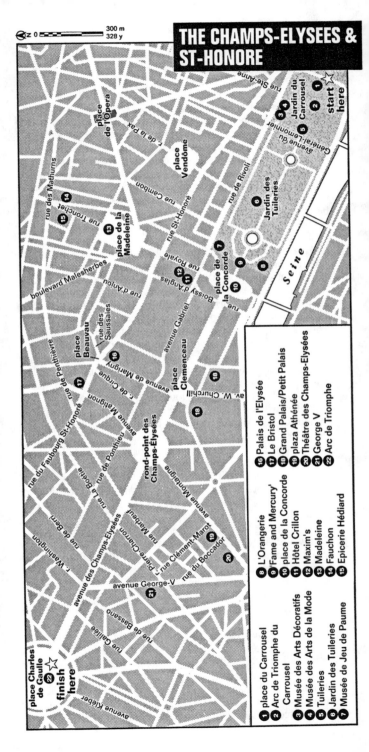

THE CHAMPS-ELYSEES & ST-HONORE

1 place du Carrousel
2 Arc de Triomphe du Carrousel
3 Musée des Arts Décoratifs
4 Musée des Arts de la Mode
5 Tuileries
6 Jardin des Tuileries
7 Musée de Jeu de Paume
8 L'Orangerie
9 'Fame and Mercury'
10 place de la Concorde
11 Hôtel Crillon
12 Maxim's
13 Madeleine
14 Fauchon
15 Epicerie Hédiard
16 Palais de l'Elysée
17 Le Bristol
18 Grand Palais/Petit Palais
19 plaza Athénée
20 Théâtre des Champs-Elysées
21 George V
22 Arc de Triomphe

national game of France and had evolved into a highly explosive and dangerous game. In fact, several nobles and kings are said to have dropped dead from the strain.

The Jeu de Paume originally housed the Royal Tennis Courts and was constructed under Napoléon III for the recreation of the Prince Imperial. Not long after lawn tennis (the next logical step from the *jeu de paume*) came into existence, the building was used to display Impressionist paintings.

From 1947 to 1986 the Jeu de Paume hosted a permanent exhibition of Impressionist works, which have since been moved to the Musée d'Orsay (see Walking Tour 4, stop 1 for more information about the Musée d'Orsay). Presently the building is being used as a show space for changing exhibitions of contemporary art and design.

To your left is:

8. L'Orangerie, formerly the orange nursery of the Jardin des Tuileries. The building now permanently houses, and is the official museum for, the Walter-Guillaume collection. Paul Guillaume, art dealer and collector, was extremely interested in the work of new and unknown artists, and in 1914, at the age of 23, he opened a gallery on rue de la Boetie that specialized in the work of such then-contemporary artists as Picasso, Modigliani, and Renoir. The Walter part of the collection was the extension of Guillaume's collection by Guillaume's widow and her new husband, Jean Walter. The total collection, consisting of 144 masterpieces and ranging from the Impressionist period all the way through the 1930s, was donated to the Louvre in 1977.

Well worth a visit, L'Orangerie is small and easily managed in an hour or less. Within you'll find Monet's *Water Lilies;* several pieces by Chaim Soutine (see Walking Tour 3, stop 20); a whole room devoted to Paul Cézanne which includes the still life *Fruit, Napkin, and Milk Can* (1880); a large number of Renoirs, including *Young Girls at the Piano* (1890); works by Henri Rousseau and Maurice Utrillo; *The Bathers* (1921) by Picasso; and finally, *The Young Apprentice* (1917) by Amedeo Modigliani.

Just as you go out of the Jardin des Tuileries are two statues:

9. *Fame* and *Mercury*, on your left and right, respectively. Both are by Antoine Coysevox, the most successful French sculptor of Louis XIV's reign. In addition to these two, he did a number of statues for the gardens and interior of Versailles. More baroque in style than his contemporaries, he appealed more to Louis XIV.

Now, as you pass between the two statues, you'll find yourself in the:

10. Place de la Concorde. The building of this square was begun in 1755 to honor Louis XV, and it took 20 years to complete. A statue of Louis XV on his horse was placed in the center of the square, but in 1792 it was overturned, and the square was renamed place de la Révolution. In 1793 the guillotine was moved from the place du Carrousel to place de la Concorde (then place de la Révolution) for the execution of Louis XVI on

January 21. Just before he lost his head he was heard to say, "Frenchmen, I die innocent." After the blade fell, the executioner lifted the king's head to the crowd, and he was met with the roar of "Vive la République!" Shortly thereafter, the councillors dipped their handkerchiefs and pikes in his blood and the executioner took the liberty of selling locks of Louis XVI's hair to onlookers. After the execution of Louis XVI, 1,234 others were guillotined here, including Marie Antoinette and Charlotte Corday (murderer of Marat). In July 1794, Robespierre's execution here ended the Reign of Terror.

It wasn't until the reign of Louis Philippe that the obelisk which hails from the temple at Luxor, was chosen as the centerpiece for the square. A gift from Mohammed Ali, the obelisk weighs over 230 tons and is made entirely of pink granite. It is over 3,300 years old and stands 75 feet tall. The hieroglyphs on the sides represent the "epic deeds" of Ramses II. Before the obelisk was erected a box of medallions with Louis Philippe's likeness on them was placed in the ground.

Built between 1836 and 1846, the fountains on either side of the obelisk are copies of the fountains in Saint Peter's Square in Rome. Around the square are statues representing the eight great towns of France. Erected during the reign of Louis Philippe, they include *Bordeaux* and *Nantes* (diagonally to the left and in front of the obelisk, facing the Champs-Elysées) by Caillonette; *Lyons* and *Marseille* (diagonally to the left and behind the obelisk) by Petitot; *Rouen* and *Brest* (diagonally to the right and in front of the obelisk) by Cortot; and *Lille* and *Strasbourg* (to the right and behind the obelisk) by Pradier.

Now, as you head out of the square in the direction of the Champs-Elysées, you'll see the Marly horses, sculpted by Guillaume Coustou for a drinking trough in Marly, Louis XIV's castle, which is located near Versailles. The statues you see today are replicas—the originals were removed in 1984 and are housed in the Louvre.

As you leave place de la Concorde, instead of heading straight down the Champs-Elysées, go out between the statues of Brest and Rouen, diagonally to the right in front of the obelisk. Cross the avenue Gabriel (which can be quite hazardous at this intersection, so watch your step) and you'll be in front of the:

11. Hôtel Crillon. Designed for the Count of Crillon in 1758 by Jacques-Ange Gabriel (1698–1782), Hotel Crillon is one of the most prestigious hotels in all of Paris. It was here that the Treaty of Friendship and Trade between the infant United States and France was signed on February 6, 1778; both Benjamin Franklin and Louis XVI were in attendance. This treaty was significant because it meant that France officially recognized the United States as a free and independent nation.

Benjamin Franklin only begins the long list of Americans who have stayed at the Hôtel Crillon. Others include Mary Pickford and Douglas Fairbanks, said to have honeymooned here in 1920; Fred and Adele Astaire, who vacationed here in

1924; and William Randolph Hearst and his mistress Marion Davies, guests in 1928.

Go right in front of the Hôtel Crillon and take a left onto rue Royale. On the left side of the street, affixed to the side of the hotel, you'll find a plaque commemorating the signing of the aforementioned Treaty of Friendship and Trade. A bit farther on you'll come across some of the city's most renowned shops and restaurants; first, on the left side of the street, is:

12. **Maxim's**—need I say more? Well, probably not, but I'm going to anyway. Some of the most interesting incidents that have occurred at Maxim's involve Americans, among them a man from California known only as Mr. L.; his real name has never been disclosed. Mr. L. used to perform a strange ritual, since dubbed the Liturgy of the Golden Calf. It began with the gathering and lining up of all the Maxim's staff, whereupon this Mr. L. would walk down the line carrying a plate stacked with piles of gold coins. As he passed each person he would place on his or her tongue one gold coin. Before he moved to the next person he would make the sign of the cross.

Another American, one Mr. Todd (a New Yorker) proceeded in a much less ceremonial manner. He would simply throw piles of louis d'or around the restaurant and amuse himself by watching the staff and resident courtesans as they fell all over each other to get at it.

After you pass Maxim's you'll come to Christofle, one of the most exclusive silverware manufacturers in the world; Cristal Lalique is next, with its Art Nouveau frosted glass. Cross the rue St-Honoré and Gucci will also be on your left.

REFRESHMENT STOP If you'd like to have a snack with some of Paris's richest citizens and devour some of the city's best croissants, stop at **Ladurée** (diagonally to the right, across the street from Gucci at number 16 rue Royale), a wonderfully elegant turn-of-the-century café/salon du thé. Try the almond cakes (*financiers*) or the chocolate macaroons. You won't be disappointed.

If you decide not to go into Ladurée, cross the street anyway and continue walking up rue Royale into place de la Madeleine, where you can't miss the:

13. **Madeleine,** with its 52 Corinthian columns. Intended as a church (with absolutely no windows and no crosses), the Madeleine has been variously a bank, a theater, a banquet hall, a monument to Napoléon's army, and the national library before it became, finally, a church dedicated to Saint Mary Magdalene. Built to look like a Greek temple, it was begun in 1764 and wasn't completed until nearly 100 years later. The structure is 355 feet long, 141 feet wide, and 60 feet tall. Inside you'll find

some beautiful rose marble, as well as a bronze door by Lemaire that depicts the Ten Commandments.

In 1975 Josephine Baker's funeral was held here. She was the first woman ever to receive a 21-gun salute. Other major events have included the playing of the organ by Saint-Saëns and the premiere of Chopin's *Funeral March*—at the composer's own funeral!

Continue around the place de la Madeleine to the flower market. Go through the market and you'll come to:

14. Fauchon, at number 26. Founded in 1886 by Auguste Fauchon, this is probably the city's most elite "grocery store." A trip inside is, for adults, like a child's trip to a candy factory. You can look, but you cannot touch. You are supposed to place your order, and then someone will bring it to you—there will be no squeezing of the produce here. Everything is beautifully displayed, and you're sure to find just about anything you could possibly want in their selection of 4,500 spices and over 20,000 other products. If you're not interested in going inside, or you're afraid you might faint from overstimulation, just take a peek at the window display (if you can even get to the window—there's usually a large crowd outside).

The two extensions of Fauchon are situated directly ahead of you at the end of the square. The first (on the right) is Fauchon's cake shop; at the second (on the left) you can purchase a bottle of fine olive oil, or even the madeleines Proust writes about in his *Remembrance of Things Past.*

When you're finished at all the branches of Fauchon, continue around, past La Maison de la Truffe, a truffle specialty store, to number 21:

15. Epicerie Hédiard. Another elite grocery store, Hédiard is a lot less commercial than Fauchon and, it seems to me, a store where French "old money" shops. You're likely to find equally good produce as you would in Fauchon, but I think you'll find less haughty service here. Pop in and judge for yourself.

JOSEPHINE BAKER

In 1925 Josephine Baker (1906–75) appeared in Paris at the Théâtre des Champs-Elysées in La Revue Nègre and was an immediate success. Everyone loved her. For that first show she made her entrance completely nude, except for a pink flamingo feather between her legs. Janet Flanner described her as "an unforgettable female ebony statue." It was during another performance, some time after that, that she came out wearing her banana skirt and was then hailed as the biggest American star in Europe. She maintained a loyal following throughout her career in Paris.

Continue along, passing Baccarat and Lucas Carton. Go to the other side of the Madeleine back onto rue Royale to the Gucci store you passed earlier. Turn right on rue du Faubourg-St-Honoré. Cross rue Boissy d'Anglas. You'll see Hermès at number 24 (in case you're interested, there's a small Hermès museum located on the top floor of this building). Just ahead on the right side is Givenchy and Guy Laroche. Just after the rue d'Anjou on the right is Cour aux Antiquaires. It's worth taking a look down this little passageway, the home of 18 fine antique shops.

Come back out of Cour aux Antiquaires and go right on rue du Faubourg-St-Honoré, passing, on the right, Ungaro, Chloé, and Gianni Versace. Just beyond, across the street from rue des Saussaies, (on the left side) is the:

16. Palais de l'Elysée. Built in 1718 by Mollet for the Comte d'Evreux, it has been the official residence of the French president since 1873. During the Revolution it housed the national printing press and at one time was home to Napoléon's sister. You can't go inside, but you should know that France's present president, François Mitterrand, does not call the Palais de l'Elysée home—he still lives in his private residence on rue de Bièvre (see Walking Tour 5, stop 10).

Continue past the palace and cross avenue de Marigny. (As you do, be sure to check out the hats in the window of Pierre Cardin. Also, if you need to sit down for a minute or two, there are some benches off to the left here.) Continue along rue du Faubourg-St-Honoré and as you walk, note some of the galleries of fine art—this is probably the only place in the world where you might find a Utrillo or something similar displayed in a shop window. Soon you'll come to number 112 rue du Faubourg-St-Honoré, the hotel:

17. Le Bristol. Being so close to the Palais de l'Elysée, this very classy hotel has played host to a long line of VIPs, among them Ulysses S. Grant, who was a guest here for almost a month in 1887. Sinclair Lewis lived here in 1925, during which time his book, *Arrowsmith,* was selected for the Pulitzer (which he turned down). And it was also here that Josephine Baker celebrated her 50th anniversary in show business.

Go left on avenue Matignon. Walk past the offices of the newspaper *Le Figaro* and some expensive art galleries to the Champs-Elysées. Go left at the Champs-Elysées and cross the street at place Clemenceau. Cross place Clemenceau to avenue Winston-Churchill. As you head down avenue Winston-Churchill you will find yourself between the:

18. Grand Palais and the Petit Palais. The Grand Palais is on your right, the Petit Palais is on your left. Both palaces were built for the Universal Exhibition of 1900 and are exceptional examples of Art Nouveau architectural design. In the Grand Palais, designed and built by three architects, you'll find 54,000 square feet of floor space. The Grand Palais often plays host to major exhibitions and retrospectives. The Petit Palais, originally built to hold a retrospective of French art for the Universal Exhibition, now holds collections from various museums all around the city of Paris. It is now Paris's Beaux Arts Museum.

The exteriors of both buildings are covered with bas-reliefs and sculptures—a Classical style of architecture that is completely contrary to the Art Nouveau iron and glass interiors.

Retrace your steps and head back to the avenue des Champs-Elysées. Go left, then make a left onto avenue Montaigne. Stay on the right side of the street. On the left side of the street you'll pass Chanel and Christian Dior, on the right you'll see Nina Ricci. No doubt you've realized that you're walking down Paris's Fifth and Madison avenues all rolled into one. Continue along across rue Clément-Marot. Eventually you'll come to number 25 avenue Montaigne, the:

19. Plaza Athénée, located on the right side of the street. This is where George Patton lived in December 1918. He gave a series of talks regarding the importance of tanks to the infantry. Only one French officer—Charles de Gaulle—believed him. The rest thought him a bit mad. It was also here, in the bar of the hotel, that Mata Hari was arrested for her work as a spy.

A bit farther on, just across rue du Boccador, is number 15, the:

20. Théâtre des Champs-Elysées, built in 1913. The bas-reliefs of Isadora Duncan on the exterior were sculpted by Antoine Bourdelle (see Walking Tour 3, stop 3). This is also the theater where *La Revue Nègre* with Sidney Bechet and Josephine Baker opened. It was her first performance in the city of Paris, and as mentioned earlier, it was a complete success.

Adrienne Monnier wrote of Josephine Baker after seeing her here that "with her get-ups, her grimaces, her contortions, she kicks up a shindy that swarms with mocking enticements—she's a Queen of Sheba who turns into a frog, into a mischievous chicken with its feathers plucked; she passes from an enamored expression to a frightful squint, she even succeeds in a squinting with her behind. . . ."

Further, it was also here that on June 19, 1926, George Antheil's *Ballet mécanique* was performed. The orchestra included six electric player pianos, six electrically run airplane propellers, car horns, whistles, and a multitude of other modern noise makers. Janet Flanner wrote: "It's good but awful."

When you get to avenue George-V, go right to number 31, the hotel:

21. George V. Duke Ellington stayed here in July 1933. The hotel opened in 1928, and between that time and 1968 the owner amassed a huge collection of art (something like $7 million worth). If for no other reason, go inside and have a look at the portions of the collection that hang in the public rooms.

Continue up avenue George-V to the Champs-Elysées. Go left on the Champs-Elysées to the end of the tour, the underground passageway to the:

22. Arc de Triomphe. Warning: Do not try to cross the street above ground to get to the arch—if you do, you're likely to end up in the hospital.

This huge Second Empire–style arch standing in the middle of an intersection took 30 years to create; conceived in the mind of Napoléon in 1806, it wasn't actually completed until 1836. It stands 163 feet high and is 147 feet wide. The arch itself is 48 feet wide—wide enough for one Sergeant Godefroy to fly his plane through in 1919. Underneath the arch is the Tomb of the Unknown Soldier and the "Eternal Flame," over which it has been reported that some jokester cooked himself an omelet. You can read the inscription, "Ici repose un soldat français mort pour la patrie, 1914–1918." (Translated, "Here lies a French soldier who died for his fatherland.") The flame is relit every evening around 6pm.

Inside the arch is a museum that documents the different stages of its construction. It is open Monday, and Wednesday through Saturday from 10am to 6pm. If you're not interested in how the arch was built you should at least go up and have a look at the magnificent view.

WALKING TOUR 9

The Palais Royal, the Opéra & the Grands Boulevards

Start: Place du Palais-Royal. (Métro: Palais Royal.)
Finish: Jardin du Palais Royal.
Time: Three to four hours.
Best Time: Monday through Saturday during business hours.
Worst Time: Monday through Saturday after 5pm, and Sunday.

This walk will take you through landmarks of Second Empire and Belle Epoque Paris and bring you back to the cloistered gardens of the Palais Royal.

Today it's hard to imagine the scenes that are associated with the Palais Royal, particularly during the regency of Louis XV, when it was notorious for debauchery and orgies of all sorts. Crowds were drawn to the entertainments in the galleries—shadow-theaters, wax works, and optical illusions—and to the cafés, like the Café de Foy, where Camille Desmoulins stirred up the revolutionary mob. A statue of him stands in the gardens.

The Grands Boulevards stretch from the Madeleine to the place de la Bastille. They were originally laid out by Louis XIV, but the boulevards as we know them were created by Baron Haussmann under Louis-Napoléon. These broad avenues and boulevards provided access to the railroad stations of the 19th century, and Parisians and provincial French people flocked to them to enjoy their cafés, theaters, and restaurants, especially on the Boulevard des Italiens between rue de Richelieu and rue de la Chaussée d'Antin. The most famous were the Café Tortoni, the Café Anglais, the Café de Paris, and the Café Riche, to which all of fashionable Paris went during the Second Empire and La Belle Epoque. The Opéra was nearby on the site that Haussman had laid out and where Charles Garnier built his huge masterpiece, which opened in 1875. Today cafés and cinemas remain, but fashionable society has departed, except around the place de la Madeleine (see Walking Tour 8, stop 13). It's hard to imagine what the scene must have been like, although a visit to the Opéra will help recapture some of the spirit of the area in its heyday.

Come up out of the Métro station at place du Palais-Royal and go left (as you're facing the Conseil d'État). Go right on rue de Richelieu (the first intersection after you pass the Conseil d'État) to the first building on your right, the current location of the:

1. Comédie Française (it wasn't always located here). In 1673, Molière, actor unto the very end, died at the age of 51 on stage while performing in his play *La Malade Imaginaire.* His troupe of actors was hence left leaderless. Seven years later Louis XIV decided to establish the Comédie Française with Molière's old troupe. Ever since then the Comédie Française has been Paris's most renowned theater group. One of its greatest talents was Sarah Bernhardt. At her debut at age 17 in the title role of Racine's *Iphigénie* she suffered a bad case of stage fright. The audience heckled her, jeering that Achilles might "impale [himself] on her toothpicks," a reference to her skinny arms, but she persevered and eventually became one of Paris's best loved actresses. In fact, she became so well respected that she was often told, backstage before the curtain rose, "Madame, it will be eight o'clock when it suits you." She had gone from being a skinny, frightened girl to, in the words of Oscar Wilde, "the divine Sarah."

Retrace your steps to the rue St-Honoré. Go right along rue St-Honoré to rue de l'Echelle. Note that to your left is the:

2. Sèvres showroom. Sèvres is the French national porcelain factory. It made the premier porcelain in Europe from about 1760 to 1815. The factory has a long, august history. Founded in 1738 in Chateau de Vincennes, Sèvres was granted a 20-year monopoly in 1745 for "porcelain in the style of the Saxon . . . painted and gilded with human figures." In 1752 Louis XV became the principle shareholder, and in 1753 the manufacture of porcelain and white pottery was prohibited unless it came from his factory. In 1756 the factory moved to Sèvres; three years later it was being run entirely by the king, to the extent that all sales of porcelain were held right in his dining room at Versailles.

Sèvres figurines are famous, and many of the models were supplied by Pigalle and Houdon. Other pieces ranged in size from plates to enormous urns, and Napoléon commissioned such large and complex pieces that the architects Percier and Fontaine had to be consulted as designers.

On your right, at number 7 rue de l'Echelle is the:

3. Hôtel Normandy, where Mark Twain lived from April to July of 1879. He was very annoyed during his stay because it rained the entire time, and all he could do was read, sleep, and write. Imagine finding yourself in Paris with nothing to do but read, sleep, and write—*quel désastre!*

Continue along rue St-Honoré to rue St-Roch. At the corner is:

4. **St-Roch,** 398 rue St-Honoré, one of Paris's largest and most prestigious churches. Here on October 5, 1795, a battle took place between Le Pelletier's rabble and Napoléon Bonaparte (you can still see the bullet holes in the facade). It marks one of the most significant events in the history of Paris, for it is here Bonaparte came to power.

St-Roch holds one of the most spectacular collections of religious art (in spite of the Revolution). As you enter, go to the right, where you will come to the *Bust of Fr. de Crequi* by Antoine Coysevox. A bit farther on is a statue of Cardinal Dubois, by Coustou. Make your way around the church, in the direction of the Communion Chapel. Go around (in a half circle). On your right you will come to *Jarius's Daughter* by Delormé. Head back toward the entrance, noting along the way, the bust of Le Nôtre (on your right) by Coysevox, and the *Monument to Mignard* by Girardon. Exit through the center door, noting the memorial to Pierre Corneille on your way.

When you leave the church, go right along St-Honoré to rue St-Roch. Go left down rue St-Roch to rue de Rivoli. Go right to:

5. **Number 206 rue de Rivoli** (you'll know it by the green tile pattern outside the door). Formerly the Hôtel du Jardin des Tuileries, writer Henry Adams (1838–1918, grandson of President John Quincy Adams) spent six weeks here from December 1879 to early February 1880. He claimed to hate everything about Paris; however, one of his best works as an historian was a medieval study, *Mont-Saint-Michel and Chartres,* (1904). You'll also see the plaque that commemorates Leo Tolstoy's stay here.

Continue on rue de Rivoli until you get to rue du 29 Juillet. Go right on rue du 29 Juillet. Continue to the corner of rue St. Honoré. Go right to:

6. **Number 211,** located on the right side of the street. Sinclair Lewis (1885–1951) and his wife and son stayed here at the Hôtel St-James d'Albany in October 1921. Lewis, a graduate of Yale University, is considered the greatest satirist of his era. His book *Arrowsmith* won him a Pulitzer in 1925, and in 1930 he became the first American ever to win the Nobel Prize in literature. While he was at the Hôtel St-James d'Albany he spent a little time working on *Babbitt,* in which he ridicules the values, life-styles, and mannerisms of the money-grubbing members of society. Most consider it to be his chef d'oeuvre. When he wasn't writing he spent a lot of time getting drunk at various bars and cafés.

Turn around and go back in the other direction on rue

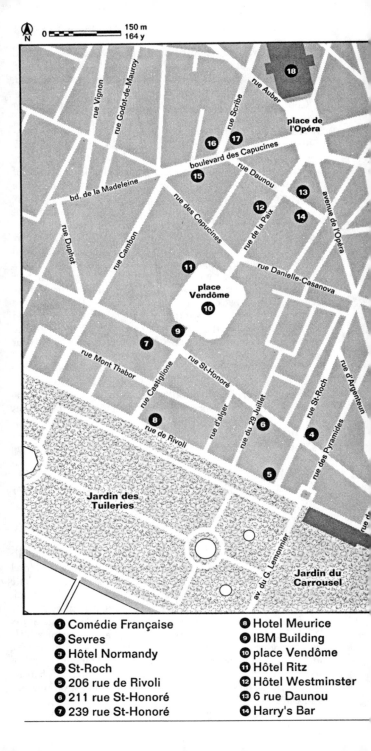

0 ——— 150 m / 164 y

place de l'Opéra

rue Vignon · rue Godot-de-Mauroy · rue Scribe · rue Auber

boulevard des Capucines · rue Daunou

bd. de la Madeleine · rue des Capucines · rue de la Paix · avenue de l'Opéra

rue Duphot · rue Cambon

rue Danielle-Casanova

place Vendôme

rue Mont Thabor · rue Castiglione · rue St-Honoré · rue d'alger · rue du 29 Juillet · rue St-Roch · rue des Pyramides · rue d'Argenteuil

rue de Rivoli

Jardin des Tuileries

av. du G. Lemonnier

Jardin du Carrousel

❶ Comédie Française	❽ Hotel Meurice
❷ Sevres	❾ IBM Building
❸ Hôtel Normandy	❿ place Vendôme
❹ St-Roch	⓫ Hôtel Ritz
❺ 206 rue de Rivoli	⓬ Hôtel Westminster
❻ 211 rue St-Honoré	⓭ 6 rue Daunou
❼ 239 rue St-Honoré	⓮ Harry's Bar

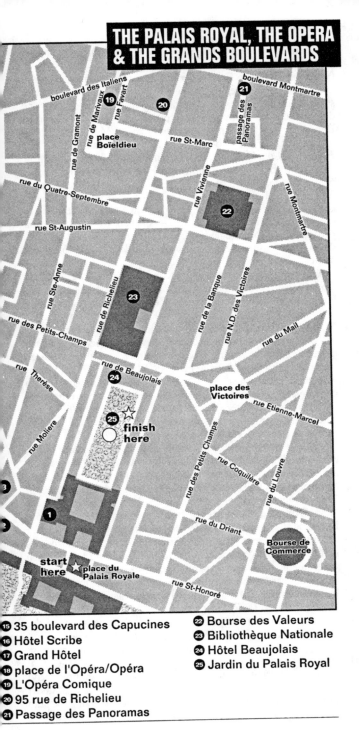

THE PALAIS ROYAL, THE OPERA & THE GRANDS BOULEVARDS

15 35 boulevard des Capucines

16 Hôtel Scribe

17 Grand Hôtel

18 place de l'Opéra/Opéra

19 L'Opéra Comique

20 95 rue de Richelieu

21 Passage des Panoramas

22 Bourse des Valeurs

23 Bibliothèque Nationale

24 Hôtel Beaujolais

25 Jardin du Palais Royal

St-Honoré, crossing the intersection of rue 29 Juillet once more. At:

7. **Number 239 rue St-Honoré** is the hotel in which Franklin and Eleanor Roosevelt spent their honeymoon in 1905. He was staying here when he visited a psychic who predicted that one day he would become president of the United States. Later, in December of 1946, American author Carson McCullers (1917–67) stayed here for about a year. McCullers, famous for *The Heart is a Lonely Hunter* (1940), simply loved her time in Paris, and even though she didn't speak a word of French she communicated well, primarily because she and her French friends all had one thing in common—they loved their whiskey and wine. Unfortunately, it was the drink that forced her to return to the United States in 1947—she had drunk so much on two occasions that she had to be hospitalized. The second time, she and her husband decided that it would be best if they went home.

Continue along to rue Cambon, and turn left to rue de Rivoli. Go left again. Note that number 218, the Hôtel Brighton, was one of Mark Twain's favorite hotel's in Paris. Later, at number 228 rue de Rivoli, the:

8. **Hôtel Meurice** was said to be the only hotel in Paris in the early 19th century that provided its guests with soap. As you can imagine, because of this singular creature comfort, it hosted many Americans, including Herman Melville, Wilbur Wright (when he came on a trip to sell his airplane to the French government), Henry Wadsworth Longfellow in the summer of 1836, and, much later, Walter Lippmann, who in 1967 stayed here while waiting for the completion of his new home, which turned out to be a veritable money pit.

Go left up rue Castiglione. Note as you walk (on your right), rue Mont Thabor, the street where the brassiere was supposedly invented. As you head into the place Vendôme, note that Fred Astaire and his wife stayed at number 1, the Hôtel Vendôme, in 1936. At number 3 you'll find the:

9. **IBM Building,** formerly the Hôtel Bristol. John Pierpont Morgan (1837–1913), a United States financier and investment banker, spent every spring here from 1890 to 1910. During the Franco-Prussian War Morgan loaned $50 million to the French government. In addition to his French exploits, he set up the United States Steel Corporation in 1901 and International Harvester in 1902; he also played a vital role in stabilizing the U.S. economy in 1907. Morgan was an avid art collector, and it is said that whenever he was in Paris art dealers came out of the woodwork at the Hôtel Bristol, hoping to make a sale.

As you continue, you'll find yourself entering the sprawling:

10. **Place Vendôme,** one of the city's most imposing architectural designs. Go right around the square, window shopping and reading as you walk. Around 1670, Jules Hardouin-Mansart purchased the palace of the duc de Vendôme, including the land stretching north of the rue St-Honoré, which was meant to be

subdivided. Instead, a minister to Louis XIV decided to build a square, in the center of which would be an enormous statue of the king; work stopped when the minister died. About 18 years later the land was turned over to the city and Mansart, the original owner, was asked to finish the square. What you see today is his design. A statue of King Louis XIV was placed in the center as was originally planned, and the square was called place Louis-le-Grand.

The houses you see surrounding the octagonal square were built in the early 18th century. When Napoléon came to power, the statue of Louis XIV was torn down and replaced with the column you see today, which celebrates the victory at Austerlitz. The 144-foot-high column is covered with bronze taken from the 1,200 cannons that were captured during Napoléon's victory at Austerlitz, and on it is a series of bas-reliefs showing battle scenes from Austerlitz. Presently, the statue at the top is a reproduction of the original statue of Napoléon I; however, in the French tradition, there have been several different sculptures placed there over the years (and torn down), including a giant fleur-de-lis.

The mansions around this square were originally sold to very wealthy financiers (including John Law, a Scotsman who became Controleur General des Finances and bought several of these houses), and the place Vendôme quickly became the most prestigious address in the city. If you go around the square to the right, you'll come to number 12, where Chopin died in 1849. The Comtesse de Castiglione lived at number 26. Apparently she was dubbed the Madwoman of the place Vendôme, because as she got older she refused to go outside during the day for fear that people would see her and think that she had become ugly with age.

Farther around the square, after you cross rue de la Paix, head around the other side of the square where you'll find the:

11. Hôtel Ritz, founded in 1898 by César Ritz. Stories about the numerous guests of the Ritz are legion. Hemingway frequented the place—indeed, one of the hotel's bars is named after him. The small bar located off rue Cambon used to be the women's bar back in the days when women weren't allowed to drink, but now it has been decorated to look like a jolly old English pub.

One story about Hemingway and the Ritz says that he once left his luggage here for nearly 30 years. Legend has it that when he finally did remove it, upon examining the contents, he found notes for the beginnings of *A Moveable Feast*, the novel that made him one of the most hated men in all of Paris. Of course, there are some who say that the story is completely untrue.

Other Americans who enjoyed spending time at the Ritz (if not for a room, for a drink at least) included F. Scott Fitzgerald (who was seen stumbling out on more than a few occasions), Fred Astaire, J. P. Morgan, and Theodore Roosevelt. Cole Porter and his wife Linda Lee Thomas took an apartment here in 1919. They drove a Rolls-Royce, owned about a dozen dachsunds, and partied with Tallulah Bankhead, Irving Berlin, George Gershwin, and the Barrymores.

Return to rue de la Paix, and as you go, look for number 13, the:

12. Hôtel Westminster, on your left, where a preteen Henry James stayed with his parents while they looked for an apartment in 1856.

When you get to rue Daunou, keep an eye out for:

13. Number 6. Oliver Wendell Holmes stayed here in August 1886 (the building then housed the Hôtel d'Orient) during his visit to Louis Pasteur, the French chemist and microbiologist. Holmes simply wanted to shake the hand of the inventor of the vaccination that would eventually be used as protection against rabies. Its discovery also led to the creation of the Institut Pasteur here in Paris in 1888. Pasteur is also renowned for pasteurization, the process, based on his discoveries, that rids dairy products of any tuberculosis bacteria.

Across the street is:

14. Harry's Bar, at number 5 rue Daunou. This bar actually opened in 1911, but it wasn't until a little later that the place really started jumping. Of course, where there was alcohol you were bound to find those crazy American expatriates. Hemingway couldn't resist a mahogany bar that was tended by an American jockey called Harry, and neither could F. Scott Fitzgerald. Even Sinclair Lewis couldn't resist "Sank Roo Doe Noo," as Harry's sign translates into franglais for Americans who become too drunk to know where they are. It was here that the Bloody Mary and the Sidecar were born, and it's where many Parisians discovered the only American-born alcoholic beverage—bourbon.

Turn around, heading back in the direction from which you came. Cross rue de la Paix and head along rue Daunou until you reach boulevard des Capucines. Go left on boulevard des Capucines and look for:

15. Number 35, on your left. Here, at today's Les Impressionistes restaurant, is the former studio of Nadar. On May 15, 1874, Nadar donated his studio to the Impressionists for their first exhibit. The exhibit was very badly received by the public—many people thought it made a mockery of true art. Renoir was very disappointed with the reviews and said, "The only thing we got out of it was the label 'Impressionism'—a name I loathe."

Across the street at number 14 is where the Lumière brothers held a public showing of the first movie in 1895. A bit farther down, at number 43, is where the first shot that sparked the revolution of 1848 was fired. Retrace your steps back to rue Daunou. Directly across from rue Daunou is the entrance to rue Scribe. At 1 rue Scribe is the:

16. Hôtel Scribe, which was the press headquarters for Allied forces from August 1944 until the fall of 1945. John Dos Passos was one of the lucky newsmen who was able to secure a job.

On your right look for the Olympia music hall (the entrance

is at 28 boulevard des Capucines), a prerequisite performance hall for all who aspire to be top pop music artists. Edith Piaf, the Beatles, Lou Reed, and Elvis Costello are among those who have played here.

Continue to the:

17. **Grand Hôtel,** at number 2 rue Scribe. This hotel has indeed been one of Paris's grandest since its opening in 1860, and is one of the oldest five-star hotels in Paris. Charles Garnier, who was also the architect of the Opéra building, submitted his plans, which were drawn up in order to provide rooms for visitors during the International Exhibition of 1867. Fifteen years later, Henry James was one of its guests after he returned from a whirlwind tour of France during which time he took notes for his book *A Little Tour in France* (1885).

Continue along rue Scribe to rue Auber. Go right along rue Auber, which will bring you almost immediately to the:

18. **Place de l'Opéra** and **the Opéra,** at one of the busiest intersections in Paris. The Opéra, decked out in Second Empire style, is wildly embellished (with what was probably considered at the time it was built to be too much of everything). When Charles Garnier (1825–98) built the Opéra, he introduced Paris and the world to Napoléon III style. Construction began in 1862 and continued until 1875. The end result is one of the most stunning buildings in all of Paris. Inside you'll find a sweeping marble staircase with an onyx balustrade, as well as the incredibly ornamented Grand Foyer, which is about 177 feet long. The walls of the Grand Foyer are bejeweled with mirrors, paintings, mosaics, and pieces of marble that hail from the Italian island of Murano (where the famous glass-blowing factory is located).

The auditorium boasts the famous 6-ton chandelier, as well as a series of paintings done by Marc Chagall in 1964.

Note: The best time to visit the Grand Foyer and the Auditorium is between the hours of 1 and 2pm when both are open.

After you come out of the Opéra, go left (facing away from the Opéra) on boulevard des Capucines, which turns into boulevard des Italiens shortly afterward. (The composer Offenbach died at number 8.) Go right on rue de Marivaux. You'll see the:

19. **Opéra Comique** on your left as you approach place Boïeldieu. The Opéra Comique is still called the Salle Favart (after the 18th-century singer). The present building opened in 1898 (there were two before it, including one by Claude Charpentier), and its back faces the boulevard, which is no accident—the actors didn't want to be confused with the mountebanks who worked the streets. The American soprano opera singer Mary Garden gave a stunning performance here when called upon to finish the final act of the opera *Louise,* for which she was an understudy at the time. The audience loved her and she sang the next hundred performances.

Alexandre Dumas, the French author, was born in 1824 at number 1 place Boïeldieu. Go left around the front of the Opéra Comique onto rue St-Marc. Follow it to rue de Richelieu. On the left is:

20. Number 95, formerly the Hôtel des Patriotes Etrangers. Gouverneur Morris arrived in 1789, prepared to serve as American ambassador to France. He was a redoubtable character who sported a wooden leg and a withered arm. During the Reign of Terror his carriage was stopped by a mob. They were about to kill him, but he stuck his wooden leg out the door and yelled, "Goddamn you—me, an aristocrat! Who lost his leg in the cause of American liberty!" The mob cheered and allowed him to continue on his way. Other ambassadors fled Paris, but he remained, and while in this very hotel he kept a 12-volume diary of what it was like to be in Paris during the Revolution. He also allowed royal treasures to be stored in the American embassy until they could be smuggled to England.

Go left up rue de Richelieu and turn right onto boulevard Montmartre. Shortly after you cross rue Vivienne you will come to the:

21. Passage des Panoramas, on your right. Originally there were two huge towers on either side of this passageway. Under the direction of American inventor Robert Fulton, who had received a patent for panorama painting from the French government, Pierre Prévost painted eighteen panoramas in the towers. Parisians would come to the towers and pay just to look at the paintings. With the money he made Fulton was able to work on his submarine (the reason he came to Paris was to try to sell the idea to Napoléon) and his steamboat. The first steamboat he tried out—on the Seine—was 66 feet long and had a flat bottom. Unfortunately, when the engine and boiler were put on board it split in two. The second boat ran at an amazing clip of about 4.5 miles an hour.

Regrettably, the towers were destroyed (and the paintings with them) in 1831, but this wonderful little passageway remains.

When you come out of the passageway, go right to rue Vivienne. Go left on rue Vivienne. Just before you get to rue du 4-Septembre you'll find yourself alongside the:

22. Bourse des Valeurs, or Paris Stock Exchange. The idea of the creation of a stock exchange emerged in 1720, when it was forbidden for anyone who was not a broker to make financial deals in a public building. In 1724 brokers were required to work in a stock exchange. For almost 100 years after this government ruling, the Bourse was housed in several different buildings. Finally, Napoléon I commissioned Aléxandre-Théodore Brongniart, who began this building in 1808 and finished it (64 Corinthian columns and all) in 1826. The Bourse then became permanently settled. You can go inside and watch the traders in action from the spectators' gallery (entrance is on the rue du 4-Septembre).

Continue down rue Vivienne to the:

23. Bibliothèque Nationale, on your right. The story of the French national library dates back to the royal collections. They became official libraries when the copyright law of 1537 went into effect. The law required that one copy of every book ever printed in France be "deposited" in what would eventually become the library you see today.

Every year approximately 40,000 volumes are added to this already immense collection. There are more than 12 million books housed in the Department of Printed Books alone. In addition, the library houses one of the largest collections of maps in the world; the Department of Manuscripts holds original manuscripts by Victor Hugo, Marcel Proust, and Marie Curie; and the Music and Record Library holds an enormous collection of original musical scores, records, and tapes.

You can't go into the great Reading Room, designed by Labrouste (1801–75), but you should definitely try to look in through the windows at the cast-iron columns and the nine square-vaulted bays within. In the Salle d'Honneur you'll find a wonderful statue of Voltaire (his heart is in the pedestal) by Houdon.

When you come out of the library, turn right on rue Vivienne to rue des Petits-Champs, then go right again on to rue de Richelieu. Turn left on rue de Richelieu to number 52 and the entrance to rue (or passage) de Beaujolais. If you go straight out of the passageway, continuing on rue de Beaujolais you'll find the entrance to the gardens of the Palais Royal (which we'll visit in just a few minutes). At number 15 rue de Beaujolais is:

24. Hôtel Beaujolais, where Margaret Anderson lived in 1923. She was fined and fingerprinted for publishing a review with reprints of portions of James Joyce's *Ulysses,* which was considered obscene at the time.

Sylvia Beach and her sister had rooms here in 1917, but the street's most famous resident was Colette, who lived at number 9 rue de Beaujolais and spent a great deal of time sitting enjoying the beauty of the lime grove in the gardens of the Palais Royal. She also enjoyed dining at the restaurant Le Grand Véfour (17 rue de Beaujolais), which was once frequented by Napoléon and Josephine, Victor Hugo, and Jean Cocteau, among others. Today it has been restored by the Taittinger family, complete with carved *boiserie* ceilings and black and gold Directoire chairs that return one to the days when the Palais Royal was in its glory.

Head into the:

25. Jardin du Palais-Royal. Cardinal Richelieu is responsible for the building of the Palais Royal, which was designed by architect Jacques Lemercier in 1642. When Cardinal Richelieu died he left the palace to Louis XIII, who died shortly thereafter; Anne of Austria then took up residence here, and at that time the Palais Royal received its name. In 1781 the palace was given to the Orléans family by Louis XIV, and after the Revolution

Napoléon established the Tribune here. It housed the Bourse for a brief time; not long after, gambling houses were opened in the palace that remained popular until they closed in 1838. The palace was burnt down during the Commune and rebuilt. It has become progressively quieter as the cafés, restaurants, and famous jewelers that once occupied the galleries have moved out.

The actual gardens and square were designed by Victor Louis under the direction of Philippe, the duc d'Orleans (to whose family the palace had been granted by Louis XIV), who came up with the idea of creating the pavilions and allotting space for apartments and shops. The streets surrounding the gardens were named after the sons of the duc d'Orleans—Beaujolais, Montpensier, and Valois.

It was in one of the cafés here, the Café de Foy, that on July 12, 1789, Camille Desmoulins (whose statue is located in the gardens) gave the speech that began the Revolution:

"Citizens . . . the time for talking has gone, the time for action has come. The people must take up arms, they must show by their cockades to which party they are pledged." And they did.

WALKING TOUR 10

Montmartre

Start: Place Pigalle. (Métro: Pigalle.)

Finish: Place Blanche.

Time: Four to six hours, depending on how long you spend in the churches, museums, and cemetery.

Best Time: It's best to get an early start on this tour because you don't want to end up at the cemetery after dark.

Worst Time: Monday, when the Musée de Vieux Montmartre is closed.

The history of Montmartre goes all the way back to the third century, when its name was still Mont de Mercure. Saint Denis and two of his prelates were tortured and taken to the top of Mont de Mercure, where they were beheaded. A miracle then happened— Saint Denis is said to have picked up his own head, carried it to a nearby fountain, washed the blood from his face, and then walked for four miles before he collapsed. Not long after this incident the hill was renamed Mont des Martyrs. Over time the hill has become known to all as Montmartre.

Much later the hill was used for its quarries, from which plaster of paris was mined. The mining continued until well into the 19th century, at which point a colony of artists began to settle here.

Today, the hill is known for the Moulin Rouge, and the great white Basilique du Sacré-Coeur, the presence of which seems to swallow the "mountain" whole. Here you'll walk through the place du Tertre where Utrillo and his mother, Suzanne Valadon, lived and worked. Rather than good restaurants and glamorous shops, in Montmartre you'll find quiet streets, old cafés, the last remaining windmills on the hill, and haunts of artists like Toulouse-Lautrec.

1. Place Pigalle. Aside from being the center of a 19th-century writers' and artists' colony, place Pigalle was built on the site of an old Montmartre tollgate by Jean Baptiste Pigalle in the 19th century. Pigalle was a sculptor and painter who specialized in pictures and sculptures of the Virgin Mary. However, he wasn't completely pious—he sculpted Voltaire in the buff.

Edith Piaf, "the little sparrow," used to sing in the alleys off the place Pigalle, hoping to earn enough money for a hot meal. She went on to be one of France's beloved entertainers.

As you come out of place Pigalle, go right on boulevard de Clichy to:

2. Number 10. The composer Darius Milhaud (1892–1974) lived here. He conducted his initial studies at the Paris Conservatory, but he also spent some time in Brazil working with Paul Claudel, the French minister to Brazil and brother of Camille Claudel (see Walking Tour 2, stop 24 for more information about C. Claudel); this experience had a profound influence on his music.

In 1940 Milhaud became a professor of music at the all-women's Mills College in California. Ultimately he became a professor of composition at the National Conservatoire in Paris. Among his most famous operas are *Le Pauvre Matelot* (1927) and *Christophe Colombe* (1930), which features a libretto by Paul Claudel.

Continue along. On the other side of the street are two of Picasso's former residences (nos. 11 and 13). A bit farther on, at number 6, is the building in which Degas died. Keep walking until you reach boulevard de Rochechouart, which was named after Marguerite de Rochechouart, abbess of Montmartre from 1717 to 1727. The intersection of boulevard de Rochechouart, boulevard de Clichy, and rue des Martyrs is where the famous:

3. Cirque Montmartre was established. In 1873 a man by the name of Fernando began a circus here (he called it Cirque Fernando) featuring high-wire acts, jugglers, trapeze artists, and clowns. In 1897, one of the circus's very famous clowns, Medrano, or Boum Boum as he was known to his admirers, took over management, and the circus changed names. Parisians loved Cirque Medrano, and it was an inspiration to many of Paris's artists, including Toulouse-Lautrec, Picasso, Degas, Renoir, and Seurat, who painted the trapeze artists and Boum Boum himself.

One of the most famous high-wire acts of the 1920s was Barbette, who liked to wear Chanel gowns, ostrich feather hats, and leotards. Not too unusual, right? Well, Barbette was a man—an American named Vander Clyde who hailed from Texas. So brilliant was his artistry that Paul Valéry described him as "Heracles transformed into a swallow." He was toasted by the rest of Paris and was a fixture of café society. Sadly, Barbette took a nasty fall at the Moulin Rouge one night and was forced to stop performing. He returned to Austin, Texas, and died in obscurity.

Go left onto rue Dancourt to place Charles-Dullin where you'll find the:

4. **Théâtre de l'Atelier,** set up by Charles Dullin (1885–1949) in 1921 in the old Théâtre de Montmartre (renamed in 1957 for Dullin). Dullin was an actor, director, and producer who was famous for his "experimental" dramas and was responsible for introducing the works of Pirandello to French audiences.

Cut through place Charles-Dullin onto rue des Trois-Frères to rue Yves-le-Tac. Turn left to:

5. **Place des Abbesses,** built on the site of Montmartre's old town hall. Verlaine was married here on August 11, 1870 (before he had an affair with his protégé, Arthur Rimbaud). On your left is the church of St-Jean-l'Evangéliste (1904), the first church to be built entirely of reinforced concrete. Note also to your right the Art Nouveau Métro station, designed by Hector Guimard. For more about Hector Guimard see Walking Tour 2, stop 5.

Exit from the church and go right across the street to passage des Abbesses. When you get to rue des Trois-Frères, go left. Soon you'll come to:

6. **Place Emile-Goudeau and the Bâteau-Lavoir,** which is on your right. Before you go into the square look down the hill to your left—there's a great view. At number 13 place Emile-Goudeau is the Bâteau-Lavoir, a small building that many artists have called home, including Picasso from 1904 to 1909 (it was here that he painted his famous portrait of Gertrude Stein, *The Third Rose,* as well as *Les Demoiselles d'Avignon);* Juan Gris from 1906 to 1922; Modigliani in 1908; Max Jacob in 1911; and Charpentier in 1912. Look at the photographs, including one of a very young Picasso. In 1970, the original building burned, but it was rebuilt in 1978; the studios are now homes for 25 artists and sculptors.

Go up the hill turning right out of place Emile-Goudeau onto rue Berthe. As you walk along rue Berthe note that it turns into rue André-Barsacq, and note the window treatments of numbers 11 and 13. When you reach rue Chappe you can choose one of three ways to get to the Sacré-Coeur. You can head up the stairs of rue Chappe; this is a strenuous climb for anyone who isn't in good physical shape, but it's the quickest way up. (There's a soda machine at the top of the stairs on the right if you need an incentive to go this way.) Your second option is to continue to the stairs at the end of rue André-Barsacq and go down to the Funiculaire (the shortest Métro line in Paris), which will carry you to the top of the hill (for the price of a Métro ride). Or finally, you can go down the stairs as if you were headed for the Funiculaire, but instead, go around it, check out the Carousel, take a small breather, and then head straight up the hill. This route will afford a magnificent view of the great white basilica.

Note: On your way into the church don't get bamboozled by the nice women who put cards and pendants in your hand—they're not giving you presents, they're gathering alms.

Whichever route you choose, the end you tend toward is the:

7. Basilique du Sacré-Coeur, certainly one of the most spectacular-looking churches in Paris. During the Franco-Prussian War Alexandre Legentil and Rohault de Fleury made a pact to build a church dedicated to the Sacré-Coeur (the Sacred Heart) at the top of this hill. The church was to be built as a symbol of hope for the city's Catholics. Work on the church began in 1876, and it was consecrated on October 16, 1919. Unfortunately, during World War II most of the stained-glass windows were shattered during an air attack on Gare de la Chapelle, but there are some wonderful mosaics throughout the church. You can go on a tour of the Dome with a guard who is stationed on the first terrace.

When you come out of the church, go right, and then right again onto rue du Cardinal-Guibert. Take your first left on rue du Chevalier-de-la-Barre to the corner of rue du Mont-Cenis. Go left to the entrance of:

8. St-Pierre de Montmartre. Consecrated in 1147, this church also claims (along with St-Julien-le-Pauvre) to be the oldest in Paris, and it is, in fact, the last trace of the original abbey that stood here. Among its parishioners have been Saint Thomas Beckett, Saint Ignatius of Loyola, and Dante. Jean-Baptiste Pigalle is buried in its tiny cemetery. The stained-glass windows date from 1954; earlier ones were destroyed by a bomb during World War II.

Go back out of the church and go left to:

9. Restaurant La Bohème du Tertre where from 1919 to 1935 Suzanne Valadon and her son, Utrillo, used to eat. Valadon was famous in her own right as a painter. She began her career as a circus acrobat, then began modeling for artists such as Renoir, Toulouse-Lautrec, and Degas. Degas encouraged her to take up painting. Her favorite subjects were nudes and still-lifes and her work is easily identified by the bold use of color, punctuated with heavy black outlines. Degas once commented that she and Mary Cassatt were the only two female painters he knew who had any talent (and he didn't really believe in women painters). She helped start her son's career as a painter by giving him a set of paints, hoping that painting would curb his drinking problem. As you'll see later in this walking tour, Utrillo did begin painting, but unfortunately he didn't stop drinking.

Go right at the end of rue du Mont-Cenis and you'll find yourself in the:

10. Place du Tertre, one of the most-frequented tourist spots in the city. Many artists scrape for a living here by doing tourist portraits or scenes of Montmartre. In earlier times, instead of artists and tourists, the abbey gallows and stocks stood here.

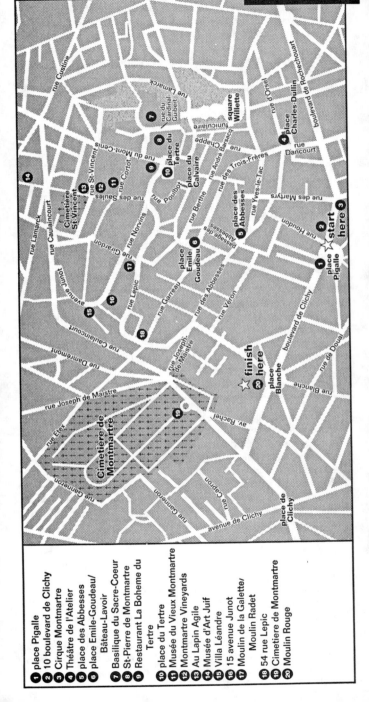

MONTMARTRE

- ① place Pigalle
- ② 10 boulevard de Clichy
- ③ Cirque Montmartre
- ④ Théâtre de l'Atelier
- ⑤ place des Abbesses
- ⑥ place Emile-Goudeau/ Bâteau-Lavoir
- ⑦ Basilique du Sacre-Coeur
- ⑧ St-Pierre de Montmartre
- ⑨ Restaurant La Boheme du Tertre
- ⑩ place du Tertre
- ⑪ Musée du Vieux Montmartre
- ⑫ Montmartre Vineyards
- ⑬ Au Lapin Agile
- ⑭ Musée d'Art Juif
- ⑮ Villa Léandre
- ⑯ 15 avenue Junot
- ⑰ Moulin de la Galette/ Moulin Radet
- ⑱ 54 rue Lepic
- ⑲ Cimetiere de Montmartre
- ⑳ Moulin Rouge

Utrillo used to hang out here in place du Tertre, and it might well have been here that he and Modigliani (see Walking Tour 11, stop 15 for more information about Modigliani) had their first meeting. Their mutual admiration, rather than creating a harmonious union, led to a fight that started with one of them announcing, "You are the world's greatest painter."

"No, you are the world's greatest painter," contradicted the other.

"I forbid you to contradict me," said the first.

"I forbid you to forbid me," said the other.

"If you say that again, I'll hit you," threatened the first.

"You are the greatest—," and the fight began.

After the fight they decided to be friends and went to a nearby restaurant, where they downed several bottles of wine. When they finally emerged and walked out into the street, one said, "You are the world's greatest painter."

"No, you are," contradicted the other.

And the fists flew again. They beat each other until they fell in the gutter, where they both fell asleep, and woke in the morning (or probably the afternoon), to find that their pockets had been emptied.

REFRESHMENT STOP It is possible (or at least you can imagine) that Utrillo and Modigliani drank away those hours at number 6 place du Tertre, which houses the restaurant **La Mère Catherine.** Founded in 1793, it is the oldest restaurant in the place du Tertre. Dine on the terrace or have a seat on one of the red velvet benches and enjoy a leisurely lunch amidst all the activity of the place.

Continue around place du Tertre and go through to place du Calvaire, where you'll find a spectacular view. Continue around to the right, head down the steps onto rue Poulbot to rue Norvins. Cross rue Norvins onto rue des Saules. When you get to rue Cortot, go right to number 12 to 14, the:

11. **Musée du Vieux Montmartre,** which will be on your left and can be visited in approximately 30 minutes. It houses a wide collection of mementos of Old Montmartre and was formerly occupied by van Gogh, Renoir, Suzanne Valadon, and Utrillo. The museum charts the history of Montmartre, houses a re-creation of the workroom of Gustave Charpentier (composer of the opera *Louise*), and has an entire room devoted to Emile Bernard of the Pont-Aven group. You'll also find a reconstruction of Café de l'Aubrevoir, which was another of Utrillo's favorite spots, and some caricatures by Steinlen (1853–1923). An extensive collection of china from the Cligancourt Pottery is also of interest.

Come back out of the museum and go left to rue du Mont-Cenis. Go left on rue du Mont-Cenis and down the stairs to rue St-Vincent. Go left on rue St-Vincent, and a little way down the road you'll come upon the:

12. **Montmartre Vineyards,** one of two remaining vineyards in the city of Paris. This vineyard produces approximately 500 bottles of Clos Montmartre red annually, and every year there is a celebration, the "harvest fête," on the first or second Saturday of October. If you're lucky enough to be in Paris at harvest time, it's quite a party—there's even a parade.

The famous cartoonist Francisque Poulbot (1899–1946), who used to do caricatures of children and street scenes of Montmartre, so loved the vineyards that he helped save them from destruction by developers in the 1930s.

On your right is:

13. **Au Lapin Agile,** the original Cabaret des Assassins. Legend has it that the cabaret got its first name because a band of assassins broke in and killed the owner's son. It was renamed in 1880 because of a sign that featured a rabbit in a bow tie, painted by André Gill. People began saying that it was the "Cabaret à Gill," which eventually became "Agile."

Belonging originally to a famous Parisian singer by the name of Aristide Bruant, the building was given, by Bruant, to a man named Father Fred, who used to entertain his clientele by playing the guitar and singing along. Because Montmartre was the heart of artistic Paris at the time, there was much discussion here that centered around the "meaning of art," and a man by the name of Roland Dorgeles (a popular writer at that time) took it upon himself to make somewhat of a mockery of all the debate by dipping the tail of Father Fred's donkey into some paint, smearing it on a canvas, and exhibiting the canvas, which he called *Le coucher du Soleil sur l'Adriatique* (or, The Setting of the Sun over the Adriatic). Much to his amusement, the critics actually liked it. Of course, he did eventually tell them (to the further amusement of many Parisians) that it was merely a joke.

The Cabaret des Assassins was often painted by Utrillo, and today this corner is one of the most visited and photographed in all of Paris.

Go right on rue des Saules and you'll see the Cimetière St-Vincent on your left, where Emile Goudeau, Utrillo, composer Arthur Honegger, and Inghelbrect are buried. To get into the cemetery continue down the stairs to rue Caulaincourt. Go left on rue Caulaincourt to the entrance. When you come out of the cemetery, backtrack to rue des Saules. Go left on rue des Saules down the stairs to number 42, where you'll find the:

14. **Musée d'Art Juif** (Jewish Art Museum) on your right. Located on the third floor, the museum was founded in 1948 to promote Jewish art. Contributions to the museum include architectural models, drawings, engravings, and paintings by Marc Chagall, Max Lieberman, and Chaim Soutine.

When you're finished at the museum, go back up the stairs to rue Caulaincourt. Go left on rue Caulaincourt to the fork at rue

MARC CHAGALL

A Russian-born painter, Marc Chagall (1887–1985) original-ly studied at St. Petersburg. In 1910 he came to Paris, where he became a part of the avant-garde set. Chagall's work reflects an element of fantasy that seems to border on surrealism, but in his biography, he claims that his work is not surreal at all, but comes directly from memories of his early childhood. Many of those memories were filled with Jewish tradition and Russian folklore. Besides painting, he also created a great deal of stained glass, and his costume designs included those used in a 1945 production of Igor Stravinsky's *Firebird*.

Caulaincourt and avenue Junot. Continue along the avenue Junot fork to:

15. **Villa Léandre,** located at number 25 avenue Junot, a short cul-de-sac that seems an oasis in the middle of a fairly busy area of the city. It probably won't come as a surprise as you walk along that many artists have called this little alley home.

Continue along to:

16. **Number 15,** the former home of Tristan Tzara (1896–1963), a Romanian-born French poet. He is best known as the founder of the dadaist movement. Tzara and André Breton (1896–1966) collaborated briefly before Breton broke with the dadaist movement to found the surrealist movement. Adolf Loos, the architect of Tzara's house, had a modernist's disdain for architectural ornamentation. This appealed to Tzara's dadaist sensibilities, and he brought Loos to Paris from Vienna and commissioned him to build this house.

Continue along avenue Junot to rue Girardon. Go right on rue Girardon to rue Lepic. Go right on rue Lepic and look back across the street to:

17. **Moulin de la Galette and the Moulin Radet,** two wind-mills that were built in 1622; the former is the one you see before you, and the latter is just a bit farther down rue Lepic (to your left as you face Moulin de la Galette). In the 19th century, they were owned by the Debray brothers, who were killed while defending them from the Prussians. Some say they were tied to the sails of their windmills and killed. Their graves are located in the small cemetery of St-Pierre de Montmartre. These two are the only survivors of the 30 windmills that once dotted the hill, and they are the subject of many paintings, the most famous of which is Renoir's *Moulin de la Galette* (1876). The windmill before you was originally named Moulin Blute-Fin, but its name changed when it became a dance hall and began serving *galettes*—cakes that were made with the flour ground inside the windmills. In the 1860s it became one of the favorite venues of

the Impressionists, including Toulouse-Lautrec, Van Gogh, Renoir, and Utrillo. Renoir's painting is greatly responsible for its worldwide fame.

Face Moulin de la Galette, then turn left and walk to:

18. **Number 54 rue Lepic.** Currently in a state of disrepair, this is the building in which Vincent van Gogh and his brother Theo lived from 1886 to 1888. Vincent and Theo had an extraordinarily strong relationship; Theo helped support Vincent, both financially and emotionally, throughout his life, but particularly during his art career. Theo ran an art gallery, which at the time exhibited very traditional art, but he believed in the talents of his brother. When Vincent shot himself Theo was so destroyed by his brother's death that many think he died of grief.

Continue along to rue Joseph-de-Maistre and go right to rue Caulaincourt. Go left on rue Caulaincourt to the entrance (at number 20 avenue Rachel) of:

19. **The Cimetière de Montmartre,** founded in 1798. You can pick up a map at the main office as you enter (it's not a great one, but it will give you a general idea of where to find gravesites not mentioned here).

Begin by going around the circle to the left, and go up the stairs, where you will find the grave of: **Emile Zola** (1840–1902), the French novelist who earned his living in journalism. As a novelist, he took a very scientific approach to his writing, describing everything down to the minutest detail. He didn't always make an adequate living as a journalist and often suffered in poverty. On one occasion he was so poor that he had to sell his raincoat and his pants and stay home working in only his shirt. His remains have been moved to the Panthéon.

Continue around the circle and go right on avenue Dubuisson to avenue Berlioz. Go left on avenue Berlioz to **Louis-Hector Berlioz's** grave, located just beyond Chemin Artot on the left side of the street. Berlioz (1803–1869) was a French composer who started out in medicine, but gave that up to go to the Paris Conservatory. His music is composed in a loose form and has a highly personal and emotional style. He won the Prix de Rome in 1830, and over the next decade composed *Romeo and Juliet.*

Cross avenue Berlioz and go left on avenue Cordier to **Jean-Honoré Fragonard's** grave, on the left side of the street. (If you get to the next intersection, you've gone way too far. It's actually located fairly close to the intersection of avenue Berlioz and avenue Cordier, but it's about four rows back and the gravestone is very plain. You might have to ask someone for help in finding it.) Fragonard (1732–1806), a French painter, won the Prix de Rome and studied in Italy from 1756 to 1761. Much of his painting consists of scenes of erotic love, but after he married his works lost their sensual qualities. A sad commentary!

Continue along avenue Cordier to **Théophile Gautier's** grave, on the right side of the road. Gautier (1811–72), a French poet and novelist who sidelined as a critic, was a member of the group that believed in "art for art's sake." In his writing he adhered to a theory of "plasticity," by which he meant that a writer should create works of art by manipulating words in the same way a painter manipulates paint, or a sculptor manipulates clay. His best-known novels include *Le Capitaine Fracasse* (1863), and *Emaux et Camées* (1852).

Continue along to avenue du Montebello. Go right on avenue du Montebello and up a flight of stairs to the grave of **Hilaire-Germain-Edgar Degas.** Degas (1834–1917) the Impressionist painter, is buried here in his family tomb; as you'll see from the tomb, the original family name was de Gas. Degas may have become one of France's most well-known artists, but he began as a student of law. A student of Ingres, his career as an artist began at l'Ecole des Beaux-Arts. Later he broke from traditional style and joined the Impressionist movement. He especially enjoyed painting (and sculpting) ballet dancers and women at their toilette, but he dabbled with painting different scenes depicting café life. As his eyesight began to fail and make painting in oils difficult for him (because of the detail required of oil painting), he began to use pastels and charcoal. He greatly influenced Toulouse-Lautrec and Picasso, and aided in the development of the career of Mary Cassatt. Once when Degas was present at an auction where one of his paintings was being sold to a bidder for an astonishing amount of money, someone asked him how he felt (supposing that he would think it a great honor) and he said, "I feel as a horse must feel when the beautiful cup is given to the jockey."

Come back down the stairs and go around to avenue du Tunnel. Go right on avenue des Carrières. When you get to avenue des Anglais, go left to **Léo Delibes's** grave. A French composer, Delibes (1836–91) attended the Paris Conservatory. He became an accompanist at the Paris Opéra, and enjoyed success with *Mallets Coppelia* (1870), *Sylvia* (1876), and his most famous work, the opera *Lakme* (1883).

Continue down avenue des Anglais to **Jacques Levy Offenbach's** grave. Offenbach (née Jacob Eberst, 1819–80), was a famous composer of operettas and a darling of the Second Empire. He was conductor at the Théâtre Française in 1849 and was particularly successful as a composer of French operettas. During his lifetime he composed over a hundred of them, including *La Belle Hélène* (1864), and *La Vie Parisienne* (1866). He spent every waking moment with his music, as is evidenced by the following anecdote: Offenbach once had a personal servant that he fired; shortly thereafter he gave the man a glowing reference to a friend who was considering hiring him. The friend was confused by this and asked him why he would give such a good reference to a man after he had just fired him. Offenbach's explanation was, "Oh, he's a good fellow, but he won't do for a composer. He beats my clothes outside my door every morning and his tempo is non-existent."

Continue down avenue des Anglais to avenue Samson. Go right on avenue Samson across avenue du Tunnel. Avenue Samson turns into avenue Travot. Follow along avenue Travot and cross avenue de Montmorency. Just across avenue de Montmorency is **Stendhal's** grave. Stendhal (born Marie-Henri Beyle, 1783–1842) traveled to Italy as a dragoon in Napoléon's army and in fact launched his literary career in Milan in 1814 by writing one of his two great novels, *The Red and the Black* (1831). The other, *The Charterhouse of Parma* (1839) was written while Stendhal was traveling around France during a leave of absence from his work as a consul.

Follow avenue de la Croix (which you walked onto when you crossed avenue de Montmorency) straight out to the circle at the entrance to the cemetery. Go right around the circle back to avenue Rachel and exit the cemetery. Follow avenue Rachel out to boulevard de Clichy. Go left on boulevard de Clichy to the:

20. Moulin Rouge, at 82 boulevard de Clichy. Founded in 1889, it still claims to have the best show in town. Once one of the favorite spots of Paris artists who had settled in Montmartre—thanks to its low cost of living and decadent mix of pleasure and vice—these days it's most popular with tourists.

The Moulin Rouge is most famous for the cancan; the "chahut," a high-kicking dance that was a forerunner of the numbers performed by today's Rockettes; and appearances by

---

TOULOUSE-LAUTREC'S WOMEN

Jane Avril (1868–1943). The daughter of an Italian emigrant and a French mother, Jane Avril danced at the Moulin Rouge at age 20 and was called "the dance incarnate" by her admirers. She died in relative obscurity, in spite of the fact that Toulouse-Lautrec immortalized her in several of his posters.

Marie-Louise Fuller (1862–1928). Originally from Illinois, Marie-Louise Fuller abandoned vaudeville and opera to become a dancer, making her debut in Paris at the Folies Bergère (located in the Rue Richer). Fuller was known for her performances on a glass platform that was floodlit from underneath. The mirrors she had set up behind and around her reflected only a silhouette so that as one critic wrote, she looked like a "genie who dances." During her time in Paris she is said to have met and had an affair with Auguste Rodin.

Yvette Guilbert (1867–1944). Appearing at the Moulin Rouge, she became famous for her silhouette of green satin and her long black gloves. Toulouse-Lautrec enjoyed painting her, and when she wasn't available but her gloves were, he painted just her gloves.

"La Goulue," a stage name of Louise Weber, whose performances in the late 1880s were talked about all over Paris. She is featured in many of Toulouse-Lautrec's paintings.

Today, the Moulin Rouge's shows still feature the world-famous bare-breasted cancan dancers, provocatively draped with ostrich feathers and covered in rhinestones (but you probably won't find it to be nearly as racy or as interesting as you thought it would be). The dinner and show are very expensive, and probably not worth the $100 to $200 it will cost you.

The Père-Lachaise Cemetery

Start: Boulevard de Ménilmontant and avenue Principale. (Métro: Père-Lachaise.)
Finish: Boulevard de Ménilmontant and avenue Principale.
Time: Two to three hours, depending on how many detours away from the tour you take.
Best Time: Anytime during the day.

The Cimetière du Père-Lachaise hasn't always been a cemetery. Its name arises from its origins as the country retreat of Père François de la Chaise d'Aix, confessor to Louis XIV. Nicolas Frochot purchased the property almost 200 years ago from Jacques Baron (the man who'd owned it after Père François) and began to promote it as a cemetery for famous or wealthy people. Needless to say, he was not pleased when his first customer turned out to be an errand boy.

Frochot puzzled over his dilemma and eventually pounced on an opportunity to purchase the supposed bones of Molière and Jean La Fontaine. He buried them side by side hoping that their presence would help to attract a better crowd. These celebrities did generate some interest, but business didn't really get any better until he acquired the bones of the famous lovers Héloïse and Abélard. All of a sudden plots began selling like hotcakes.

Now you have the opportunity to visit the resting place of all the famous people who have since been interred here. In working up this tour I tried to stop at all the major luminaries, but there are a few who had to be left out because of where they were located. Get a map at the entrance to the cemetery and you might find others you'll want to visit. This is a wonderful place. Parisians love their cemetery, and I hope you will too.

In case you're wondering—Père de la Chaise is not buried here.

Go straight up avenue Principale to the sign that says "Chapelle." Go left onto avenue Circulaire. The third stone on the right, a black stone with gold lettering, is the grave of:

1. Sidonie-Gabrielle Claudine Colette, (1873–1954). Known simply as Colette, this writer was the first woman president of the Goncourt Academy, and the second woman to be made a grand officer of the French Legion of Honor, and was married three times. Most of her writing is for and about women. Some of her most famous novels are *Gigi* (1945), *The Cat* (1933), and *Chéri* (1920). Colette attributed her success as a writer (and her powers of observation) to her mother, whose oft-repeated advice to "Look, look!" taught her daughter to watch for life's wonders. On her deathbed in 1954 during Paris's worst thunderstorm in almost three-quarters of a century, Colette pointed at the sky and the lightning and said, "Look, look!" for the very last time.

Go back to avenue Principale and go left up to the grave of:

2. Gioacchino Antonio Rossini, (1792–1868). Located on the left side of the path just before the sixth tree (counting from the intersection of avenue Circulaire and avenue Principale) you'll find the grave of the Italian operatic composer who wrote *The Barber of Seville*. During the time he was composing operas he was considered a big box office draw, because his operas featured the common person. He was indeed a commoner and not a wealthy man. When he was very old but quite famous, a group of students were trying to raise money in order to have a statue dedicated to him. He told them, "Give me the twenty-thousand and I'll stand on the pedestal myself."

Just after the next tree, also on the left, is the grave of:

3. Louis-Charles-Alfred de Musset, (1810–57), a French romantic playwright, fiction writer, and poet who was infatuated with and had a short affair with George Sand. Note: His sister is buried behind him.

Go back in the direction from which you came. Go left on avenue du Puits. Take your second right, then your first left (a dirt pathway), which is avenue Rachel. Just after the eighth tree in the front row of the old Jewish section of the cemetery is the:

4. Rothschild family plot. A German-Jewish family whose history begins with Mayer Anselm (1743–1812), the Rothschilds were one of Europe's great financial powers. Mayer Anselm began as a moneylender in Frankfurt and lent great sums of money to various governments and princes. His five sons expanded the business to Vienna, London, Naples, and Paris. The youngest, Jacob (1792–1868), started the Paris branch of the business, and his capital was used to help build the French railroad. He was also a great patron of the arts; if you go to the

Louvre you'll see many pieces that were given to the museum by the Rothschilds. But the most successful branch of the business was opened by Sir Nathan Mayer, who not only lent money to Wellington and the British government during wars with Napoléon, but was the first Jewish man to be admitted to England's House of Lords.

Continue five trees down from the Rothschild plot and in the second row head to the gravesite of:

5. **Camille Pissaro,** (1830–1903), a painter and graphic artist. Born in the West Indies to a Jewish father and Creole mother, he moved to Paris in 1855. Four years later he met Monet and became a member of the Impressionist group. Of the Impressionists, Pissaro was the oldest (by about 10 years) and he became a sort of father figure to Monet, Renoir, and Cézanne. He experimented briefly with pointillism, and though he is not the most well known of the group, he was the only one who exhibited in all eight of the Impressionist exhibitions. After 1895 he was forced to stay indoors because of his failing health, but it was during this time that he managed to paint some of his finest works, including his series depicting the avenue de l'Opéra.

Go back out to avenue du Puits and go right on this avenue to the fifth tree from the corner. You'll see a gothic structure with a fence around it; this edifice is the grave of:

6. **Héloïse and Abélard,** two of the world's most famous lovers. Pierre Abélard was born near Nantes and attended the school of Notre Dame, where he had a falling out with his master and was expelled. Abélard crossed the river to the school at Ste-Geneviève, where he himself eventually became a master. By the time he was 36 years old he was recognized as a great scholar and, ironically, became canon and master of Notre Dame in 1115. He became one of Paris's great teachers and his presence attracted students from all over medieval Europe to Notre Dame.

A bit later, while Abélard was working as the assistant to the canon Fulbert, the uncle of Héloïse, he and Héloïse fell in love. They were secretly married. When their secret was discovered, Héloïse was sent to the convent of Argenteuil, and Uncle Fulbert had Abélard castrated. Abélard did not die, however, and went to a monastery. Not long afterward, he opened a school of theology in which he challenged ecclesiastical authorities. Although he remained popular with his students, his enemies charged him with heresy and persecuted him constantly.

During the time he and Héloïse were separated they maintained their romance through letters. Abélard died in 1142. Héloïse died 24 years later. Finally, after many separations, their remains were reunited here in Père-Lachaise.

Go back out to avenue du Puits, and go right to chemin Mehul (an unpaved road on your left). Go left on chemin Mehul, then take your second left (not chemin du Coq, the next one). There's no name marker, but the road is cobbled. On the right is the grave of:

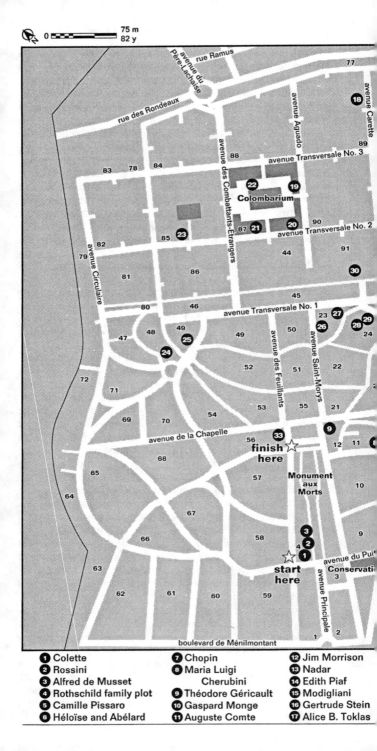

0 ⟝⟝⟝⟝ 75 m / 82 y

rue Ramus
avenue du Père-Lachaise
rue des Rondeaux
avenue Aguado
avenue Carette
77
18
89
avenue Transversale No. 3
88
83 78 84
22 **19**
Colombarium
avenue des Combattants-Étrangers
87 **21** **20**
90
avenue Transversale No. 2
85 **23**
44
91
82
79
avenue Circulaire
81 86
30
45
80 46
avenue Transversale No. 1
23 **27**
26
28 **29**
47 48 49
25
49
50
24
24
avenue des Feuillants
avenue Saint-Morys
52
51
22
72 71
53 55
21
69 70 54
avenue de la Chapelle
56 **33**
9
finish here ☆
12 11
65
57
Monument aux Morts
10
64
67
3
9
66
58
4 **2**
63
1
avenue du Pui
start here ☆
avenue Principale
Conservati
3
62 61 60 59
2
1
boulevard de Ménilmontant

1 Colette
2 Rossini
3 Alfred de Musset
4 Rothschild family plot
5 Camille Pissaro
6 Héloïse and Abélard
7 Chopin
8 Maria Luigi Cherubini
9 Théodore Géricault
10 Gaspard Monge
11 Auguste Comte
12 Jim Morrison
13 Nadar
14 Edith Piaf
15 Modigliani
16 Gertrude Stein
17 Alice B. Toklas

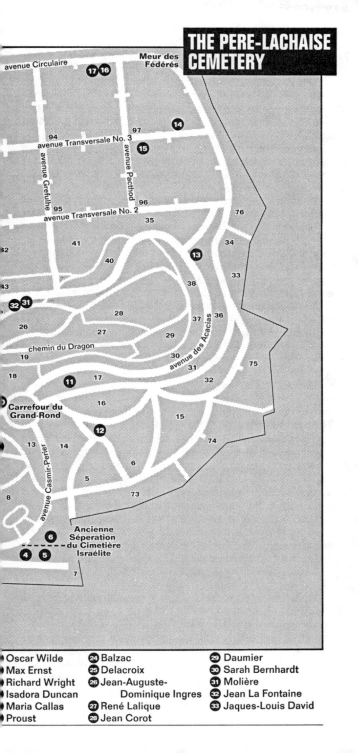

THE PERE-LACHAISE CEMETERY

avenue Circulaire

Meur des Fédérés

17 16

94
avenue Transversale No. 3

97

14

avenue Grefulhe

avenue Pacthod

15

95
avenue Transversale No. 2

96

35

76

42

41

40

34

33

38

13

43

32 31

28

37 36

26

27

29

chemin du Dragon

30

avenue des Acacias

19

31

75

18

11

17

32

Carrefour du Grand-Rond

16

15

12

13

14

avenue Casmir-Perier

74

6

5

8

73

6

Ancienne Séperation du Cimetière Israélite

4 5

7

Oscar Wilde	24 Balzac	29 Daumier
Max Ernst	25 Delacroix	30 Sarah Bernhardt
Richard Wright	26 Jean-Auguste-	31 Molière
Isadora Duncan	Dominique Ingres	32 Jean La Fontaine
Maria Callas	27 René Lalique	33 Jaques-Louis David
Proust	28 Jean Corot	

7. **Frédéric François Chopin,** (1810–49). Of Polish descent, Chopin was a child prodigy who at a young age was asked to play in the salons of Warsaw's wealthiest. When he was 21 he gave his first concert in Paris, and by the time he was 29 he had completed 24 preludes, one in each major and minor key and not one lasting more than five minutes. He has gained notoriety most for having introduced the piano to the musical world as a solo instrument, rather than an accompanying one. Oddly enough, it is interesting that Chopin preferred teaching to stage performance. Like many before and after him, Chopin also had a turbulent but significant affair with George Sand.

You might be interested to know that Chopin's heart is buried in a Warsaw church.

Continue along, and about four stones down on the right you will find another child prodigy:

8. **Maria Luigi Cherubini,** (1760–1842), the Italian composer. Cherubini particularly enjoyed religious, or sacred, music. By the time he reached the age of 16 he had already written several masses and other sacred choral works. His work is said to have profoundly affected the vocal works of Beethoven. At the age of 60, after working as a professor of composition at the Paris Conservatory for four years, he became its director. Incidentally, Cherubini apparently hated the flute and was at one time heard to say that he believed the only thing worse than one flute was two flutes.

Turn right at avenue Laterale du Sud. Go up two staircases and take a right on avenue de la Chapelle. On the right just beyond the bench behind the bush is the grave of:

9. **Théodore Géricault,** (1791–1824), the Romantic painter. On the grave marker is a statue of a sculpture of an artist with his palette, and if you go around the side you'll see a bronze bas-relief of one of his paintings, *Mounted Officer of the Imperial Guard* (1812). Géricault studied in Paris with Carle Vernet and Pierre Guérin and spent time copying the old masters at the Louvre. His most famous work, *The Raft of the Medusa,* was one of the first paintings of its size to reflect a contemporary newsworthy event—the shipwreck of the *Medusa* in 1816. He was also one of the first to break traditional form in technique and is thought to have influenced Eugène Delacroix (see below).

Return to the road and continue along to carrefour du Grand-Rond.

Go left around the circle. On your left you'll see the grave of:

10. **Gaspard Monge, comte de Péluse** (1746–1818), a French mathematician, physicist, public official, and friend to Napoléon. He is particularly well known for his geometrical research and was instrumental in the founding of Paris's Ecole Polytechnique in 1794. Gaspard Monge's research helped lay the foundations of modern geometry, which is essential to the mechanical drawings produced by today's architects.

Follow the road around the circle to the second left. Go along to the second tree on the left after the first possible right.

On the left you'll see a black statue in the posture of a Madonna and Child. In front of that headstone is the grave of:

11. **Auguste Comte** (1798–1857), the French philosopher. Comte was the founder of positivism, a philosophy whose goal was to create a peaceful and harmonic society. His system for social reform is described in *The Course of Positive Philosophy* (1830–42), and his book the *System of Positive Polity* (1851–54) describes his belief in a society that makes a religion out of worshiping humanity. Comte is credited with coining the term *sociology*, and his research contributed to what is now known as modern sociology.

Confronting his impending death in 1857, the modest and humble Comte is reported to have said, "What an irreparable loss!"

Head back to the right turn you passed on your way to Comte's grave, chemin Lauriston (now on your left). Go left down chemin Lauriston. When you get to the fork in the road, take the left fork (chemin de Lesseps) to the grave of the illustrious:

12. **Jim Morrison** (1943–71), the American rock singer and sixties icon. This one is a little tricky to find because it is a small grave site, tucked away amidst the many larger tombs. The first thing you should look for is the crowd of people that is always gathered here. Then look for two large trees (on the right), one of which has "God Bless America" carved into it; the other, a bit closer to the road, says, "Elvis is king."

Morrison, the now cult figure, and former vocalist of the Doors rock group is quite controversial within the confines of the cemetery. Because of the number and type of visitors his grave site attracts, the area is heavily trafficked and heavily grafittied. It will come as no surprise to anyone who sees the headstones and tombs surrounding his grave that the French (particularly those who have family plots near his) don't want him here and would even like to have him exhumed and moved to another location. The headstone you see today is a new one—the original had a marble bust of Morrison on it.

In case you're wondering how it is that Jim Morrison came to be buried in this very prestigious French cemetery, it's because he fit one of the three requirements for burial—you have to be born in Paris, die in Paris, or live in Paris. Morrison died of a drug overdose while touring with the Doors in France.

Go back the way you came to carrefour du Grand-Rond. Go right to your first right off the circle—avenue des Acacias. This one is a bit of a walk, but follow this road up and around. Not far after the sign for section #38 you'll see a cement bench on your right. Just behind the cement bench is the grave of:

13. **Nadar** (1820–1910). Nadar (whose real name was Gaspard Félix Tournachon) was one of the greatest, if not the greatest, photographer of the 19th century. He is remembered as a portrait photographer who made stunning photographs of Hugo, Sand, Baudelaire, Delacroix, and Bernhardt. He pre-

ferred not to make portraits of women (with a few exceptions) since the resulting picture was "too true to nature to please the sitter, even the most beautiful." Eventually Nadar gave up photography and took up hot-air ballooning instead. It was during one of those hot-air balloon rides that he became the first to make a bird's-eye view photograph of Paris.

Take your first right after Nadar onto chemin Abadie. Go right on avenue Transversale #2 to avenue Circulaire. Go left to avenue Transversale #3 and go left. Before you get to the next grave site, you should definitely take note of the two monuments to the victims of Nazi concentration camps on your right—one from Manthausen, the other from Flossenberg. The grave of:

14. **Edith Piaf** (1915–63) is located down the first dirt pathway off the right side of avenue Transversale #3. Take the dirt pathway, then take your first right (another dirt pathway) almost immediately after you get off the main road. Look for the grave site of the Famille Gassion-Piaf in the second row back from the street. Edith Piaf was a world-famous cabaret singer who was loved for her powerful, emotional voice. Dubbed "the little sparrow," she began singing in cafés and on the streets of Paris at the tender age of 15, and was so loved by her fans that there was even a play written for her by Jean Cocteau.

Go back out to the road and continue in the direction you were headed before the detour to Edith Piaf's grave. Go left on the pathway just before the intersection of avenue Transversale #3 and avenue Patchod. Just after you take the dirt pathway, go left again down to the seventh row. Go right to the second grave on the left. A very plain stone marks the grave of:

15. **Amedeo Modigliani** (1884–1920), a wonderfully individualistic Italian painter and sculptor who is famous for his sculpture of elongated forms. He became passionate about sculpture as a medium after he met Brancusi in 1909; however, the most notable influence on his work is that of African sculpture. In spite of (or probably because of) his unique style he remained unknown until well after his death of tuberculosis—a condition that he only made worse with his abuse of drugs and alcohol.

Go back out to avenue Transversale #3 and go left to avenue Patchod. Go right on avenue Patchod and head up to avenue Circulaire. First make a detour to the right to the other monuments of concentration camp victims. Just walk along and look at the immense sculptures that certainly speak much louder than any words that could be inscribed on the monuments themselves.

When you've finished meditating on the monuments here, head back in the other direction, crossing avenue Patchod. Just after the fourth tree on the left you'll find the grave of:

16. **Gertrude Stein** (1874–1946) who is perhaps most famous for her line, "A rose is a rose is a rose." Friends with Ernest Hemingway, Sherwood Anderson, Pablo Picasso, Sylvia Beach, and many others, Stein held one of the most famous weekly salons in Paris. She and her brother Leo were trendsetters in the

art world, and she had one of the best private collections in Paris at the time. Stein claimed to have discovered Picasso, and she so loved his work that she used to say of the two Picassos that hung on her wall that if her apartment were on fire and she "could take only one picture, it would be those two." She worked alongside Picasso and attempted to create the written equivalent of cubism. The ideology might have worked in her mind, but most people find her writing absolutely unintelligible.

Although *The Autobiography of Alice B. Toklas* (1933) brought her the fame that she had been trying to gain by constantly entertaining famous and talented people, it was not taken very seriously by many people—among them, her own brother, Leo. In regard to the book, Leo said that it was "a ferrago of rather clever anecdote, stupid brag, and general bosh . . . I simply cannot take Gertrude seriously as a literary phenomenon." Some of her acquaintances (including Matisse, Braque, and Tzara) followed Leo's lead by pointing out that there were many lies and/or mistakes in the book. Braque said, "Miss Stein understood nothing of what went on around her. But no superegoist does . . . she has entirely misunderstood cubism . . . which she saw simply in terms of personalities."

Next to Stein is what looks like an empty plot, or a plot without a stone, but in reality, it is the ever-present, ever-silent:

17. Alice B. Toklas (1877–1966), Gertrude Stein's famous-by-association lover. As always, Alice has taken a back seat to Stein and is duly noted on the backside of Stein's headstone. Even in death Toklas stands behind Stein—a fitting but melancholic ending.

Continue along avenue Circulaire and take your second left onto avenue Carette to the grave of the witty writer:

18. Oscar Fingal O'Flahertie Wills Wilde (1854–1900). You can't miss his headstone—it's a massive Art Deco Egyptian-like sphinx that looks like it might just take flight. First and foremost a dandy and an aesthete (and always a comedian), Wilde himself was once quoted as saying that he put his "genius into [his] life and [his] talent into his work." Some of his most famous works are *The Picture of Dorian Gray* (1891), *A Woman of No Importance* (1893), *The Importance of Being Earnest* (1895), and his collections of fairy tales. In the late 1890s Wilde was found guilty of homosexual practices and was sentenced to two years' hard labor. One day while standing handcuffed in cold rain he declared, "If this is the way Queen Victoria treats her prisoners then she doesn't deserve to have any."

At one time, his aesthetic sense made him the central figure of a group that believed in beauty for the sake of itself. His fixation with aesthetics followed him all the way to his deathbed, where he quipped, "Either that wallpaper goes, or I do." He died in Paris of cerebral meningitis. I assume the wallpaper stayed.

Continue along to the next intersection. Go right on avenue Transversale #3. At the next intersection go left on avenue

Aguado (there is no name marker here). Go right into the Colombarium and make your first right under the covered walkway. Just before the second staircase in the first row of the second section, fourth row from the bottom, is the marker for:

19. Max Ernst (1891–1976), a German-born surrealist painter who was originally a psychology student at Bonn University. The man who called himself Dadamax took up painting because of his interest in the painting of psychotics. Ernst came to Paris in 1922 and joined the surrealist movement of Paris two years later. He lived in the United States from 1941 to 1949 and was briefly married to the famous Peggy Guggenheim, but returned to France in 1949 and remained there until his death.

Turn around and cross the entry road that you came in on to the other side (as if you had gone left, rather than right on entering the Colombarium). Go straight to the end and make a right when you can't go any farther. Behind the third stair on your left is the marker of:

20. Richard Wright (1908–60), an African American writer. Wright was born on a Mississippi plantation and joined the Federal Writer's Project in the 1930s. His many books include *Uncle Tom's Children* (1938) and the most famous of his novels, *Native Son* (1940).

In December 1945 Wright was invited by the French government to come to Paris as its guest. He had a horrible time getting a passport from the U.S. State Department, but when he finally did get one he and his wife set out, by ship, for Paris. When they finally got there, they were met by the American ambassador and none other than the Mother of them all, Gertrude Stein. Stein had, in her usual way, already managed to gain the praises of Wright in a letter she sent him before his trip. It read, "Dear Richard: It is obvious that you and I are the only two geniuses of this era." Wright died at the age of 52 in Paris. He was cremated with a copy of his book *Black Boy*.

Continue around to the next block. Just before the first staircase, second row up, last stone on the right, is the marker of:

21. Isadora Duncan. Dora Gray Duncan (1878–1927) was born in San Francisco and became famous for her flamboyant expressionism as a dancer. She danced barefoot to music not written to be danced to in a scant Greek tunic draped in a multitude of flowing scarves. She didn't receive very warm reviews in the United States, but was adored in Paris from the time of her arrival in 1922. By the time she died, that adoration had spread all over Europe. Her last performance was held in Paris.

While in Paris she spent a good deal of time in the Louvre studying the vases as examples of grace. She was complimented by Rodin when he said, "she has attained sculpture and emotion effortlessly . . . has properly unified Life and The Dance."

Duncan died in a way that was most fitting to her persona— she was accidentally strangled to death when her favorite red scarf became entangled in the wheel of her brand new Bughatti race car. Her last words as she began to drive off were, "Je vais à la gloire!" Five thousand people attended her funeral.

Continue around, through the courtyard and around to the stairs between the two structures on the other side (those facing the one with Isadora Duncan's marker). Go down the stairs and make a right. At the end of the hallway go left to the stone numbered 6258 on your right. It is the grave of:

22. **Maria Callas** (1923–77), a Greek American soprano opera singer who was born in New York City. At age 13 she moved to Greece and studied at the Royal Conservatory in Athens. Loved for her versatility as an opera singer and her dramatic intensity, she debuted in 1947 at Verona and made her first appearance at the Metropolitan Opera in 1956. Callas had a fairly short career and retired at age 42. Several recent biographies have uncovered her obsession with Aristotle Onassis, who dumped Callas in order to marry Jackie Kennedy.

From Callas's stone continue straight ahead and go up the main stairs, to your right. Go left down avenue Combattants-Etrangers (the one that is directly ahead of you). When you get to avenue Transversale #2 go right. At the first dirt pathway go right to the fourth grave on the left, which is that of:

23. **Marcel Proust** (1871–1922). The sickly son of wealthy parents, Proust is considered one of the truly great literary figures of modern history because of his ability to communicate the link between a person's external and internal consciousness. His writing culminated in the creation of his multivolumed masterpiece, *Remembrance of Things Past,* which he began writing—in his bed—shortly after the death of his mother in 1906.

Proust wanted to be buried with his friend and lover Maurice Ravel, but their families would not allow it.

Go back out to avenue Transversale #2 and go right (in the direction you were headed before you turned off to see Proust), then go left at the first intersection onto avenue des Thuyas. Continue along to avenue Transversale #1. Cross avenue Transversale #1 and continue going straight. On the right just before the next corner is the grave of:

24. **Honoré de Balzac,** (1799–1850), who began his adult career studying law at the Sorbonne but decided that he would rather devote his life to writing. And devote he did, spending all day and most of the night writing, sleeping in the late afternoon for only a few hours. Not unlike many writers throughout history, he spent much time attempting to avoid starvation and so, to support himself, he wrote what would today be the equivalent of "trashy" novels and had them published under a pseudonym.

During the time of his greatest poverty Balzac lived in a stark, unheated room. He kept a sense of humor about it, writing on the walls, "Rosewood paneling with commode," "Gobelin tapestry with Venetian mirror," and, above the fireplace, "Picture by Raphael." One of his greatest wishes was to "be so well-known, so popular, so celebrated, so famous, that it would permit [him] . . . to break wind in society, and society would think it a most natural thing."

Only a few months before his death he married the Polish countess Evelina Hanska, with whom he had been exchanging love letters for an incredible 18 years.

Go left at the next intersection onto avenue Eugène-Delacroix to the grave of:

25. **Eugène Delacroix** (1798–1863), one of the greatest French painters of the Romantic movement. He, like Géricault, spent a great deal of time copying old masters at the Louvre and was an admirer of Rubens. Quoted as having said, "If you are not skillful enough to sketch a man falling out of a window during the time it takes him to get from the fifth story to the ground, then you will never produce a monumental work." Well, Delacroix produced many monumental works, among them, *The Bark of Dante* (1922) and *The Massacre at Scios* (1824). During his lifetime his body of work grew to over 9,000 paintings, drawings, and pastels. He was an inspiration to many of the Impressionists, including van Gogh, Seurat, and Renoir. Today, his old studio in the rue de Furstemberg has been turned into a museum of his work (see Walking Tour 4, stop 13).

Directly on your right is chemin de la Cave. Follow it, crossing avenue Feuillant. Chemin de la Cave turns into chemin Cabail. Follow it to avenue Saint-Morys. Go right on the path just past the second tree and you'll find a white stone, situated about three rows back, facing away from avenue Saint-Morys. It is the grave of the painter:

26. **Jean-Auguste-Dominique Ingres** (1780–1867). Ingres entered David's studio (see below) at age 17 and won the Prix de Rome only four years later. His work has a fluid, sinuous, rhythmical quality that broke with traditional classical form. In 1806 because he distorted the human figure (in his portrait of Madame Rivière) in favor of the linear rhythm of his painting, he was alienated from the Académie. That same year, in frustration, he returned to Rome, where he remained until 1820.

Ironically, when Ingres returned to Paris in 1824 (after a brief period in Florence), he was named president of the École des Beaux-Arts. Delacroix didn't like that very much, and he criticized Ingres again, saying that Ingres taught "beauty as one teaches arithmetic." Because of this, there was so much animosity between the two that Ingres refused Delacroix's handshake until well into his old age.

He left again for Rome in 1834 when yet another of his pictures was rejected for not following classical rules. He returned to Paris in 1841 and lived out the rest of his life here.

Some of his greatest works include *Bather of Valpincon* (1808, Louvre), and *Odalisque with the Slave* (1842).

Go back to avenue Saint-Morys and go left. Take your first left onto chemin Adonson (the left fork) to the grave of:

27. **René Lalique** (1860–1945), one of France's most talented Art Nouveau jewelers and glassmakers. Most know him only for his

clear crystal glass engraved with different frosted patterns— flowers, figures, or animals—which he began designing after 1902. However, the jewelry he made after he established his workshop in Paris in 1885 focused not on the stone but on the design. He particularly enjoyed using semiprecious stones— most notably, the opal—and brought them back into fashion. He enjoyed crafting his pieces using the Art Nouveau motifs of dragonflies, peacocks, and female nudes.

Continue out. The pathway veers right, and from the path you can see the tops of the heads of two sculpted busts. The black one is:

28. Jean-Baptiste-Camille Corot (1796–1875). Born in Paris and the son of a shopkeeper, this landscape painter worked in textile shops until around 1822 and didn't even begin to study painting until he was 30 years old. Only five years after he commenced his study, he began exhibiting regularly at the Barbizon School's Salon. The Barbizon School was a group of artists who focused primarily on landscape painting, but the only outdoor work they did was considered to be nothing more than sketches.

Corot was greatly respected by his contemporaries and influenced many younger artists. He did not receive great acclaim until he was well into his fifties. He was very down to earth and loved having his paintings around him. If he had no money and had to sell one he would exclaim in despair, "Alas, my collection has been so long complete, and now it is broken!"

Three rows behind Corot, directly in front of the big tree is:

29. Honoré Daumier (1808–79). It is appropriate that Daumier is buried so near Corot, for it is Corot who gave Daumier a house at Valmondois-sur-Seine-et-Oise when he was old, poor, nearly blind, and threatened with eviction. Most famous for his spontaneous caricature sculptures of political figures, Daumier was even imprisoned once for six months for his 1832 Gargantua cartoon that shows Louis Philippe swallowing bags of gold that have been extracted from his people.

Daumier produced approximately a hundred lithographs a year in addition to his sculpture and painting. A member of the realist school, he was admired by Delacroix, Balzac, Baudelaire, and Degas. In fact, Balzac was once heard to say of Daumier, "this boy has some Michelangelo under his skin."

Go back to the main path and cross avenue Transversale #1. To the left of the back of the big tomb in front of you is the grave of:

30. Sarah Bernhardt (née Henriette-Rosine Bernard, 1844–1923), the Paris-born actress who for the first 13 years of her life was raised in a convent. A graduate of the Paris Conservatory, her debut at 17 was unsuccessful. However, she persevered and eventually became one of Paris's best-loved actresses. Janet Flanner said after her funeral that "for days after what seemed like Bernardt's last public performance, mourners stood in line in the cemetery to get a view of where she lay dead, just as they had made the box-office queue to see her alive on the stage."

She is especially well known for her performances in Victorien Sardou's *Fédora, Théodora,* and *La Tosca,* and in 1912 she became a silent-film star.

Go back to avenue Transversale #1. Go left on it to the dirt pathway on the right, just before the sign marking the 39th division. You'll come to chemin Molière et La Fontaine. Go right on it to the grave of:

31. Molière (née Jean-Baptiste Poquelin, 1622–73). Born in Paris, Molière, a writer and actor, was the king of French high comedy in the 17th century. His satirical plays, including *La Tartuffe* (1664) and *Le Misanthrope* (1666), aimed at pointing out the hypocrisies in society and were often attacks on the church. Hence, there were many problems when it came to the issue of his burial. The church officials decided that he couldn't be buried in consecrated ground, which was said to run 14 feet deep. Louis XIV ordered that the grave be dug to 16 feet so as to avoid Molière's being buried in consecrated ground. Unfortunately, no one knows where the great dramatist was really buried because legend has it that he disappeared before he could be buried in that 16-foot-deep grave, so Mr. Frochot (the man who started the cemetery) was most likely taken for a ride when he bought Molière's bones.

32. Jean La Fontaine (1621–95) is right next to Molière. They're side by side and surrounded by a wrought-iron fence. La Fontaine was a French poet who is famous mainly for his books of fables (12 in all) that feature animals behaving like humans. The fables, modeled after those written by Aesop, were so successful that 137 editions were printed before he died. It's probably safe to assume that if Frochot was duped in regard to the bones of Molière he was probably duped about the bones of La Fontaine as well, but it's the thought that counts, right?

Keep going to the end, take the left fork and follow it all the way back down to avenue de la Chapelle. Go right on avenue de la Chapelle. Pass Géricault's grave (on your left) and go left on the other side of the park to the fifth grave on the right, that of:

33. Jacques-Louis David (1748–1825), a neoclassicist French painter who is known to most just as David. His first attempt at the Prix de Rome failed and led to a suicide attempt. Fortunately, he was saved by some fellow students at the Académie who found him in his room at the Louvre before it was too late.

Later, in 1774, he did win the Prix de Rome and left to study in Italy. He returned to Paris in 1780 and became very politically involved. He even actually voted for the execution of Louis XVI in 1793.

David revolutionized art with his paintings on huge canvases that were allegories or commentaries on current events. He even liked to sketch prisoners on their way to the guillotine from the terrace outside the Café de la Régence. Among those he sketched was Marie Antoinette. Napoléon recognized David's potential as a propagandist and appointed him to the position of official painter. Between 1802 and 1805 he painted a series of paintings for Napoléon, including the *Coronation of Napoléon* (1805–07; displayed at the Louvre). When Napoléon fell, David went into exile in Brussels. His influence can be seen in the work of Ingres, Gérard, and Gros.

Continue down the steps to avenue du Puits. Go left to avenue Principale. Go right on avenue Principale to the exit.

APPENDIX

Recommended Reading

GENERAL HISTORY

Bennett, Arnold. *Paris Nights and Other Impressions of Places and People* (George H. Doran, 1913).

Bierman, John. *Napoleon III and his Carnival Empire* (St. Martins Press, 1988).

Braudel, Fernand. *The Identity of France* (Harper & Row).

Bury, J. P. *France 1814-1940* (Routledge, Chapman & Hall, 1985).

Callaghan, Morley. *That Summer in Paris: Memories of Tangled Friendships with Hemingway, Fitzgerald and Some Others* (Coward-McCann, 1963).

Carpenter, Humphrey. *Geniuses Together: American Writers in Paris in the 1920s* (Houghton Mifflin, 1988).

Cobban, Alfred. *A History of Modern France* (Penguin, 1965).

Cooper, Duff. *Talleyrand* (Fromm, 1986).

Dark, Sidney. *Paris* (Macmillan, 1936).

Duras, Marguerite. *The War: A Memoir* (Pantheon, 1986).

Edwards, George Wharton. *Paris* (Penn, 1924).

Febvre, Lucien. *Life in Renaissance France* (Harvard University Press, 1979).

Fitch, Noel Riley. *Sylvia Beach and the Lost Generation: A History of Literary Paris in the Twenties and Thirties.* (W.W. Norton, 1983).

Flanner, Janet. *Paris Was Yesterday 1925–1939* (Harcourt Brace Jovanovich, 1988).

Gibbings, Robert. *Trumpets From Montparnasse* (J.M. Dent & Sons, 1955).

Hampson, Norman. *Danton* (Basil Blackwell, 1988).

Hemingway, Ernest. *A Moveable Feast* (Macmillan, 1988).

Hibbert, Christopher. *The Days of the French Revolution* (Morrow, 1981).

Hobsbawn, E. J. *The Age of Revolution 1789–1848* (New American Library).

Huddleston, Sisley. *In and About Paris* (Methuen & Co., 1927).

Liebling, A. J. *The Road Back to Paris* (Paragon House, 1988).

Longstreet, Stephen. *We all Went to Paris: Americans in the City of Light 1776–1971* (Macmillan, 1972).

Lucas, E. V. *A Wanderer in Paris* (Methuen & Co., 1925).

McDougall, Richard. *The Very Rich Hours of Adrienne Monnier* (Scribner's, 1976).

Maurois, Andre. *A History of France* (Methuen & Co., 1987).

Paul, Eliot. *The Last Time I Saw Paris* (Random House, 1942).

Phelps, Robert. *Belles Saisons: A Colette Scrapbook* (Farrar, Straus & Giroux, 1978).

Pinkney, David H. *Napoleon III and the Rebuilding of Paris* (Princeton University Press).

Rearick, Charles. *Pleasures of the Belle Epoque: Entertainment and Festivity in Turn-of-the-Century France* (Yale University Press, 1986).

Russell, John. *Paris* (Harry N. Abrams, 1983).

Schama, Simon. *Citizens: A Chronicle of the French Revolution* (Knopf, 1989).

Thompson, J. M. *The French Revolution* (Basil Blackwell, 1985).

Thompson, J. M. *Napoléon Bonaparte* (Basil Blackwell, 1988).

Thompson, J. M. *Robespierre* (Basil Blackwell).

Weber, Eugen. *France, Fin de Siecle* (Harvard University Press, 1986).

Wedgwood, C. V. *Richelieu and the French Monarchy* (Macmillan, 1965).

Zeldin, Theodore. *France 1848–1945* (Oxford University Press, 1981).

Zeldin, Theodore. *The French* (Pantheon, 1982).

ART & ARCHITECTURE

Bernadac, Marie-Laure. *Picasso Museum Paris: The Masterpieces* (Reunion des Musees Nationaux, 1991).

Bernard, Denvir, ed. *Impressionists at First Hand* (Thames and Hudson, 1987).

Blunt, Anthony. *Art and Architecture in France 1500–1700* (Penguin, 1973).

Brassai. *The Secret Paris of the 30's* (Patheon, 1977).

Delacroix, Eugene. *The Journal of Eugene Delacroix* (Crown, 1948).

Elderfield, John. *Henri Matisse: A Retrospective* (Metropolitan Museum of Art, 1992).

Freches-Thory, Claire, et al. *Toulouse Lautrec* (Reunion des Musees Nationaux, 1992).

Herbert, Robert. *Impressionism: Art Leisure and Parisian Society* (Yale University Press, 1988).

Lecoque, A. L. *Renoir My Friend* (Edition Mona Lisa, 1968).

Paris, Reine-Marie, and Arnaud de la Chapelle. *L'Oeuvre de Camille Claudel* (Editions d'Art et d'Histoire Arhis, 1990).

Reff, Theodore. *Manet and Modern Paris* (National Gallery of Art, 1982).

Rewald, John. *The History of Impressionism* New York Graphics Society (New York).

Rewald, John. *Post-Impressionism: From Van Gogh to Gauguin* (Museum of Modern Art, 1978).

Van Gogh, Vincent. *Vincent van Gogh: Lettres à Theo* (Editions Gallimard, 1956).

FICTION

Bowen, Elizabeth. *The House in Paris* (Knopf, 1936).

Colette. *The Vagabond* (Ballantine, 1982).

Dickens, Charles. *A Tale of Two Cities* (Penguin, 1970).

James, Henry. *The Ambassadors* (Penguin, 1987).

Miller, Henry. *Tropic of Cancer* (Grove, 1987).

Stein, Gertrude. *The Autobiography of Alice B. Toklas* (Random House, 1955).

Index

Please Send Me the Books Checked Below.
FROMMER'S COMPREHENSIVE GUIDES
(Guides listing facilities from budget to deluxe,
with emphasis on the medium-priced)

	Retail Price	Code		Retail Price	Code
☐ Acapulco/Ixtapa/Taxco 1993–94	$15.00	C120	☐ Jamaica/Barbados 1993–94	$15.00	C105
☐ Alaska 1990–91	$15.00	C001	☐ Japan 1992–93	$19.00	C020
☐ Arizona 1993–94	$18.00	C101	☐ Morocco 1992–93	$18.00	C021
☐ Australia 1992–93	$18.00	C002	☐ Nepal 1992–93	$18.00	C038
☐ Austria 1993–94	$19.00	C119	☐ New England 1993	$17.00	C114
☐ Austria/Hungary 1991–92	$15.00	C003	☐ New Mexico 1993–94	$15.00	C117
☐ Belgium/Holland/ Luxembourg 1993–94	$18.00	C106	☐ New York State 1992–93	$19.00	C025
☐ Bermuda/Bahamas 1992–93	$17.00	C005	☐ Northwest 1991–92	$17.00	C026
☐ Brazil 1993–94	$20.00	C111	☐ Portugal 1992–93	$16.00	C027
☐ California 1992–93	$18.00	C112	☐ Puerto Rico 1993–94	$15.00	C103
☐ Canada 1992–93	$18.00	C009	☐ Puerto Vallarta/ Manzanillo/Guadalajara 1992–93	$14.00	C028
☐ Caribbean 1993	$18.00	C102	☐ Scandinavia 1993–94	$19.00	C118
☐ Carolinas/Georgia 1992–93	$17.00	C034	☐ Scotland 1992–93	$16.00	C040
☐ Colorado 1993–94	$16.00	C100	☐ Skiing Europe 1989–90	$15.00	C030
☐ Cruises 1993–94	$19.00	C107	☐ South Pacific 1992–93	$20.00	C031
☐ DE/MD/PA & NJ Shore 1992–93	$19.00	C012	☐ Spain 1993–94	$19.00	C115
☐ Egypt 1990–91	$15.00	C013	☐ Switzerland/Liechten- stein 1992–93	$19.00	C032
☐ England 1993	$18.00	C109	☐ Thailand 1992–93	$20.00	C033
☐ Florida 1993	$18.00	C104	☐ U.S.A. 1993–94	$19.00	C116
☐ France 1992–93	$20.00	C017	☐ Virgin Islands 1992–93	$13.00	C036
☐ Germany 1993	$19.00	C108	☐ Virginia 1992–93	$14.00	C037
☐ Italy 1993	$19.00	C113	☐ Yucatan 1993–94	$18.00	C110

FROMMER'S $-A-DAY GUIDES
(Guides to low-cost tourist accommodations and facilities)

	Retail Price	Code		Retail Price	Code
☐ Australia on $45 1993–94	$18.00	D102	☐ Israel on $45 1993–94	$18.00	D101
☐ Costa Rica/Guatemala/ Belize on $35 1993–94	$17.00	D108	☐ Mexico on $50 1993	$19.00	D105
☐ Eastern Europe on $30 1993–94	$18.00	D110	☐ New York on $70 1992–93	$16.00	D016
☐ England on $60 1993	$18.00	D107	☐ New Zealand on $45 1993–94	$18.00	D103
☐ Europe on $45 1993	$19.00	D106	☐ Scotland/Wales on $50 1992–93	$18.00	D019
☐ Greece on $45 1993–94	$19.00	D100	☐ South America on $40 1993–94	$19.00	D109
☐ Hawaii on $75 1993	$19.00	D104	☐ Turkey on $40 1992–93	$22.00	D023
☐ India on $40 1992–93	$20.00	D010	☐ Washington, D.C. on $40 1992	$17.00	D024
☐ Ireland on $40 1992–93	$17.00	D011			

FROMMER'S CITY $-A-DAY GUIDES
(Pocket-size guides with an emphasis on low-cost tourist
accommodations and facilities)

	Retail Price	Code		Retail Price	Code
☐ Berlin on $40 1992–93	$12.00	D002	☐ Madrid on $50 1992–93	$13.00	D014
☐ Copenhagen on $50 1992–93	$12.00	D003	☐ Paris on $45 1992–93	$12.00	D018
☐ London on $45 1992–93	$12.00	D013	☐ Stockholm on $50 1992–93	$13.00	D022

FROMMER'S WALKING TOURS
(With routes and detailed maps, these companion guides point out the places and pleasures that make a city unique)

	Retail Price	Code		Retail Price	Code
☐ Berlin	$12.00	W100	☐ Paris	$12.00	W103
☐ London	$12.00	W101	☐ San Francisco	$12.00	W104
☐ New York	$12.00	W102	☐ Washington, D.C.	$12.00	W105

FROMMER'S TOURING GUIDES
(Color-illustrated guides that include walking tours, cultural and historic sights, and practical information)

	Retail Price	Code		Retail Price	Code
☐ Amsterdam	$11.00	T001	☐ New York	$11.00	T008
☐ Barcelona	$14.00	T015	☐ Rome	$11.00	T010
☐ Brazil	$11.00	T003	☐ Scotland	$10.00	T011
☐ Florence	$ 9.00	T005	☐ Sicily	$15.00	T017
☐ Hong Kong/Singapore/			☐ Thailand	$13.00	T012
Macau	$11.00	T006	☐ Tokyo	$15.00	T016
☐ Kenya	$14.00	T018	☐ Venice	$ 9.00	T014
☐ London	$13.00	T007			

FROMMER'S FAMILY GUIDES

	Retail Price	Code		Retail Price	Code
☐ California with Kids	$18.00	F100	☐ San Francisco with Kids	$17.00	F004
☐ Los Angeles with Kids	$17.00	F002	☐ Washington, D.C. with		
☐ New York City with Kids	$18.00	F003	Kids	$17.00	F005

FROMMER'S CITY GUIDES
(Pocket-size guides to sightseeing and tourist accommodations and facilities in all price ranges)

	Retail Price	Code		Retail Price	Code
☐ Amsterdam 1993–94	$13.00	S110	☐ Miami 1993–94	$13.00	S118
☐ Athens 1993–94	$13.00	S114	☐ Minneapolis/St. Paul		
☐ Atlanta 1993–94	$13.00	S112	1993–94	$13.00	S119
☐ Atlantic City/Cape May			☐ Montreal/Quebec City		
1993–94	$13.00	S130	1993–94	$13.00	S125
☐ Bangkok 1992–93	$13.00	S005	☐ New Orleans 1993–94	$13.00	S103
☐ Barcelona/Majorca/			☐ New York 1993	$13.00	S120
Minorca/Ibiza 1993–94	$13.00	S115	☐ Orlando 1993	$13.00	S101
☐ Berlin 1993–94	$13.00	S116	☐ Paris 1993–94	$13.00	S109
☐ Boston 1993–94	$13.00	S117	☐ Philadelphia 1993–94	$13.00	S113
☐ Cancun/Cozumel/			☐ Rio 1991–92	$ 9.00	S029
Yucatan 1991–92	$ 9.00	S010	☐ Rome 1993–94	$13.00	S111
☐ Chicago 1993–94	$13.00	S122	☐ Salt Lake City 1991–92	$ 9.00	S031
☐ Denver/Boulder/			☐ San Diego 1993–94	$13.00	S107
Colorado Springs			☐ San Francisco 1993	$13.00	S104
1993–94	$13.00	S131	☐ Santa Fe/Taos/		
☐ Dublin 1993–94	$13.00	S128	Albuquerque 1993–94	$13.00	S108
☐ Hawaii 1992	$12.00	S014	☐ Seattle/Portland 1992–		
☐ Hong Kong 1992–93	$12.00	S015	93	$12.00	S035
☐ Honolulu/Oahu 1993	$13.00	S106	☐ St. Louis/Kansas City		
☐ Las Vegas 1993–94	$13.00	S121	1993–94	$13.00	S127
☐ Lisbon/Madrid/Costa			☐ Sydney 1993–94	$13.00	S129
del Sol 1991–92	$ 9.00	S017	☐ Tampa/St. Petersburg		
☐ London 1993	$13.00	S100	1993–94	$13.00	S105
☐ Los Angeles 1993–94	$13.00	S123	☐ Tokyo 1992–93	$13.00	S039
☐ Madrid/Costa del Sol			☐ Toronto 1993–94	$13.00	S126
1993–94	$13.00	S124	☐ Vancouver/Victoria		
☐ Mexico City/Acapulco			1990–91	$ 8.00	S041
1991–92	$ 9.00	S020	☐ Washington, D.C. 1993	$13.00	S102

Other Titles Available at Membership Prices
SPECIAL EDITIONS

	Retail Price	Code		Retail Price	Code
☐ Bed & Breakfast North America	$15.00	P002	☐ National Park Guide 1993	$15.00	P101
☐ Bed & Breakfast Southwest	$16.00	P100	☐ Where to Stay U.S.A.	$15.00	P102
☐ Caribbean Hideaways	$16.00	P005			
☐ Marilyn Wood's Wonderful Weekends (within a 250-mile radius of NYC)	$12.00	P017			

GAULT MILLAU'S "BEST OF" GUIDES
(The only guides that distinguish the truly superlative from the merely overrated)

	Retail Price	Code		Retail Price	Code
☐ Chicago	$16.00	G002	☐ New England	$16.00	G010
☐ Florida	$17.00	G003	☐ New Orleans	$17.00	G011
☐ France	$17.00	G004	☐ New York	$17.00	G012
☐ Germany	$18.00	G018	☐ Paris	$17.00	G013
☐ Hawaii	$17.00	G006	☐ San Francisco	$17.00	G014
☐ Hong Kong	$17.00	G007	☐ Thailand	$18.00	G019
☐ London	$17.00	G009	☐ Toronto	$17.00	G020
☐ Los Angeles	$17.00	G005	☐ Washington, D.C.	$17.00	G017

THE REAL GUIDES
(Opinionated, politically aware guides for youthful budget-minded travelers)

	Retail Price	Code		Retail Price	Code
☐ Able to Travel	$20.00	R112	☐ Italy	$18.00	R125
☐ Amsterdam	$13.00	R100	☐ Kenya	$12.95	R015
☐ Barcelona	$13.00	R101	☐ Mexico	$11.95	R016
☐ Belgium/Holland/ Luxembourg	$16.00	R031	☐ Morocco	$14.00	R017
☐ Berlin	$13.00	R123	☐ Nepal	$14.00	R018
☐ Brazil	$13.95	R003	☐ New York	$13.00	R019
☐ California & the West Coast	$17.00	R121	☐ Paris	$13.00	R020
☐ Canada	$15.00	R103	☐ Peru	$12.95	R021
☐ Czech and Slovak Republics	$15.00	R124	☐ Poland	$13.95	R022
☐ Egypt	$19.00	R105	☐ Portugal	$16.00	R126
☐ Europe	$18.00	R122	☐ Prague	$15.00	R113
☐ Florida	$14.00	R006	☐ San Francisco & the Bay Area	$11.95	R024
☐ France	$18.00	R106	☐ Scandinavia	$14.95	R025
☐ Germany	$18.00	R107	☐ Spain	$16.00	R026
☐ Greece	$18.00	R108	☐ Thailand	$17.00	R119
☐ Guatemala/Belize	$14.00	R010	☐ Tunisia	$17.00	R115
☐ Hong Kong/Macau	$11.95	R011	☐ Turkey	$13.95	R027
☐ Hungary	$14.95	R118	☐ U.S.A.	$18.00	R117
☐ Ireland	$17.00	R120	☐ Venice	$11.95	R028
			☐ Women Travel	$12.95	R029
			☐ Yugoslavia	$12.95	R030